Skilled Dialogue

STRATEGIES FOR RESPONDING TO
CULTURAL DIVERSITY IN EARLY CHILDHOOD
SECOND EDITION

by

Isaura Barrera, Ph.D.
Our Lady of the Lake University
San Antonio, Texas

Lucinda Kramer, Ph.D.
National University
Costa Mesa, California

and

T. Dianne Macpherson, M.S.W., LCSW, CAS

·P·A·U·L·H·
BROOKES
PUBLISHING C.⁰ ®

Baltimore • London • Sydney

Paul H. Brookes Publishing Co.
Post Office Box 10624
Baltimore, Maryland 21285-0624
USA

www.brookespublishing.com

"Paul H. Brookes Publishing Co." is a registered trademark
of Paul H. Brookes Publishing Co., Inc.

Typeset by Auburn Associates, Inc., Baltimore, Maryland.
Manufactured in the United States of America by
Sheridan Books, Inc., Chelsea, Michigan.

Poem "Warrior Child" (appearing on pages 209–211) by Nanci Presley-Holley from *Children of Trauma* by Jane Middelton-Moz, copyright © 1989. Published by arrangement with Health Communications Inc.

The individuals described in this book are composites or real people whose situations are masked and are based on the authors' experiences. In all instances, names and identifying details have been changed to protect confidentiality.

Library of Congress Cataloging-in-Publication Data
Barrera, Isaura.
　Skilled dialogue : strategies for responding to cultural diversity in early childhood / by Isaura Barrera, Lucinda Kramer and T. Dianne Macpherson.—2nd ed.
　　p.　cm.
　Includes bibliographical references and index.
　ISBN-13: 978-1-59857-164-6 (pbk.)
　ISBN-10: 1-59857-164-8 (pbk.)
　1. Multicultural education. 2. Early childhood education. I. Kramer, Lucinda. II. Macpherson, Dianne. III. Title.
　LC1099.B39 2012
　370.117—dc23　　　　　　　　　　　　　　　　　　　　　　　　　　　2012002640

British Library Cataloguing in Publication data are available from the British Library.

2016　2015　2014　2013　2012

10　9　8　7　6　5　4　3　2　1

Contents

About the Authors

Isaura Barrera, Ph.D., grew up on the U.S. side of the Texas–Mexico border speaking only Spanish until the age of 6. The subsequent challenges and gifts of communication across diverse perspectives, languages, and cultures sparked her interest in what has now become Skilled Dialogue. She received her doctoral degree in educational evaluation from the University of New York at Buffalo, with concentrations in early childhood education, bilingual education, and special education. Dr. Barrera is currently Professor Emerita at the University of New Mexico in Albuquerque and Chair of the Education Department at Our Lady of the Lake University in San Antonio, Texas.

Lucinda Kramer, Ph.D., earned her doctoral degree in special education with a concentration in early childhood special education from the University of New Mexico. As Associate Professor in Special Education at National University in Costa Mesa, California, she coordinates the credential and graduate programs in special education. She has served as Chair of the Multicultural Committee for the Council of Exceptional Children's Division of Early Childhood and has worked with teachers, families, schools, and agencies in Texas, Arizona, and California.

T. Dianne Macpherson, M.S.W., LCSW, CAS, is a clinical social worker in private practice in Arizona. Ms. Macpherson has more than 30 years' professional experience with direct clinical care involving a wide range of mental health and addictive disorders in a variety of settings, including chemical dependency programs, forensic mental health services, child protective services, outpatient mental health clinics, and behavioral health managed care. She has provided clinical consultation and training for mental health professionals at various local, state, national, and international conferences. Ms. Macpherson has been a guest lecturer/consultant teaching undergraduate and graduate college-level special education courses with a focus on mental health issues in the classroom and strategies for identification, intervention, and risk reduction.

Foreword

"It is how we interact rather than what we know that ultimately determines the outcome of our interactions with those who hold diverse values and beliefs and who speak and behave differently from ourselves."—*Skilled Dialogue*, Chapter 3

It is unusual to find a book that in its voices and structure invites readers of diverse beliefs, funds of knowledge, and lived experiences to engage deeply with challenging ideas. Readers of *Skilled Dialogue: Strategies for Responding to Cultural Diversity in Early Childhood, Second Edition* will quickly realize that what they are encountering is not mere exposition and communication of ideas by disembodied experts. Instead, they will find an invitation to bring themselves—their personal and professional histories, identities, and commitments—to join the authors in considering powerful ideas about engaging with equally complex others on behalf of all children.

These are not trivial features in a book such as this one. There are important parallels here between the message and the stance of the messengers. The message—the importance of individuals' contexts, histories, identities, beliefs, and values—is conveyed by authors who reveal themselves in stories of their own contexts, histories, and identities. In other words, the authors are respectfully and persistently present.

How the authors engage readers is consonant with the book's content as well. The authors establish early on that we each embody cultural and linguistic characteristics that are valid in our own contexts and should be honored as such. Implicit in this message is that each reader will bring different perspectives to reading and that these perspectives will be recognized and respected. The authors present concepts that may be unfamiliar or uncomfortable and knowledge that may challenge readers' commitments to their own beliefs and values as offerings rather than requirements of the reader. The authors invite readers into engagement with the book's content without dominating or silencing.

Two structural features of the book—the use of vignettes and the recursive pattern of concept development—acknowledge the diversity of pathways readers may take as they engage with the content. Vignettes included throughout the text place the central concepts of Skilled Dialogue into contexts familiar to many in early childhood fields. The vignettes serve to bridge the new and the familiar as they provide opportunities to see the concepts of Skilled Dialogue instantiated in settings and events they may recognize. Further, these rich and multifocal vignettes permit readers to see events and the diverse players in ways that Maxine Greene (1995) calls "seeing big." Seeing big involves seeing others in the concreteness and particularity of their lives and as intentional participants in events. Seeing big complicates and enriches our perceptions of others while offering multiple points of contact for readers to find their own stories in the stories of others.

The recursive structure of this book leads readers back again and again to the central concepts of Skilled Dialogue, each time allowing readers to build deeper and more nuanced understanding of the process. The vignettes, too, are revisited and reconsidered in light of increasingly sophisticated understandings. Unfolding slowly as they do, readers have a chance to reconsider their initial perceptions and to expand their repertoire of responses. This recursive structure also serves to slow down and hold ideas and events still for closer examination, communicating by example that there is always more to see and more to understand. It allows readers a chance to experience other powerful elements of Skilled Dialogue as well: staying with the tension, resisting the urge to freeze assumptions, and remaining open to surprise.

The message, the stance of the authors, and the structure of this book all serve to welcome a diverse audience of readers. Like the Skilled Dialogue books that preceded this one, this book speaks to readers across the professional life span and the range of roles and contexts that those in early childhood education, leadership, and advocacy find themselves. Readers in undergraduate, graduate, and professional development courses in early childhood education, leadership, and advocacy have engaged deeply in Skilled Dialogue. Traditional-aged undergraduates who are finding their own voices and identities and negotiating rapidly changing relationships and responsibilities will find immediate application in their own lives. Differences of values and behaviors in students' widening circles of friends, classmates, roommates, partners, family members, professors, children, cooperating teachers, and employers are part of their daily experience and will find immediate application. The undergraduates with whom I have worked have been eager to share their own stories of striving to listen openly, understand behaviors differently, and begin to question their familiar ways of engaging with others.

Practicing professionals will appreciate the complexities and challenges presented in the vignettes that serve as points of connection with their own rich personal and professional histories and present realities. As they grapple with the concepts of Skilled Dialogue, they find alternative ways of interpreting past experiences and invitations to deeply examine their approaches to current challenges. I have observed significant but often subtle changes in program administrators, mentors, coaches, technical assistance providers, home visitors, and others in the field of early care and education who have engaged with this text. For some, the questions they pose in the face of challenge shift from "What shall I say?" and "What shall I do?" to "How can I better understand?" and "How can *we* address this situation?" For some, the very definition of a challenging situation expands. Situations that may have gone largely unnoticed because they posed no challenge to their own values, beliefs, and purposes are appreciated as posing challenges to others who do not share their perspectives or those on which programs, policies, and routines are based.

Those who are familiar with the previous Skilled Dialogue books may experience both a comforting sense of the familiar and the satisfaction of finding many of those familiar ideas deepened and connected in new ways in this second edition. The authors are careful to bring such readers along. They explicitly address how and why their thinking evolved—in many cases as a result of their interactions with the many readers of their work and participants at Skilled Dialogue workshops.

Welcoming all readers—those new to Skilled Dialogue and those who are more familiar—does not mean that all readers will find this a comfortable read, one that confirms prior knowledge or perspectives. This is a demanding book. It requires emotional as well as intellectual engagement. It requires a willingness to examine one's own beliefs, values, and actions fearlessly. And it may require readers to be patient while trying on new frames for hearing the voices of others, seeing behaviors that differ from one's own, and practicing a process of engaging with others that requires one's full presence.

I confess to a challenge in reading this book, albeit a challenge I have come to welcome. It interrupts my very American East Coast 21st century drive to take in and use new information rapidly. I have had to learn to permit myself significant pauses to allow time to follow lines of thought from the text into my own experience and back again. I have learned to turn backward and forward through the text to gather up and reexamine my thoughts. I have learned to anticipate looking in unfamiliar and sometimes uncomfortable ways at my teaching and the voices and quality of interactions it supports, my research and the forms of agency and identity it assumes, and my interactional competency in all areas of my life.

My advice to readers is to allow time to respond to the invitations in this book, to persist in examining ideas that are unfamiliar or uncomfortable, and to marvel at your own new ways of seeing, understanding, and acting. Stay with the tension, as the authors say. And know that the authors are a patient presence throughout.

Cynthia L. Paris, Ph.D.
Associate Professor, Department of Human Development and Family Studies
University of Delaware, Newark

REFERENCE

Greene, M. (1995). *Releasing the imagination: Essays on education, the arts, and social change.* San Francisco, CA: Jossey-Bass.

Acknowledgments

This revised edition is dedicated to J., E., and S., whose continuing willingness to engage with me respectfully, reciprocally, and responsively, lightens and brightens my life beyond measure. I also wish to acknowledge all the graduate students and practitioners who continue to share their insights and stories with me, as well as all those who have so graciously invited Lucinda and me into their schools and agencies so that we could share Skilled Dialogue with them. I wish to also acknowledge Rob Corso for his work on the first edition, without which this second would not be possible, and Lucinda Kramer for her work and support in the writing of this second edition—and her patience with all my ideas and requests for rewrites.

—I.B.

With love to Francis and Elliotte Clifton, Ben, Adam, Sam, Lori, Zalman, and Laya.

—L.K.

Introduction

Welcome to the new and updated edition of *Skilled Dialogue: Strategies for Responding to Cultural Diversity in Early Childhood.* In the years since the first edition published in 2003, we have listened to practitioners' concerns and reflected on our materials as well as on the Skilled Dialogue process itself. Our first response to what we learned was the publication of a companion book, *Using Skilled Dialogue to Transform Challenging Interactions: Honoring Identity, Voice, and Connection,* devoted to providing practitioners with more concrete guidance for using Skilled Dialogue when any type of diversity presented challenges (Barrera & Kramer, 2009). As we continued presenting and training, however, we noticed that many of the situations practitioners wanted us to discuss continued to focus primarily on cultural linguistic diversity. It became evident to us that the more specific challenges posed by cultural linguistic diversity had not diminished. If anything, they had become more problematic in the face of increasingly limited resources and other changes in the educational climate. Questions such as the following continued to be asked.

- How can I communicate with Sally's family and ensure that they understand what I am saying about their child in ways that do not penalize them for limited familiarity with the language and culture of testing?

- How can I respect Mr. and Mrs. Quentin's cultural beliefs and practices about carrying Alred when I feel that these beliefs and practices are not in the best interests of Alred's learning to walk?

- This family does not seem to understand the importance of working with me when I am in their home. How can I increase their engagement during my sessions with their child?

- This is my third appointment with Mrs. Brown to observe her child. We have already had to reschedule twice. The first time she said she forgot. The second time she had to go to her sister's to help her with something and did not call me to let me know she would be gone. How can I communicate the importance of keeping appointments as scheduled?

- Ahmed apparently does not want to work independently on the lesson activities. He constantly requests my presence and will not start until I approach him and watch what he is doing. How can I teach him to be more independent?

Other equally challenging questions emerged from families themselves as they met diversity in early childhood environments. Though often unspoken, these questions nevertheless reflected real concerns that affected the outcome of practitioners' interactions. Examples of these questions include the following:

- How can we communicate with the people who come into our home to help us and ensure that they understand what we mean, and not just our language?

- When we disagree with what practitioners tell us about our child, how can we be respectful yet also let them know that they are not respecting us (e.g., our cultural child-rearing practices and expectations)?

- The therapists who work with our child do not seem to understand the importance of teaching our child to respect her elders in ways that we value. How can we get them to support this need for our child instead of focusing so much on her use of words?

- We have had several appointments with our child's teacher. Each time, a family issue has prevented us from getting there in time. We know that the teacher does not like this, but how can we tell him that we cannot simply interrupt our family members and tell them we have to leave?

- Our child is caring and likes to be with us. We like to do things for him that make his life easier. How can we communicate that the autonomy that practitioners value so much is not so important to us? We believe that people should do for each other and be close to each other.

The situations described by practitioners were not limited to general communication and collaboration interactions across diverse values and perspectives, which we discussed in our 2009 book. They were more often specifically focused on interactions associated with planning and conducting appropriate and valid assessment and instruction for children who are culturally and linguistically diverse (e.g., How can I address dual language instruction when we no longer offer that at our school?). The persistence of these questions reflected an ongoing need not only for learning Skilled Dialogue in general, but also more specifically for learning to apply its dispositions and strategies to assessing these children's learning needs and developing appropriate instructional responses within what seemed to be more restrictive educational contexts. This revision is written in response to that need.

CHANGING CONTEXTS

Although the questions just discussed remained largely unchanged, the educational contexts in which they need to be answered have changed significantly. Three of these changes were particularly relevant to our work: a greater acknowledgment of the role of culture and cultural diversity in educational settings, a trend toward greater curricular and instructional standardization, and increasing attention to new research on learning and the brain. Simultaneously, the Skilled Dialogue context itself evolved to include specific dispositions and more concrete strategies.

The Evolution of Skilled Dialogue

It is helpful to briefly discuss the evolution of Skilled Dialogue in order to under-stand the differences and connections between this book and our 2009 book. This evolution can be thought of in three phases: 1) the beginnings, as we started to discover the need for a different mindset; 2) the first steps, as we began to intuit the key beliefs, qualities, and skills of Skilled Dialogue; and 3) the operationaliza-tion of the Skilled Dialogue process, leading to the current model, presented in the 2009 text.

The challenge in writing this revised edition was to bridge its content with that in the later text. The 2003 edition was, in a way, the culmination of the first two phases. It focused primarily on Skilled Dialogue as a tool for optimizing our response to cultural linguistic diversity. Our 2009 book emerged following the demand for operationalizing the Skilled Dialogue process. Threaded throughout this evolution was an evolving understanding of the power of Skilled Dialogue as more than technique or procedure for helping others to change. Our current understanding of Skilled Dialogue, which has guided the changes in this revised text, would define its purpose as follows: To set the stage for miracles as we en-gage with others in ways that honor our identities, our voices, and our connection within a mutual and interdependent reality. We believe that its full potential can be realized only when focused toward this purpose.

The Beginnings: From Knowledge to Process   The need for a different mindset for dealing with cultural diversity emerged from our early work at the University of New Mexico with a very diverse group of graduate students that in-cluded Navajo, Pueblo, and Hispanic (various groups) students as well as students who identified themselves as either "White," "Anglo," or at times as "not having a culture." We remain thankful to those students for their roles in leading us toward a different mindset as they interacted with each other and with us.

In our initial work, their responses quickly led us to realize that simply acquir-ing knowledge (i.e., learning *about* other cultures) did not significantly change the students' beliefs or practices about those different from themselves. We observed that, at times, the facts learned about other cultures actually served to confirm or create stereotypes, however benign. In other words, such teaching did not result in what we hoped it would—a curious and open perspective that invited con-nection and partnership. As we listened further, we discovered that specific facts tended to become lenses that limited how individuals saw each other rather than springboards for connection across their differences. It was then that we started to take our first steps toward formulating Skilled Dialogue.

First Steps: Beliefs, Qualities, and Skills   Anchored Understanding of Diversity (AUD) and 3rd Space were the two elements that first emerged as we started to conceptualize Skilled Dialogue. The first, AUD, addressed the need to anchor understanding of diversity experientially; the second, 3rd Space, focused on the need to integrate rather than polarize perspectives. The element of 3rd Space was reinforced when studying information on various cultures presented in a two-column format (i.e., Column A = characteristics of Group A, Column B = characteristics of Group B). "But we don't fit into only one column" was a frequent refrain that led to discussions of "either-or" frameworks as compared with what became known as 3rd Space frameworks. The refrain, "There is always a third choice" became a popular one. I (Barrera) will always remember the first time I was asked, "We have a test on Thursday and I can't be here, what is my third choice?"

Discussions of identities also led to the realization that a different kind of knowing resulted from face-to-face interactions as compared with those that resulted from learning about diversity in less personal ways. One particular instance stands out. In an intensive course in which religion and spirituality were discussed and which was coincidentally composed of approximately one third American Indian students, one third Hispanic students (Mexican American and Native New Mexicans) and one third nonethnically identified students, each group discussed their perspectives. At one point, the American Indian students were discussing their spiritual perspective that all of nature was sacred and "church" was not a single place. A non–American Indian student said, "That's true for me also," to which the American Indian students said, "But you worship inside a building." Several minutes later, as fixed ideas about each other emerged and were discussed, each group had a new and truer understanding of the other group's spirituality, as well as the awareness that stereotypes were not the property of any one population. The concept of AUD began to form as we struggled to find understandings that honored everyone's perspectives (after all, wasn't that our first and primary goal?).

Formulation of the Skilled Dialogue model presented in our 2003 text continued over several years. The two elements of AUD and 3rd Space remained the primary focus of Skilled Dialogue as we started to use it in teaching and staff development. We understood the significance of the two elements for working with culturally linguistically diverse populations, but we did not yet fully grasp how they might be taught or learned most effectively.

The Current Model: Operationalizing the Process   After the first edition of this book was published in 2003, the "fuzziness" of the two elements and of the entire Skilled Dialogue process was brought to our attention multiple times. We could communicate its spirit but did not yet have any really specific "how-to's." The questions provided in Chapters 5 and 6 of the original edition were as close as we could come.

"What does Skilled Dialogue look like?" "How does it work?" "Can it be made more concrete?" were questions asked repeatedly by practitioners at our workshops and in our classes. It was in response to these questions that we started to write our 2009 book.[1]

We continued to study practitioners whom we believed to be exceptionally skilled at working across diverse cultural parameters, testing various strategies and slowly crystallizing what subsequently became the strategies presented in the 2009 book. In doing that, we moved toward discussing Skilled Dialogue as an approach to diversity of all types and placed less emphasis on the source of that diversity. We enhanced its technology, specifying concrete strategies for each quality. As we increased our focus on these "how to's," though, we also felt that we risked making something that was intended to be an open and creative process

---

[1]Lucinda Kramer was the second author for the first book until approximately 2008, when she was unable to continue. She was, however, consistently involved in the training on Skilled Dialogue as much as possible.

into a prescriptive procedure, thus losing the spirit of Skilled Dialogue. And, in some cases, we saw that very thing happening.

The Current Revision   The current revision reflects our intent to integrate both the spirit of Skilled Dialogue, which was so much more present in the first edition, and the technology of Skilled Dialogue, which was so much of the 2009 text. Only through both can Skilled Dialogue meet its purpose as previously stated. The dispositions into which the original skills have been absorbed (see Chapters 5 and 6) play a critical role in this integration. They are, in many ways, the strongest bridge between spirit and technology. These dispositions are not simply good intentions, however. They are an ethic as defined by Kendrick: "values that have taken hold in people in some enduring way rather than just being abstract preferences" (2000, p. 5).

Ultimately, Skilled Dialogue is much more about a set of values than a set of skills, although the latter are essential to the expression of its values. We assert in the first deposition—Choosing Relationship over Control—that it is relationship, not expertise or status, that must set the context for the strategies. We extend that assertion in the second deposition—Setting the Stage for Miracles—by emphasizing that all perspectives are, ultimately, only facets of a single reality.

Our understanding and teaching of Skilled Dialogue continues to deepen and evolve, which is as it should be. It is our hope that your understanding and use of Skilled Dialogue will also continue to evolve as you study it and apply it to a range of situations in your work and your life.

Greater Acknowledgement of the Role of Culture and Cultural Diversity in Educational Settings   The past few years have witnessed a growing acknowledgment that culture and cultural diversity are significant variables not only in the children and families with whom practitioners work, but also across the individual practitioners themselves, even though there is still not enough of the latter. More sophisticated information on these topics has appeared in texts and materials on the market. Culture and cultural diversity have become common topics in early childhood texts (e.g., Trawick-Smith, 2010). In contrast to when we wrote our first edition, it is now almost rare to find a text on child development that does not somehow address culture and cultural diversity. In addition, the primary concern once focused mainly on the number of discrete ethnicities represented in a single school or classroom, and now there is a growing recognition that the equation of culture with singular ethnicities can no longer serve the practical needs of early childhood practitioners.

Parallel to this recognition is the acknowledgment that early childhood practitioners, many of whom teach in classrooms containing up to 15 different cultures, can no longer simply learn and reference specific cultural content (e.g., customs, foods) associated with discrete cultures or ethnicities. A simple revision of content is slowly being replaced by a deeper revision of strategies and implicit EuroAmerican Normative Culture (ENC)–based perspectives. Recognizing the multicultural nature of families, which has been long acknowledged outside of the educational arena (Seelye & Wasilewski, 1996), supports this shift in curricular design. Although listings of the perspectives, values, and behaviors of specific cultural communities remain useful, it is now more widely recognized by educators that few if any families can be characterized by listings restricted to singular cultural identities.

It is no longer enough to remain focused on ethnicity yet blind to culture. Nor is it any longer enough to think of cultural diversity as an exception triggered by the influx of this or that population into early childhood settings. The need to emphasize the pervasive nature of culture and to address it whenever one is discussing ethnic diversity has become imperative (Derman-Sparks, Ramsey, & Edwards, 2003). Similarly, every discussion of children's development, whether or not it is targeted to a specific population, must acknowledge culture's role in development if inclusion is to become the reality it is meant to be (Barrera & Corso, 2000; Rogoff, 2003).

Increasing Trend Toward Curricular and Instructional Standardization, Including the Use of Scripted Curricula Paradoxically, this second trend stands in tension to the first (i.e., greater recognition of diversity). It reflects an increased emphasis on uniformity and, consequently, an unexamined diminishment of tolerance for diversity in general. This development has significant, albeit mostly unacknowledged, implications for acceptance of cultural and linguistic diversity. Ironically, assessment practices are simultaneously moving toward less standardized formats that are more explicitly tuned into diversity (e.g., response to intervention [RTI]).

It is important to explicitly state that cultural diversity cannot and must not be divorced from diversity in general. There is a Zen saying and a book titled *How You Do Anything Is How You Do Everything* (Huber, 1988). These words reflect an important psychological truth. Cultural diversity is not a phenomenon divorced from diversity in general; it is, in fact, a manifestation of that very diversity. As we stated in our 2009 book, what people tend to find most challenging about cultural diversity is its very diversity (i.e., the fact that it deviates from familiar values and expectations). Our response to cultural diversity is, in fact, largely rooted in our responses to differences in general. A resistance to diversity of one sort (e.g., use of scripted curricula) inevitably contaminates responses to diversity of other sorts (e.g., curricula reflective of diverse communities). It sends, however unintentionally, a strong message that differences are not valued. When differences are valued, however, there is a tendency to value all differences, or at least, to reserve initial judgments.

Both the trend toward an understanding of culture as a pervasive dynamic and the one toward standardized curricula and instruction have significant implications for collaboration across cultures as well as for the use of Skilled Dialogue in the assessment and instruction of children identified as culturally and linguistically diverse in inclusive settings. Although we do not claim to resolve this dilemma, its presence has shaped our revisions, especially in the chapters on assessment and intervention.

New Research into Learning and the Brain Research into development and learning (e.g., brain function, social intelligence, mirror neurons, perception) has also influenced the need for this revision. Findings yielded by that research provided significant insights into the impact of practitioner–child/family interactions that are less than respectful, reciprocal, and responsive. Research into socioemotional intelligence, brain and biochemical functioning, and mirror neurons (Cozzolino, 2006; Goleman, 2006, Jaffe, 2007; Rizzolati, Fogassi, & Gallese, 2006), for example, is increasingly substantiating the fact that respect, reciprocity, and responsiveness are not just subjective qualities whose absence has minimal, if any, impact on children's behaviors and development. Rather, such research is finding that these qualities are external social markers with proven impact on internal biophysiological chemistry and, consequently, on development and learning.

Our response to these changing contexts, although not always explicitly addressed in this revision, has nevertheless significantly shaped its content. Although the first edition was the prequel to our 2009 book, *Using Skilled Dialogue to Transform Challenging Interactions,* this new edition can now be used as a sequel to that book. The more thorough description of Skilled Dialogue in the 2009 book remains essential, though, providing the backdrop and larger context for this revision's discussion of challenges more specific to cultural linguistic diversity. Each book thus provides its own perspective, yet is best understood when complemented by the other.

SPECIFIC CONTENT REVISIONS

The changing educational contexts as well as the changes in Skilled Dialogue model itself have all influenced the changes made in this second edition. Some of the more significant changes include the following.

- Clearer linkages between the Skilled Dialogue strategies explained in the original edition and those identified in the second 2009 text

- Inclusion of new material related to recent research and changes in education

- Reorganized material on the Skilled Dialogue process as applied to assessment and instruction

- Rewritten chapter on instruction

- Expanded material on culture and cultural diversity in relation to childhood trauma

- Updated references

Readers will note that we have also kept many of our original citations, even though many are now more than 10 years old. It was our decision to do this as the information they contain is still relevant and not available in newer editions or alternate sources.

DEFINITION OF KEY TERMS

Shared understanding of terms is a critical component of Skilled Dialogue. Common understanding of terms and concepts should never be assumed even when there is no evident diversity. Such understanding is even more critical when cultural linguistic diversity is present. Key terms are, therefore, briefly defined here as well as discussed in detail when addressed in subsequent chapters.

- *Cultural competence:* The ability to skillfully address communication and learning across diverse cultural parameters. It is more specifically defined by the authors as the ability to craft respectful, reciprocal, and responsive interactions across diverse cultural and linguistic parameters. It is their understanding that such competence is ongoing and not a static skill set to be mastered once and for all.

- *Cultural diversity/cultural linguistic diversity:* Behavioral, value, linguistic, and other differences ascribed to people's cultural backgrounds. Cultural diversity almost invariably includes some level of diversity in how language is understood and used whether a different language is spoken. The authors therefore use *cultural diversity* and *cultural linguistic diversity* synonymously.

- *Culture:* "The abstract values, beliefs, and perceptions of the world that lie behind people's behavior, and which are reflected in their behavior" (Haviland, 1993, p. 29). If human nature is the hardware, then culture could be considered the software that shapes behaviors and interactions.

- *Culture bumps:* The dissonance experienced when differing values, beliefs, perceptions, or behaviors come into contact (Archer, 1986; Barrera & Kramer, 1997). This dissonance can occur when one person behaves in a culturally influenced way that is unanticipated or judged as inappropriate by another (e.g., does not arrive at a scheduled appointment on time, does not ask direct questions).

- *Dispositions:* "A value, commitment, or an ethic that is internally held and externally demonstrated" (Cudahy, Finnan, Jarusiewicz, & McCarty, 2002).

- *Early childhood education:* Programs and services provided to young children from birth to age 8 years, including children with developmental delays/exceptionalities. May be inclusive (i.e., in typical early childhood settings) or segregated (e.g., in clinical settings).

- *Enculturation:* The process of learning the behaviors, language(s), beliefs, and roles common to one's first or home culture(s).

- *EuroAmerican:* Used by the authors in place of terms such as *White* to refer to native speakers of English with Northern European heritage who identify ENC as their primary cultural framework. Although EuroAmerican tends to include people with English, Scandinavian, and other such backgrounds, it can include people from French or Scottish backgrounds to the degree they would identify ENC as their primary cultural framework. An additional reason for using this term in place of *White* is that the latter is not culture specific and can refer to various groups of people, regardless of their cultural backgrounds (e.g., American Indians refer to all non-Indians as White).

- *EuroAmerican Normative Culture (ENC):* The institutionalized cultural norms against which cultural linguistic diversity is defined in the United States. This term has been chosen by the authors instead of more common terms, such as *White* or *European,* to highlight its reference to institutionalized cultural norms rather than to the personalized cultural frameworks of particular individuals.

- *Forestructure:* "What one has already learned and internalized in life, and the manner in which the learning has been organized in preparation for the future assimilation of something new" (Nakkula & Ravitch, 1998, p. 5).

- *Guiding beliefs:* Statements of beliefs that underlie and guide the Skilled Dialogue process.

- *Intercultural competency:* Competency not only in a particular culture(s), but also the ability to "translate" meanings/behaviors/words from one culture into another. Three particular skills have been identified by Fantini: 1) "the ability to establish and maintain relationships [across cultures]," 2) "the ability to communicate [across cultures] with minimal loss or distortion," and 3) "the ability to collaborate [across cultures] in order to accomplish something of mutual interest or need" (2001).

- *Minority:* People and/or communities that are accorded less social and political power by the group considered to be the majority or normative group within a particular country. Loosely related to actual demographic numbers.

- *Privilege:* When used as a verb, refers to the act of attributing more power or higher status to a behavior, value, or attribute than to another, as in "to privilege verbal skills over nonverbal skills."

- *Skilled Dialogue:* The process described in this book for communicating and interacting across diverse cultures or mindsets.

- *Skilled Dialogue dispositions:* Refers to two intentions prerequisite to the use of Skilled Dialogue strategies—Choosing Relationship over Control and Setting the Stage for Miracles.

- *Skilled Dialogue strategies:* The set of explicit attitudes and behaviors that give concrete expression to the Skilled Dialogue dispositions—Welcoming, Allowing, Sense-Making, Appreciating, Joining, and Harmonizing.

OVERALL TEXT ORGANIZATION

The organization of this edition's sections and chapters parallels that of the first edition and reflects Barrera's ways of thinking, which are rooted in a culture other than ENC, the culture common to academic and special education disciplines (cf., Kalyanpur & Harry, 1999). Figure 1 illustrates the organization of the sections and chapters of this edition.

The first aspect of this diverse perspective on organization is reflected in the nonlinearity of this text. Professional writing in academic and special education disciplines tends to mirror ENC's preference for linear and deductive organization (Hall, 1977; Stewart & Bennett, 1991). Written material from these disciplines is typically presented sequentially, one step at a time, with initial parts acting as building blocks for subsequent parts. This edition, however, is organized like the first in a less linear and more reiterative fashion, which some readers may find unfamiliar and/or uncomfortable. Ideas in one chapter are often revisited in subsequent chapters; the full substance of some ideas may not be clear until all of the material is read. Material in each chapter is cross-referenced to material in other chapters to facilitate links between ideas.

The extensive use of direct quotes, both within chapters and as initial thought-provoking introductory notes, is a second aspect of the book's organization that reflects Barrera's culturally diverse ways of thinking. Using quotes in this

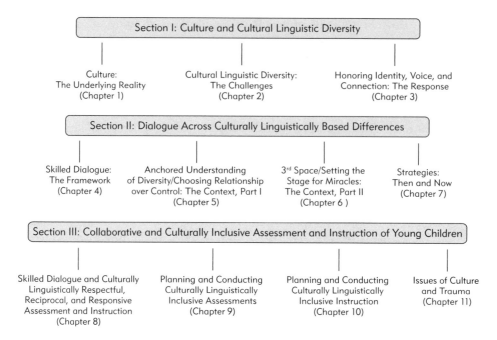

Figure 1. Organization of *Skilled Dialogue: Strategies for Responding to Cultural Diversity in Early Childhood.*

way reflects a culturally based perspective that privileges "distributed knowledge" (Goleman, 2006; Salomon, 1993). This perspective 1) understands knowledge as embodied and 2) recognizes that each person holds only one piece of a multifaceted truth. Although some readers may be unfamiliar with this type of organization, its consonance with the Skilled Dialogue model becomes clear as the text progresses.

CONTENT OVERVIEW

The overall content of this second edition contains much of the information from the first edition, with some significant differences in Section III. As a whole, it addresses three needs the authors have found to be critical to responding to culture and cultural linguistic diversity in ways that are not only respectful (i.e., honor diverse identities) but also reciprocal (i.e., honor diverse voices) and responsive (i.e., honor connection—the fact that diversity connects rather than divides). These needs can be briefly summarized as follows.

- *The need to understand culture before seeking to understand and address diversity.* It is all too common to assume a shared understanding of culture without checking to see if in fact that assumption is correct and/or to assume that culture can be accurately determined according to ethnic identity. Both of these assumptions unfortunately limit our subsequent ability to establish respectful, reciprocal, and responsive interactions with those diverse from ourselves.

- *The need to shift our understanding of differences from a polarized either-or perspective to an inclusive perspective with room for paradox.* Less recognized than the need just described, this need is nevertheless a critical one for which there is grow-ing scientific evidence. Either-or perspectives as well as their close relative—the both-and perspective—either do not connect differences or leave them merely side by side. Ultimately, each can gain access to or mine the contrasting and distinctive riches of one reality only at the expense of the riches of the other. Neither can move beyond compromise at best.

- *The need to learn how to craft respectful, reciprocal, and responsive interactions across diverse cultural and linguistic parameters rather than just acquiring knowledge about specific cultural communities.* This need underscores the fact that respectful, re-ciprocal, and responsive interactions across diverse beliefs, values, and per-spective cannot rely on knowledge of those beliefs, values, and perspectives alone. The challenges of diversity cannot be mastered with more knowledge because we may still be unable or unwilling to relate to someone else respect-fully, reciprocally, and responsively regardless of how much we know about their beliefs, values, and perspectives.

This edition, like the original edition, has three sections. Section I addresses the first need just described. It summarizes key information on culture, cultural di-versity, and intercultural competency. Chapter 1 focuses on culture as the reality underlying both teaching and learning in all situations and with all children and families. Chapter 2 discusses cultural diversity and its implications for creating inclusive early childhood environments that both gain access to and mine its re-sources, not just its challenges. Chapter 3 focuses on the three qualities key to Skilled Dialogue—respect, reciprocity, and responsiveness.

Section II addresses information relevant to the second need. Chapter 4 in-troduces Skilled Dialogue along with its key beliefs and qualities. Chapters 5 and 6 provide a bridge between our original conceptualization of Skilled Dialogue and the conceptualization that we discuss in our 2009 text. It focuses on AUD and 3rd Space, the two skills that originally defined Skilled Dialogue, describing them and their relationship with the newer dispositions of Choosing Relationship over Control and Setting the Stage for Miracles, which were discussed in the 2009 text. These remain important to understand, even though they are no longer explicitly addressed. Ex-amples of their use are provided. Chapter 7 is an entirely new chapter that briefly describes the strategies associated with the current Skilled Dialogue model and con-nects these with those in the first edition of this text.

Section III focuses on the third need. It addresses the application of Skilled Dialogue to specific early childhood assessment and instruction involving cultural linguistic diversity. This section has been largely rewritten and reorganized. Two of its chapters have been significantly revised to improve clarity and add new in-structional suggestions. Chapter 8 now includes more information on establishing collaborative and culturally inclusive interactions with children and families as a prequel to collecting initial assessment information. It focuses more specifically on the information gathering necessary prior to initiating assessment or instruction that involves any degree of cultural linguistic diversity, in contrast to the more typical practice of collecting the bulk of the information through assessment or instruction. Chapters 9 and 10 guide the reader through the considerations criti-cal to planning respectful, reciprocal, and responsive assessment and instruction. Both chapters provide a wealth of concrete suggestions and resources. Chapter 11 discusses issues of trauma, culture, and cultural diversity. Although these issues cannot be discussed in the comprehensive manner that they would be in a book devoted to them, the new and expanded discussion provides for a more complete exploration of issues associated with the complex interplay between culture, cultural diversity, and trauma.

Finally, this edition contains three appendixes. Appendix A, originally Appendix C in the first edition, contains photocopiable materials for practitioners' use and now includes revised as well as additional materials. Appendix B, originally Appendix D in the first edition, contains a summary of key guidelines for working with interpreters/translators and remains unchanged. Appendix C contains a new Skilled Dialogue self-assessment.

Culture and
Cultural Linguistic Diversity

Section I examines core concepts related to the challenge of communication and interactions across diverse cultural parameters. Chapters 1 and 2 focus on the foundational concepts of culture and cultural diversity respectively. Chapter 3 focuses on the idea of honoring identity, voice, and connection as a response to this challenge. This idea sets the stage for introducing Skilled Dialogue in Section II.

Culture

THE UNDERLYING REALITY

GUIDING
BELIEF
Cultural diversity cannot be adequately addressed if culture itself is not first understood.

At preschool, a EuroAmerican boy was playing with blocks. Nearby, Jasmine, the daughter of immigrant Latino parents, took one of the blocks that the boy was not using and began to play with it. The boy's response was to hit Jasmine, whereupon she began to cry. The teacher reprimanded the injured, crying Jasmine, admonishing her not to take the other children's toys.

It just happened that Jasmine's mother had been looking through a one-way window and observed the entire incident. She became terribly upset that the teacher not only failed to reprimand the boy for his act of aggression, but also scolded Jasmine for something perceived as completely normal in her household—sharing objects. (Greenfield, Raeff, & Quiroz, 1996, as cited in Rothstein-Fisch, 1998, p. 28)

DEFINING CULTURE

Although personality and temperament played some role in the interactions previously described, a deeper variable is also at work—culture and its associated perceptions of behavior. Though a detailed discussion of culture is outside the purpose and scope of this book, it is nevertheless critical to address at least those points that we have found the most useful in developing responses that honor diverse identities, diverse voices, and the connections that unite them, as in the situation just described.

The first point we need to address is a working definition of *culture*. All too often the literature related to early childhood and culturally linguistically

diverse families and children either does not define culture or equates it only
with ethnicity (Barrera & Corso, 2000). Both treatments distort its actual nature as a reality that applies to everyone in every situation, even when specific
ethnic variables cannot be identified.

Researchers listed more than 150 definitions of culture. Baldwin, Faulkner,
Hecht, and Lindsley called the definition of culture "illusive" and "a moving
target" (2006, p. 3) in their discussion on the various shifts in our understanding and study of culture from the early 1950s to today. They identified at least
seven distinct themes or foci in how culture is defined: culture as a "system or
framework of elements," culture as "a tool for achieving some end," culture as
a socially constructed process, culture defined in terms of artifacts, culture
as framed "as a sense of individual or group cultivation to higher intellect or
morality," culture as group-based power or ideology, and, finally, culture "in
terms of a place or group of people" (pp. 30–31).[1]

According to Malina,

> Culture is a system of symbols relating to and embracing people, things, and events
> that are socially symboled. Symboling means filling people, things, and events with
> meaning and value (feeling), making them [i.e., the symbols] meaningful in such a
> way that all the members of a given group mutually share, appreciate, and live out
> of that meaning and value in some way. (2001, p. 11)

Culture is the acquired learning of a group that gives its members a sense of who
they are, of belonging, of how they should behave, and of what they should be
doing; culture makes that group recognizably different from other groups.

These definitions address two points key in our discussion of Skilled Dialogue. The first is the assertion that culture is a group or social phenomenon;
that is, it is a system of symbols, behaviors, and values that operate at a social
level rather than at a purely individual level. Although culture is, of course,
expressed by individuals, its ultimate reality is social. Like gender, a tree, or
other similar categories, culture refers to a reality that cannot be defined or
contained by individual examples (e.g., a single tree cannot define or contain
the concept of treeness; a single person, male or female, cannot define or
contain the concept of gender). Malina's definition stated, "All members of a
given group mutually share, appreciate and live out of" (2001, p. 11) a given
culture's meanings and values, regardless of their individual personalities or
talents. Those personalities and talents may influence just how meanings and
values are expressed (and perhaps, which ones are favored), but they do not
create those meanings and values.

The external aspects of culture are driven by more internalized meanings.
Malina's definition explicitly addressed this symbolic nature of cultural content: "culture is a system of symbols" (2001, p. 11) (i.e., things that stand for

---

[1]Readers will find frequent references to literature outside the early childhood and education
fields. This reflects the fact that 1) much of the literature on culture comes from other fields and 2)
the perspectives from these other fields, through recognizing culture rather than merely diversity, lend
themselves to our conceptualization of Skilled Dialogue (see Chapter 2).

other things). The more visible aspects of a culture (e.g., handshakes) stand for or symbolize other less visible things (e.g., respect, friendship). Such specific behaviors and practices are part of the acquired learning that composes culture. They have value and meaning not only in themselves but also and perhaps more important in the degree to which they represent less visible things (e.g., respect, power). As such, behaviors and practices are secondary cultural artifacts; a fact that can be easily overlooked when we focus first on visible behavioral differences between people.

The seven ideas that follow expand on these points and introduce an understanding of culture from a Skilled Dialogue perspective. For additional information on culture, refer to the sources cited in the references.

1. **"All human beings are entirely the same, entirely different, and somewhat the same and somewhat different at the same time"** (Malina, 2001, p. 7).

Culture is one of three simultaneous realities within which people live: the universal, collective, and individual (see Figure 1.1). Little room for diversity exists within the universal level (e.g., human nature). Everyone is largely the same (i.e., we all have arms and legs, we all have a brain that works similarly to other brains at a physical level). The generic heart portrayed in a medical textbook reflects this limited diversity. In contrast, the individual level is the

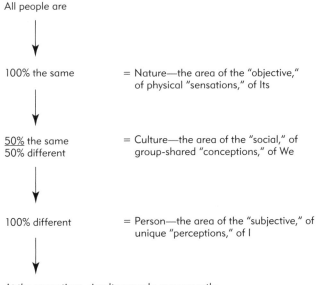

Figure 1.1. Similarities and differences spectrum. (From Malina, Bruce J. [2001]. *The New Testament world* [3rd ed., rev., p. 8]. © 2001 Bruce J. Malina; reprinted by permission of Westminster John Knox Press.)

most differentiated reality—everyone is unique, with little room for commonality (e.g., no two people's fingerprints are the same).

Culture resides at the collective level—at the interface between the almost total uniqueness at the individual level and the almost total similarity at the universal level. It is only at this level that its nature as a reality that simultaneously recognizes both uniqueness and similarity can be truly recognized. People are neither so unique that they have nothing in common, nor so human that they have only commonalities. It is at the collective level that recognizing culture facilitates, rather than impedes, avoiding stereotyping and maintaining connections (see Figure 1.1). As Malina noted,

> To understand your story adequately, I need to know not only the who, what, when, where, and how of your human nature and unique personhood, but also the whys and wherefores of our *commonly shared cultural story* [emphasis added] that gives mutually appreciable meaning and value to both [sic]. (2001, p. 9)

Following this understanding, Skilled Dialogue places great emphasis on understanding others' cultural stories as social artifacts expressed through particular behaviors though these do not totally define them.

2. There is a distinction between culture and cultures, just as there is a distinction between language and languages.

One may talk about language in general (e.g., all languages name things), or one may speak about specific languages (e.g., English uses nouns to name things). In the same way, one may talk about culture as a universal process (e.g., all cultures differentiate roles), or one may talk about specific cultures (e.g., one culture differentiates between the roles of parent and family decision makers and another does not).

Understanding both of these levels of definition is important. The first level (i.e., culture in a universal sense) emphasizes that all people are cultural beings. Everyone has a culture, whether he or she can name that culture and whether that culture can be ethnically identified.

It is at the second level, however, that the distinctive behaviors, values, and meanings shared by a particular group are found. Understanding a specific culture encourages honoring the rich gifts that diversity offers within precise contexts. All cultures, for example, develop strategies for building relationships. The gifts of diversity, however, lie in the particular strategies developed by particular cultures, which enrich our strategic repertoire as well as our understanding of diversity.

Focusing only on the uniqueness of individual cultural groups distorts the true meaning of culture as a reality shared by all human beings, just as focusing only on certain languages distorts the meaning of language as a human phenomenon. Also, focusing only on similarities across groups erases the very concept of cultural diversity, just as focusing only on commonalities across languages can blind us to the unique strengths of an individual language.

The paradox of commonality and uniqueness and similarities and differ-ences is discussed further in Chapter 6, which introduces 3rd Space—a skill essential to Skilled Dialogue that focuses on the importance of holding two dissimilar or even contradictory ideas in one's mind at the same time. This skill is relevant not only to understanding the relationship between culture and cultures and the relationship between uniqueness and similarity, but also to learning how to transform contradictions into complementarities.

3. Cultures are mental models or paradigms developed by communities over time to make sense of their physical, emotional, and social environments and to determine how best to operate within them.

Solomon and Schell referenced an early statement by Geert Hofstede, a cultural anthropologist, who called culture the "software of the mind" (2009, p. 49). This metaphor reflects the nature of culture as a mental model or para-digm for navigating the contexts in which we live rather than as just a cluster of distinctive behaviors.

There are multiple and equally valid models or cultures, just as there are multiple and equally valid languages. A culture is more than just observable beliefs, behaviors, or values, just as a language is more than just the sounds and words produced. Each culture is rooted in a deeper, less visible reality—the unique worldviews or paradigms that structure and sanction communi-ties' ways of perceiving, believing, and evaluating reality. Some cultures, for example, support a worldview in which human beings are superior to all other creatures; others support a worldview in which human beings are servants of creation. These worldviews are not directly visible but can be inferred from more visible behaviors.

The aspects of culture that are most easily perceived (e.g., foods, behav-iors) are only surface manifestations of deeper, less visible ways of perceiving, believing, and evaluating reality developed by a particular community or so-cial group. For instance, respect for elders—a valued aspect of interpersonal behavior in many cultures—can be a manifestation of a deeper worldview that understands personal experience rather than written text as a source of knowledge and wisdom. That same belief, though, could express a worldview that privileges power hierarchies. Figure 1.2 outlines the layers of culture, showing that particular funds of knowledge, including those related to per-ceptions of self and power, lie beneath surface manifestations. In turn, these funds are shaped by worldviews born of a community's shared experiences across families and generations.

Although the layers of culture can be discussed separately, they are inex-tricably linked. Any change at one level affects all other levels. A request to change a behavior such as indirect eye contact is more than a simple request to change a behavior. It simultaneously touches on the deeper realities that determine the value and meaning of that behavior (see Chapter 2). The most persistent challenges posed by cultural diversity are often linked to the deeper,

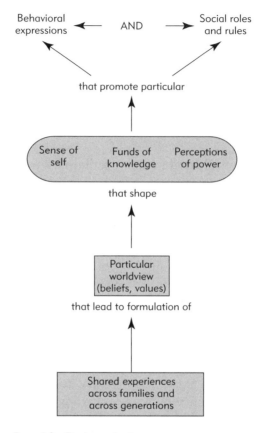

Figure 1.2.   The layers of culture.

less visible aspects of culture, which must be recognized and acknowledged if our interactions with others are to truly honor their identities and voices.

4. **People learn and internalize "sets of cultural cues that lead [them] to perceive, feel, act, believe, admire, and strive in ways that make sense to [them] as well as to others" (Malina, 2001, p. 16) who share these cues.**

People are thus enculturated into particular ways of being. Children may be enculturated into more than one culture, just as they may learn more than one language at a time. They learn particular cultural cues and ways of perceiving, believing, and evaluating reality from their primary caregivers and others whom they perceive to be significant in their early lives. For example, in early childhood, children learn from family members to perceive particular behaviors as appropriate or inappropriate. As children observe adults they perceive to be significant (e.g., mother, father, grandparent), they learn that certain characteristics are more admirable than others and that certain behaviors carry more positive or negative value than others. It is difficult to overestimate the degree to which individuals' ways of perceiving, feeling, acting, believing, admiring, and striving are based on the cues designated as important by the culture(s) of their primary environments as expressed by the significant adults in their lives. The influence of these early learnings about what is right, appropriate, or respectful persists even after children leave the environments in which these learnings occurred. Just as children learn the language(s) they speak from others almost unconsciously, they also learn the beliefs and behaviors that they "speak" and assume that these are the most appropriate.

Individuals will need to learn a different set of cues more consciously when they move out of the environments in which they were raised and into environments with different ways of perceiving, feeling, acting, believing, admiring, and striving. This process is usually termed *acculturation* rather than enculturation. Speaking a second cultural "language" with the same fluency as the first can be difficult, but it can be done with intention, persistence, and much practice. It also takes the ability to "decenter" and learn to see things from perspectives other than our own (see Chapter 6).

5.   There are levels of culture and levels of participation in cultures.

Although culture is often depicted as an iceberg with two levels, one visible and one hidden, Solomon and Schell went a step further. They identified three levels of culture: visible culture, hidden culture, and core culture. Visible culture is "the outer layer of culture: what people say and do, how they dress and speak, their architecture, offices and behavioral customs" (2009, p. 64). This tends to be the layer that first catches our attention.

Hidden culture is "the middle layer of culture: the values, beliefs, and philosophy that define a culture, such as attitudes toward time, communication, and religion and notions about good and evil" (Solomon & Schell, 2009, p. 64). Although less visible, this layer is one that is also commonly recognized by early childhood practitioners, albeit one whose specific characteristics are more difficult to identify in particular situations.

The third layer—core culture—is one that tends to be less explicitly recognized or distinguished from the second. It is the layer that is the most out of our conscious awareness and, thus, often the layer that gives rise to the strongest challenges. It is

> The invisible layer, composed of the principles that drive the middle level, principles that most people take for granted. Core or invisible culture harkens back to the essence of people's innermost beliefs about universal, nonnegotiable truths that were learned in childhood and retold generation to generation. (Solomon & Schell, 2009, p. 65)

Core beliefs (e.g., whether there is good and evil, whether the world is benign or harmful) lie at this level. An interesting example is the perception of multiple identities. Multiple identities are often laughingly disparaged in EuroAmerican Normative Culture (ENC). "I'm Heinz 57" or "I'm a mutt" are responses we often get at workshops when we introduce discussions of cultural identity. In other cultures, however, multiple identities are described much more positively. Mexican culture, for example, speaks proudly of its Spanish and Indian mix, discussing the strengths of each as the core essence of being Mexican. Core culture is the layer that defines this and other realities for people. Its content tends to be perceived not as a cultural product but as the perception of things as they really are. When challenged, people tend to respond as if truth itself is challenged.

There are, as well, levels of participation in particular cultures. That is, cultural identity is not a simple "I-am-this-or-I-am-that" phenomenon. Except for an increasingly small segment of people, everyone participates in one or more cultures to a greater or lesser degree. In fact, "many millions of people have their roots in two or more distinct cultures" (Seelye & Wasilewski, 1996, p. xvii). Ethnic labels identify some but certainly not all of these cultures. Many may have no clear labels. Kalyanpur and Harry referred to Banks when they discussed culture as

> A complex picture of micro and macro levels whereby the macrocultural framework is an overarching national frame [e.g., Hispanic, American] that includes many microcultural groups [e.g., Mexican-American, Puerto Rican] each of which participates to varying extents in the macroculture. (1999, p. 4)

The terms *Hispanic culture* or *Asian culture,* for example, refer to an overarching cluster of beliefs, values, practices, and language associated with more than a single community or heritage. In addition, individuals participate in any particular culture to varying degrees depending on a variety of factors (e.g., family history, personal experience). Compounding this participation is a simultaneous participation in one or more additional cultures outside of the overarching culture (e.g., American Indian, ENC). Individuals and communities thus reflect, but do not ever completely define, a macroculture. Such a culture, in fact, exists only at an ideal level, much as do the concepts of elm tree or cat, for example. These cannot fully define any individual elm tree or cat. Similarly, *Hispanic, Chinese,* or *American Indian* cannot define any individual Hispanic, Chinese, or American Indian person. At the same time, overall identity cannot be fully defined without reference to cultural identity anymore than an individual can be fully defined without reference to gender. This is the dialectic relationship between the collective and the individual level that was previously discussed.

6. **Culture functions to connect groups as well as to distinguish them. "In addition to the goal of guidance, culture serves other individual and social functions. It fosters a sense of belonging, which serves to maintain or build an identity among a group" (Baldwin et al., 2006, p. 38).**

Maintaining the coherence of groups, with survival as a guiding goal, is one function of culture. Cultural models are initially rooted in the practices and beliefs a group perceives as essential to their survival and welfare.

Cultures thus set parameters that connect people within a group. These very same parameters, however, also unavoidably distinguish one community from another. Speaking Spanish, for example, simultaneously serves to connect people who speak Spanish with each other and to distinguish them from those who do not speak Spanish. This dual aspect of culture makes sense when it is placed on the similarities and differences spectrum (see Figure 1.1). Like a combined centripetal and centrifugal force, culture acts to keep the necessary balance between connection and separation. The challenges posed by cultural diversity are grossly inflated when either function is addressed at the expense of the other.

7. Personal and group histories simultaneously enhance and limit the degree to which children and families gain access to and express cultural values.

Personal and group experiences shape how culture manifests in particular contexts and lives. These experiences can enhance or limit one's access to the specific ways of perceiving, believing, evaluating, and behaving within a group. For example, if these experiences include grandparents who share rich stories about family and tradition and patiently teach the ways and words of their culture, then one's access to that culture is enhanced. Conversely, if one has collectively or individually experienced trauma, then his or her access to such culturally distinct experiences may be reduced—possibly by choice.

Individuals as well as whole cultural communities experience trauma in a variety of ways, sometimes from other communities and sometimes from geophysical elements. DeVries discussed culture in this context as a "double-edged sword" (1996, p. 400). He first stated that "the power of culture as a protector, integrator, and security system is evident in studies [on] cultural assimilation" (1996, p. 400). He then went on to say,

> When the cultural defense mechanisms [e.g., mourning rituals] are lost, individuals are left on their own to achieve emotional control. Traumas that occur in the context of social upheavals, such as revolutions, create a profound discontinuity in the order and predictability that culture has brought to daily life and social situations. (1996, p. 400)

All cultural discontinuity, whether personal or collective, affects individuals' ability to gain access to and express cultural values, beliefs, and behaviors that serve as protectors, integrators, and security systems (van der Kolk, McFarlane, & Weisaeth, 1996). This loss of full access to cultural values, beliefs, and behaviors can also happen when shame or trauma becomes associated with cultural membership (e.g., when one is ridiculed for not speaking English). The interface between culture and trauma, unfortunately, has not been addressed in any extensive fashion. Chapter 11 addresses it in more detail because of its influence on access or nonaccess to individuals' cultural content.

These seven points are addressed only briefly in this text. Nevertheless, they are critical to the development of dialogic competence in situations in which culturally based values, beliefs, and behaviors are significantly different. A common theme running through all seven points is the paradox and dialectic between individual, universal, and communal variables. Coming to terms with the multiplicity of these variables and the complexity of their interplay in particular interactions is a critical aspect of Skilled Dialogue.

IMPORTANCE OF ADDRESSING CULTURE BEFORE ADDRESSING CULTURAL DIVERSITY

Discussions of culture in early childhood special education (ECSE) literature tend to make diversity rather than culture their primary focus. Barrera and Corso's (2000) extensive review of leading journals addressing early childhood issues found that few articles explicitly defined or addressed culture in any substantive manner. Most articles in this study addressed culture minimally, if at all. Readers' understanding of culture and its dynamics was most often merely assumed.

The discipline's perspective on culture was most telling in the fact that culture was seldom addressed at all unless the article specifically targeted ethnic or culturally diverse children and families. Studies on motor development, for example, contained no mention of culture unless it was their stated purpose to study motor development in diverse populations. Such neglect of cultural reality sends the implicit message that it is not a significant variable outside of these populations. Yet, studies documenting the role of culture in all areas of child development do exist.

A statement from Trawick-Smith in an early childhood text was fairly representative of this emphasis on diversity over culture itself.

> Professionals must come to understand, appreciate, and show sensitivity to those differences [in the ways children from different cultures communicate and interact with adults and peers] as they interact with children and families. They must devise ways to provide their students with knowledge of people of other cultures and with positive and significant cross-cultural experiences. (2010, p. 11)

Although these statements are absolutely correct and appropriate, an emphasis on culture itself might result in the following rewording.

> Professionals must come to understand, appreciate, and show sensitivity to cultural dynamics in the ways children from all cultures communicate and interact with adults and peers as they interact with these children and their families. They must devise ways to provide their students with knowledge of their own culture and how it affects their behavior as well as knowledge of how other cultures compare and contrast with their own and with positive and significant cross-cultural experiences.

Making only differences the focus of learning subtly conveys the idea that culture is only about differences and that, therefore, knowledge of it is not important in the absence of differences. Children learn only about others and not about how culture deeply affects their own perceptions and interactions.

In addition, focusing primarily on differences between groups and groups identified as culturally diverse, without also acknowledging the more general, shared dynamics of culture, is somewhat akin to attending to gender (differences between individual human beings) without first paying attention to being human. This inverted attention ironically risks the divisive responses that recognizing diversity is designed to eliminate.

Focusing primarily or solely on cultural diversity implicitly holds one population as constant or normative (e.g., ENC) and assesses others against its standards. Such a focus by necessity splits how "you are not like me" from how "you are like me," limiting the development of a perspective that takes both similarities and differences into account simultaneously without privileging one over the other. Although informative, a diversity-first focus literally takes differences out of context and places them center stage—limiting communication at best, polarizing diverse perspectives at worst.

Responding appropriately to cultural diversity requires that one first understand the meaning of culture and how it functions within us as well as within others. Learning about cultural diversity starts with recognizing that what one person considers normative and the truth is at the same time "entirely the same, entirely different and somewhat the same and somewhat different" (Malina, 2001, p. 7) from what others consider normative and true. Varied human behaviors and beliefs can then be better understood and accepted in their own right as valued and deeply rooted expressions of self and community, not only as contrasting behaviors and beliefs. Only when culture itself is understood can differences be respected without sacrificing the connections that unite them.

Take, for example, the behavior of not asking direct questions. It may easily be judged as less effective than the more valued ENC behavior of asking direct questions when examined out of context as an isolated diverse behavior. This behavior, however, can be perceived in its own right as a highly effective choice that expresses values held by a particular group or community when understood as one of an interconnected cluster of behaviors reflective of a community's culture. Practitioners can then acknowledge such behavior as a strategy that functions as effectively within a given cultural context as any alternative developed by another community within its context. In addition, the connection between both direct and indirect styles of communication can be better appreciated.

We cannot effectively address diversity (i.e., differences in what we learn and how we learn) until we understand culture (i.e., what we learn and how we learn). Changing individual behaviors without attention to their cultural context jeopardizes the coherence of related behaviors as well as individuals' sense of self and power, which drive their motivation and capacity to learn. Someone entering a new culture, for example, may learn to bow instead of shaking hands but, without understanding the hidden and core aspects of that behavior, may well continue to perceive bowing as a subservient behavior and never learn the cultural nuances that dictate its proper use—or the connection between both as expressions of respect. A similar phenomenon can be seen when one learns a new language and attempts to understand its puns and metaphors without having experienced the larger cultural context within which these are set.

The implicit or sometimes still quite explicit pressure on families with diverse home languages to speak only English with their young children is another example of focusing on diversity before understanding culture. This pressure ignores the cultural context that is inextricably linked with the home language. Changing one's language is about much more than merely substituting English words for other words; it changes many other things as well, such as what we talk about and how we talk about it (Chen & Starosta, 2005). Limiting a family's language usage in this way diminishes adults' ability to sing familiar lullabies to their children, tell them traditional stories and pass on wisdom from one generation to another, or share observations of the world around them. How can parents teach their children to perceive and name colors when they can no longer use familiar words for those colors, words that evoke not only labels but also the experiences of those colors, such as the blue of a butterfly's wings or the rose-tinted sky of an early dawn? The words shift but the memories and emotions remain attached to the words first learned (Fishman, 1996). Such limitations diminish the emotional, cognitive, and linguistic richness of caregivers' interactions children, which can subsequently disconnect them not only from their own identity but also from the larger contexts in which they are being asked to function. They also inevitably diminish the emotional, cognitive, and linguistic richness of varied perceptions of the world for all of us (see Chapter 2).

Only when placed within its proper context of culture can cultural diversity be appreciated for what it is—the reflection of human creativity and wisdom expressed in particular ways. Its gifts can only emerge to take their place beside its challenges as we understand its source and its function in relation to development and learning.

CULTURE'S RELEVANCE TO DEVELOPMENT AND LEARNING

As previously discussed, culture is a pervasive dynamic that influences every aspect of one's perceptions and interactions with others. The behaviors we pay attention to and the meaning we attribute to them are all culturally conditioned (Chen & Starosta, 2005). Even the colors we perceive are culturally contexted. Not all cultures, for example, have words that distinguish pink from red. They might have different words for blue and light blue instead. This aspect of culture's affect on perception and learning is seldom discussed in early childhood curriculum that lists developmentally appropriate concept development.

Where, for example, is the concept of *educación*, a Spanish word that has no association with schooling or degrees, on the developmental continuum?

Where is the development of the concept and practice of shared ownership of toys as understood in the Mexican culture? It is the lack of acknowledgment of culturally referenced development such as reflected in these examples that results in scenarios such as the one given at the beginning of this chapter.

All cultures, by their very natures, channel knowledge, values, and social mores from one generation to another (Greenfield & Cocking, 1994; Phillips, 1994; Polk, 1994). Culture shapes and patterns our ways of thinking, relating, and perceiving as well as our ways of child rearing, our teaching practices, and our selection of curricular content. Cross-cultural literature provides examples of the critical connection among culture, development, and learning. Greenfield and Cocking noted, "The key fact about human culture is its intergenerational transmission through the socialization process" (1994, p. 3). All children are socialized into particular languages, roles, and rules through the process of enculturation to prepare them for successful participation in their communities (Damen, 1987; Phillips, 1994). Values, perceptions, and beliefs are passed from one generation to another, implicitly through modeling, as well as explicitly through messages such as, "This works; it's good" or "That doesn't work; it's not good."

Goldhaber noted the relevance of culture to development and learning rather succinctly—research findings "led contextually-oriented researchers to become disenchanted with the notion of identifying universal context-free measures of development or even valid ways of making developmental comparisons across cultures" (2000, p. 327). He then added,

> Vygotsky is arguing for the recognition of the particular structure of culture as defining not only the content of an individual's development but also the very structures through which this content functions. That is, development always evolves out of an individual's immersion in specific culturally defined activities, practices, and rituals. (p. 327)

A family's template for promoting development and learning is inextricably rooted in its cultural funds of knowledge (Moll & Greenberg, 1990; Velez-Ibañez & Greenberg, 1992), which Moll and Greenberg compared with an "operations manual of essential information and strategies households need to maintain their well-being" (p. 323). These operations manuals are contained within and transmitted through a community's culture (Landrine & Klonoff, 1996; Trumbull, Rothstein-Fisch, Greenfield, & Quiroz, 2001). Some might even say that culture is a set of these manuals tailored for and by a particular community. This raises serious concerns when only one such manual is institutionalized in curricular standards and expectations.

Who is family and who is not comprises a specific fund of knowledge, for example; yet, the content of this fund differs across cultures. In some homes, children are taught to recognize and name close family friends as family (e.g., *tía* or *tío;* auntie). In other homes, even people who are biologically aunts or uncles are not tied closely to the family. In some cultures, social intelligence is valued more than linguistic competence—the size of a child's vocabulary at age 4 is valued much less than whether he or she can properly welcome and greet visitors and relatives. The variations are endless and fortunately need not all be learned behavior by behavior.

> Culture isn't random. It consists of distinct and logical behavior patterns. These patterns form the framework for analyzing culture, and once you understand that framework, you can use it to predict the [most probable] way people will respond in a variety of situations. (Solomon & Schell, 2009, p. 51)

The process of learning one's first culture in early childhood is termed *enculturation*. As previously stated, however, children often need to function in more than one culture; that is, they may need to learn how to use more than one set of cultural frameworks. Acculturation is the parallel process to enculturation. It refers to acquiring additional funds of knowledge for functioning outside of one's home culture. According to Damen, acculturation "involves the process of pulling out of the world view or ethos of the first culture, learning new ways of meeting old problems, and shedding ethnocentric evaluations" (1987, p. 140).

The difference between enculturation and acculturation roughly resembles the difference between learning a first and second language. Enculturation generally is not as stressful as acculturation. The modeling and nurturing of significant caregivers within one's home culture support learning. There are often, however, varying levels of stress associated with the process of acculturation (e.g., Igoa, 1995; Landrine & Klonoff, 1996). Asking young children to acquire funds of knowledge unfamiliar to them or not valued at home can challenge their emotional and cognitive resources. This is especially so when the degree to which children are still mastering a home culture is not adequately recognized. Although acculturation is certainly necessary in today's multicultural world, one's degree of understanding about its cognitive and emotional demands can significantly affect the difficulty or ease with which it occurs. Energy that would ordinarily be available for learning must be shifted into coping mechanisms when children feel torn between two worlds or when unfamiliar expectations are not explicitly explained.

A LOOK AHEAD

This chapter only opens the door into the aspects of culture and our approach to it, which can shift our understanding of diversity from a teaching/learning challenge to a teaching/learning asset. Chapter 2 explores the challenges of cultural diversity and discusses different components of culture common to all people and how these may differ across groups as well as within groups. A cultural data table is introduced for subsequent use in identifying cultural data for individual children and families. Chapter 3 completes this first section by focusing on how we can honor diverse identities and voices as well as the connections that unite them.

Chapter 2

Cultural Linguistic Diversity

THE CHALLENGES

Cultural diversity is a dynamic and relational reality that exists between people rather than within any single person. Its challenge lies not so much in different behaviors as in the diverse meanings attributed to those behaviors.

As Anna breast-feeds her 18-month-old child, she sees other mothers around her following the same practice. Her behavior stems from cultural templates that she learned as a child. Anna herself was breast-fed until she was 2 years old as were her sisters and the children of her neighbors and extended family. Breast feeding is a valued practice that is considered the norm in her culture. All credible people around her advocate it as a desired and valued practice.

Doris also breast-feeds her 18-month-old child. Doris's behavior, however, stems from a more conscious choice. She belongs to La Leche League International. Although other mothers in La Leche League breast-feed their older children, most of Doris's relatives and friends do not advocate this practice. Doris was not herself breast-fed after 6 months of age. Many "experts," including her own relatives, disagree with Doris's choice.

An early childhood practitioner who believes in ceasing breast feeding to develop children's self-feeding skills would face distinct challenges in working with these mothers. Decreasing or ceasing breast feeding would carry different meanings for Anna and Doris. Although both mothers might consider cessation negative, Anna would also consider this abnormal or at least contrary to accepted practice. To change her behavior would mean going against all that she believes and has experienced since childhood. It also means risking almost certain censure from her family and community. Doris, however, has a framework for understanding the argument behind cessation. She might even have access to specific literature sup-

porting an early shift to bottle feeding. In addition, Doris probably knows other
mothers who do not breast-feed their older children. Discontinuing breast feeding
would certainly go against Doris's beliefs, but it would not challenge her world-
view and would carry a small risk of censure from her family and community.

This vignette illustrates how differences between two people from different
cultures lie not only in different behaviors, but also, and perhaps more significantly, in the meaning given to those behaviors within social contexts as well
as in the actual or perceived risks associated with changing them (Barrera &
Kramer, 2003; Chen & Starosta, 2005; Landrine, 1995). The risks of changing
one part of a system without understanding the whole have been well documented in relation to ecology (Childs, 1998). The very meaning of the word
ecology refers to an interconnected system within which each part acts in con-
cert with the others. Culture is also such an interconnected system.

The most prominent challenge posed for early childhood practitioners by
cultural diversity lies not merely in understanding the specific behavioral differences between groups, but in understanding the meaning associated with
these differences and the actual or perceived risks in changing them. That
is, of course, assuming that a valid reason exists for encouraging a behavior
change in the first place (see Section III).

Learning to believe and trust that unfamiliar ways of supporting children's development and learning can be as effective as familiar ones is a second challenge posed by cultural diversity. Lack of trust is often the primary
reason for urging change. For example, pushing parents to enforce a set bedtime ignores the evidence of healthy child rearing in many cultures that do
not enforce set bedtimes. Barrera, for example, did not grow up with a set
bedtime. This practice worked within the context of other culturally determined and interconnected variables (e.g., being put to bed within earshot of
parents and grandparents talking and cleaning up the kitchen in preparation
for bed themselves).

Trusting diverse child-rearing practices can be a difficult challenge for
many early childhood practitioners, however, especially as literature in the
field tends to support a single normative way of supporting development. Yet,
assuming that there is only one way to support development and learning can
frequently—and unnecessarily—lead to miscommunication between practitioners and families. It may even end up inhibiting desired development and
learning as interactions and opinions become polarized and cultural contexts
are disrupted.

When early childhood practitioners believe that parents must change a
particular behavior(s), it is critical to first ask whether that assumption is rooted
in an ethnocentric perspective (i.e., one valued only within one culture) or
in more general developmental concerns that are valid across cultures. Sometimes, for example, a practitioner may strongly believe that parents should
stop carrying their 2-year-old child with delayed motor skills so that the child
will be motivated to learn to walk. In situations such as this, it is important

to examine whether that belief reflects best practices or an ethnocentric non–research-based assumption that carrying children past a certain age inhibits their motivation to walk. In a cultural context in which most children are carried until they become too heavy and still learn to walk, such an assumption invalidates not only the individual perspectives of the families involved; it also invalidates the larger cultural perspective within which they function.

Although it may sometimes indeed be necessary to invite family members to encourage a child's walking, such encouragement should not implicitly or explicitly communicate that the family's current culturally sanctioned practices are developmentally inappropriate. The latter encouragement, however well-intended, can lead to cultural shaming. Telling families that, "This practice is inappropriate," is quite distinct from saying, "I'm wondering what you think about encouraging Rosie to walk a bit more," or "I'm wondering whether perhaps more time walking independently would help Rosie. What are your thoughts about that?"

The first message (i.e., that culturally based practices can inhibit development) can all too easily be heard as a judgment of incompetence, a perception exacerbated within cultural contexts where the correction of adult behavior is seen as shaming and where the family involved may have experienced similar situations repeatedly. The second message, in contrast, communicates respect and opens dialogue. It invites a sharing of perspectives within which the families' voice is given equal validity to the practitioners' voices. It is in situations such as this, where seemingly opposing practices (i.e., carrying, walking) need to be simultaneously honored, that Skilled Dialogue becomes most essential (see Section II).

There are, of course, situations in which culturally sanctioned practices may indeed need to be identified as inappropriate (e.g., corporal punishment). Even in these cases, however, practitioners can respectfully acknowledge the community or cultural value placed on the practice while sharing information about alternatives and the consequences for not changing. When state law judges a practice abusive, the legal implications of continuing that practice also need to be discussed.

DEFINING CULTURAL LINGUISTIC DIVERSITY

Differences between people may be perceived and explained through a variety of lenses such as personality, trauma experiences, gender, and personal history. Culture is only one lens that can be used in seeking to explain and understand differences in behavior. It is a primary lens in that many of the other lenses acquire their value and meaning from the cultural context within which they are defined (e.g., gender is understood differently and involves different behaviors in one culture as compared with another). This book's focus on culture should not, however, be interpreted as discounting or devaluing other sources of diversity.

Many people use the term *cultural diversity*[1] to identify differences perceived to stem from racial or ethnic heritage or identity without examining or controlling for actual differences in specific behaviors, languages, values, and beliefs (Barrera & Corso, 2000). That is, cultural diversity is presumed once group identity is determined. For example, one group of researchers at a national conference reported data for African American families based on a clustering of families that had immigrated from Africa and the Caribbean, as well as families born and raised in the United States—presumably because all shared a racial identification.

At first glance, a definition of cultural diversity based solely on stated ethnic or racial identity may seem adequate. It is easy to take one's understanding of cultural diversity for granted and move on to the more urgent issue of dealing with the challenges that such diversity poses for practitioners. Doing that, however, risks perpetuating several assumptions that inhibit optimal responses to cultural diversity in early childhood environments:

1. The assumption that cultural diversity is a static quality inherent in individuals based on their ethnicity—an assumption that leads to labeling and stereotyping

2. The assumption that cultural diversity can be reliably determined by ethnicity—an assumption that ignores the nature of culture as a universal social process common to all people

3. The assumption that because only certain ethnically identified groups are discussed ethnicity is somehow the problem, posing a risk that must somehow be lessened or reduced—an assumption that limits practitioners' ability to appreciate diverse practices and gain access to their potential as a positive resource

Responding optimally to cultural diversity in early childhood environments involves questioning these assumptions. The following subsections address aspects critical to understanding cultural diversity in a more respectful, reciprocal, and responsive fashion.

Diversity Is a Relational Reality that Depends on Who Is Involved

Diversity is both relative and inclusive. That is, it depends on who is involved (e.g., are they similar or not) and it is not the property of any single person (e.g., if I am diverse from you, then you are automatically diverse from me). Deceptively simple, the statement that diversity is both relative and inclusive is a significant one in learning to respond to the challenges it poses in early childhood settings.

---

[1]As noted in the Introduction, the authors use *cultural diversity* and *cultural linguistic diversity* synonymously.

No person in and of him- or herself can be identified as diverse. The question, "Can this family be identified as culturally diverse?" cannot be answered without adding, "As compared with whom? This practitioner? That practitioner? The culture reflected in early childhood practices and curricula? The family's neighbors?" The most accurate answers to the initial question, therefore, can only be, "Perhaps, in relation to these people or that environment" or "Probably not, in relation to these other people and that other environment."

All of us are, in fact, diverse in relation to some people and some environments, just as all of us are tall or short, depending with whom or what we are compared. At the same time, all of us are also not diverse in relation to other people and other environments (e.g., girls in a group of other girls are not diverse in terms of gender). Diversity is a dynamic and relational quality, sometimes present and sometimes not, depending on context.

All too often, however, early childhood literature addresses diversity as a static characteristic that is true of only certain people (e.g., lists that discuss only certain ethnically or racially identified groups: Hispanic but not Amish or Swedish American).[2] The characteristics of these people are then defined as being diverse independent of their context (e.g., someone who is Swedish American is presumed to be nondiverse or at least not diverse enough to make it into discussions of cultural diversity in early childhood literature). A simple example illustrates the shortcomings of such a perspective.

A practitioner is introduced to an East Indian family whose members are not fully English proficient and asks, "Would you identify this family as culturally diverse?" The practitioner might say yes because this family's beliefs and behaviors differ significantly from his or her own or from those of other families with whom he or she works. The practitioner cannot truly answer accurately, however, until the family is placed next to another family or in a particular environment. If that second family or environment also conforms to East Indian culture and is not fully English proficient, then the answer would be, "No, it's probable that the two families are culturally similar" (i.e., neither can be judged to be culturally diverse from the other). If, however, the second family or environment to which this first family is compared conforms to Chinese American culture, then the practitioner could answer, "Yes, in all probability, each family can be considered culturally diverse from the other."

This example illustrates a key aspect of diversity—its relativity. No single person can be said to be diverse, culturally or otherwise, except in reference to other people or environments. Diversity, unlike some other characteristics (e.g., hair color, height), cannot exist independently of its context. Recognizing this point is essential to responding respectfully to cultural diversity and honoring those who are diverse from us.

Cultural diversity is also inclusive. When a person names particular children and families as being culturally diverse, that individual must simultane-

---

[2]This is true of much of the literature in education but not of literature in other disciplines.

ously also name him- or herself as diverse from them. Calling "them" culturally diverse without also calling "me" culturally diverse fails to recognize the
relational aspect of diversity. It implicitly assumes a hierarchy of power within
which only the namer has the privilege of setting the norm and not needing
to change. The imbalance of power inherent in such an assumption undermines cultural competency as effectively as explicit racism. A firm foundation of trust cannot be established when families and children detect that a
practitioner perceives only one context as normative (i.e., as all right and not
needing to be changed). Respectful communication is weakened or cannot
occur at all.

Ethnic Identity and Differences Are Only Indicators of Cultural Diversity

Ethnic identity is personally, socially, and politically important. Educationally,
however, specific behavior and linguistic values and characteristics, rather
than ethnic identity per se, need to be recognized and addressed. Ethnicity
is only one indicator of the possible presence or absence of particular behavior and linguistic characteristics. It is not, however, the sole or most reliable
indicator. Although cultural diversity stems from culture, which is a group
or social variable, it cannot be defined solely or reliably by membership in a
particular group or community.

For example, a university professor and father who identifies as Navajo
yet follows no traditional Navajo practices may not be similar to other parents
who identify themselves as Navajo and follow traditional Navajo practices. The
fact that this father may identify as ethnically Navajo certainly has important
implications. Yet, can he be accurately judged as culturally diverse from a parent who identifies as ENC solely on that basis? Perhaps he was adopted and
raised in New York by parents who were both Swedish; or perhaps he was
raised by biological parents who left the reservation as young children and did
not retain either the language or practices associated with the Navajo culture.

The same question could be asked of a non–American Indian parent who
does not identify as Navajo but has lived on a Navajo reservation from childhood and participates extensively in traditional Navajo practices. Would this
person be considered culturally diverse from other Navajo families simply
because he or she cannot identify as ethnically Navajo? These are not simple questions. They represent a complex reality, as explained by Seelye and
Wasilewski:

> You are stretched between cultures when you have been raised in a multicultural
> household or when you have lived for years in a second (or third) culture where you
> are dependent on doing things the local way if you are to survive. (1996, p. 6)

It is important, therefore, to look beyond ethnicity to a family's values, beliefs, and behaviors, which may or may not be consonant with that ethnicity.

The cultural or ethnic identity that an individual holds for him- or herself is relatively static. How much that identity differs from others holding the same identity, however, is more fluid. It is this comparison that determines the degree of cultural diversity that an individual or a group experiences or that is attributed to that individual or group.

A person can be ethnically diverse and yet not be culturally diverse in their neighborhood school. An example would be a Hispanic child who was adopted from Latin American parents at birth and is now being raised by monolingual English-speaking parents who identify themselves as Jewish and Scandinavian. A person might believe this child is highly culturally diverse, whereas another may not perceive him or her as significantly culturally diverse (e.g., as a child fluent in English raised within a strong traditional Jewish culture). The combination of possibilities is endless and ever changing. From this perspective, cultural diversity is present only when there is "the probability that, in interaction with a particular child or family, the [practitioner] might attribute different meanings or values to behaviors or events than would the family or someone from that family's environment" (Barrera, 1996, p. 71).

What ultimately determines the degree of cultural diversity is not so much whom a person identifies with ethnically but rather the specific behavior and linguistic characteristics exhibited in that person's interactions with others. This does not negate the person's ethnicity; it only determines the degree to which that ethnicity can be a reliable indicator of diversity. Omitting this understanding increases the probability that responses to children and families identified as diverse will be based on generalities attributed to a group rather than on individuals' specific characteristic.

Cultural Diversity Is Never the Problem to Be Addressed

Cultural diversity is often discussed as a problem that needs to be addressed. In fact, cultural diversity is never problematic in and of itself. It is instead the response of individuals and institutions to diversity, or the lack thereof, that can be problematic. For example, having little or no proficiency in English in an environment where only English is spoken is not a problem in and of itself. Limited proficiency in English only becomes problematic when accommodations are not made (e.g., not offering to translate or to seek a translator, not teaching English or learning the other language, not seeking alternative means of communication). Granted, speaking English in a monolingual English-speaking environment has a decided advantage. That does not, however, mean that not doing so is a problem.

Within a social environment where individuals—no matter how different or similar to others—are truly respected and validated, diversity's true nature as a strength and resource eclipses perceptions of it as a problem or risk factor. It is essential to perceive diversity as a rich source of multiple options.

Biologists have begun to understand the essential nature of what they term *biodiversity*. Nabhan noted the necessity of appreciating and maintaining diversity in nature, culture, and story by quoting D.M.J.S. Bowman: "So what is biodiversity? My belief is that the variety of life on the planet is like an extraordinarily complex, unfinished, and incomplete manuscript with a hugely varied alphabet, an ever-expanding lexicon, and a poorly understood grammar" (1997, p. 20). Losing that manuscript, Nabhan affirmed, shortchanges all of us as well as the planet on which we live. His plea to appreciate and sustain biodiversity speaks eloquently to appreciating and sustaining cultural diversity.

In the magazine *Cultural Survival,* MacIntosh made a striking comment that echoes this understanding of diversity: "There are nine different words in Maya for the color blue in the comprehensive Porrua Spanish-Maya Dictionary but just three Spanish translations, leaving six butterflies [whose true color] can only be seen by the Maya" (2001, p. 4). This may perhaps seem to be a minor loss, until we understand its logical extension. When we lose words, we also lose the knowledge they contain. A different word for hyperactivity, for example, might provide unimagined responses to its strengths, responses inaccessible as long as it is defined as "hyper" or "too much." How might we perceive persistent questioning if we lost the word *curiosity,* for example?

In a statement whose full power has yet to be recognized, Seelye and Wasilewski noted correlations between genetic diversity and cultural diversity. In both cases, unexpected resources can be found when templates that lie outside the norm are explored.

> Cultural diversity enriches our ability to survive. Just as "irrelevant" genetic mutations may be on call within our DNA, individuals with different cultural viewpoints may be on call within our societies to aid the group in adjusting to life's changing conditions. Diverse, multiple perspectives—even unpopular ones—offer humans an important mechanism for survival. (1996, p. 16)

PRIMARY CHALLENGES POSED TO PRACTITIONERS BY CULTURAL DIVERSITY

Cultural diversity, like all diversity, requires that practitioners exercise their abilities to appreciate variety and respond to a wide range of behaviors and beliefs respectfully and reciprocally, whether in teaching and learning situations or in social ones. This global challenge can be further broken down into more specific challenges such as communicating across different languages or needing to differentiate a behavior indicative of disability from one that reflects unimpaired ability. For easier understanding, these specific challenges can be clustered into three common types.

Practitioners face challenges of information when they have insufficient information about the cultural dimensions in which people are most likely to encounter differences. They may remain unaware of differences and the associated need to identify them. Challenges of judgment and interpretation emerge as individuals strive to understand and interpret the meanings associated with particular behaviors. Practitioners may well identify differences yet remain unaware of the varied meanings they carry. Challenges of relationship, which are acknowledged less frequently than the other two challenges, are generated when connections across differences are not recognized. In such instances, people remain unaware of or fail to acknowledge the dynamics of power and social positioning that influence every interaction and, thus, remain limited in their skills to address them. The following sections detail each of these challenges.

Challenges of Information

Dissonance and discomfort often result when insufficient or different information exists about another's behavior. Archer introduced the concept of a culture bump, which "occurs when an individual from one culture finds himself or herself in a different, strange, or uncomfortable situation when interacting with people of a different culture" (1986, pp. 170–171). Barrera and Kramer (1997) applied this idea to cultural diversity in ECSE environments, defining *culture bump* as the cognitive and emotional dissonance experienced between people when differing values, beliefs, or worldviews come into contact. It is this dissonance, rather than the differences themselves, that holds the core of this challenge.

Culture bumps signal unfamiliar territory. Some may find such territory exciting and stimulating; others may find it confusing, irritating, or even frightening. Culture bumps tend to have both visceral and cognitive dimensions because they mark the boundaries of understanding and/or tolerance. A practitioner may, for example, have a strong negative emotional reaction to a parent who asks questions that seem too personal (e.g., "How many children do you have?") or to a parent who is repeatedly late for sessions. An analysis of common experiences across cultures indicates that most culture bumps result from dissonance across one or more of three cultural dimensions that underlie how cultures frame reality—funds of knowledge (Moll & Greenberg, 1990; Velez-Ibañez & Greenberg, 1992), sense of self, and perceptions of power.

Cultures selectively support and value particular beliefs, values, languages, and behavioral expectations. Moll and Greenberg used funds of knowledge to refer to "specific knowledge of strategic importance" (1990, p. 323) to members of a community or culture. Analogous to cultural capital (Lubeck, 1994), this concept refers to the depth and breadth of knowledge associated with a particular cultural context(s).

It is through their culture's funds of knowledge that people learn who they are and how to act (i.e., acquire a sense of self). For instance, is being independent a highly valued skill? Or, is learning how to interact well with others and live in harmony a more important skill?

Perceptions of power are equally influenced by culture, though perhaps more subtly. Does being highly verbal confer power? Or, does it place one's credibility at risk? Some cultures value the first, whereas others believe the second.

Directly or indirectly, cultures shape assumptions, biases, and stereotypes about what is important and valuable within each of these dimensions. Table 2.1 illustrates the content of each dimension in relation to three areas common to early childhood curricula—communicative-linguistic, personal-social, and sensory-cognitive. Questions are provided for use in exploring each dimension in relation to self and others. Table 2.2 presents specific examples of culture bumps within each of the three dimensions, which are organized around the same three curricular areas. The cultural data table discussed later in this text (see Chapter 8) was developed around these questions and bumps as an instrument for assessing the degree and nature of cultural linguistic diversity that may be present in a particular situation.

Table 2.1. Cultural dimensions underlying common culture bumps related to developmental/curricular areas

Developmental/ curricular area	Cultural dimensions		
	Sense of self	Funds of knowledge	Perceptions of power
Communicative-linguistic	What do I consider the relationship of language to identity? How does my language and communication maintain my sense of self? What are values and rules for the use of personal and family names?	What language(s) do I speak? What do I consider the roles and rules for use of language and communication? How do I define the relative value of verbal and non-verbal communication? How is literacy perceived? To what degree is oral literacy valued? Written literacy?	How do I express/maintain power through language? What status is given to the language(s) I speak? What has been my experience as a speaker of this language (or these languages)?
Personal-social	How does my sense of self play out in social interactions and settings? Who do I believe I am (individual identity)? How do others see me (attributed identity)?	What is my understanding of social roles and rules? What do I consider appropriate behavior? What degree of importance do I give to the individual? To the community?	What has been my experience of power in relation to the larger society? Peers? Authorities? Others? In what situations do I feel competent/ powerful? In what situations do I feel unskilled/powerless?
Sensory-cognitive	What does *identity* mean to me? What characteristics do I believe are essential to sense of self? What is the relationship of self to the larger environment (i.e., one's place in the world)?	What are my values/beliefs concerning • Ways to best teach/learn • How the world works • Ways to best solve problems and make decisions What is my worldview?	How do I define *power*? How do I believe that it is acquired and exercised? What do I believe confers power on a person? To what degree am I conscious of my own power?

Table 2.2. Common culture bumps in relation to developmental/curricular areas

Developmental/ curricular area	Common culture bumps
Communicative-linguistic	The language used by practitioners and/or reflected in early childhood environments (e.g., CDs, posters) may be different from that used in the child's home, so the family may have difficulty communicating with providers and supporting desired activities and interactions. Also, the family may feel unwelcome or shamed.
	The child may have limited or no proficiency in the language used by practitioners and/or reflected in early childhood environments (typically English). He or she may be unable or limited in ability to understand and respond to verbal interactions and directions. This affects self-esteem and sense of competence as well as communication.
	The rules and strategies for using language that child and family have mastered may differ from those assumed by the practitioner, resulting in miscommunication and confusion. For example, a child or family member may fail to "speak up" because he or she is waiting for pauses that are, according to their values and experiences, long enough.
	The roles and rules for sending and receiving nonverbal messages may differ between the family and the practitioner. One common example is corrections: In some cultures, corrections between adults are always nonverbal, if at all possible. Another example are signals for entering a group conversation. In some cultures, one must wait for a silent pause of several seconds; other cultures teach listeners to listen to intonation rather than silence as a signal that it is okay to speak.
	The family's/child's culture may value nonverbal communication over verbal communication. For example, family members may send silent behavioral messages that they are confused or wish to stop interaction rather than say so in words.
	The language spoken in the child's primary caregiving environment may be perceived to have a lower status than English. Sending this message—whether intentionally or unintentionally, explicitly or implicitly—can have a negative impact on learning and intergenerational interactions.
	The definition of *family* differs across cultures. Who is in a family? What is the function of family? What roles are essential to family? All of these answers and more describe how the concept of family is structured and defined within a particular culture. Even when the same word is used in the same language, miscommunication can occur. Bumps may occur when similar concept structures and definitions are assumed. This may be particularly troublesome when translating concepts (e.g., *education* and *educación* are not equivalent words).
Personal-social	The family/child may be unfamiliar with, may not value, or may not understand behaviors and beliefs that are common to EuroAmerican Normative Culture (ENC).
	The family/child may be unfamiliar with, may not value, or may not understand professional early childhood cultures and may not exhibit expected behaviors such as arriving on time.
	The family/child may have a different understanding of what "self" is and how "self" functions. Many common early childhood concepts, such as autonomy, presume a particular sense of self. A child may, for example, appear to have trouble "detaching" from his or her mother because such detachment is not part of the child's or family's cultural repertoire related to "self" and how "self" should function.
	Identity and competence are defined differently from culture to culture. Families may have different perceptions from practitioners and, thus, may appear to have difficulty understanding or accepting intervention goals.

(continued)

Table 2.2. *(continued)*

Developmental/ curricular area	Common culture bumps
Personal-social	Developmental goals and expectations can differ significantly across cultures, as can norms for "good" parenting. Differences in beliefs and experiences in this area can trigger major difficulties between families and caregivers.
	Families/children from culturally diverse groups that have been identified as social and political minorities may have had negative or shaming experiences that influence their interactions with practitioners. Practitioners may discount the power of their own position, and, consequently, misunderstand interactions with families and children.
	The sources of assistance and support that individuals seek may be different across cultures. Reliance on extended families is one example. Families have skills for gaining access to resources within their cultural contexts—for instance, they may be quite skilled at approaching family members but have fewer skills for "interviewing" professionals to determine which one best suits their needs.
Sensory-cognitive	The areas and kinds of knowledge that are valued can differ across cultures. ENC, for example, tends to value early verbal proficiency; other cultures (e.g., Mexican American) value early social skills. Families may, for example, not value the early verbal labeling of colors or shapes found in many early childhood curricula.
	The family/child may value, and promote, certain learning strategies over others. Some cultures value and promote modeling over direct questioning strategies, for example. Family/child may be unfamiliar with, may not value, or may not understand strategies used by early childhood practitioners.
	The family/child may value certain strategies for problem solving and decision making (e.g., going to the family elder, imitating a peer) that are not common to early childhood settings and interactions and that may seem, consequently, "wrong," ineffective, or inefficient.
	The family/child and practitioners may have strikingly different conceptions of how the world works. Beliefs about health are one example. Are diseases caused by germs or by displeasing a higher power? Worldviews are seldom explicit; they are composed of what individuals take for granted as "the way it is."

Challenges of Judgment and Interpretation

Beyond the challenges posed by insufficient or conflicting information are challenges posed by the diverse meanings and values attached to specific beliefs and behaviors. Everyone depends on predictable patterns and familiar scripts for interactions with others (e.g., a script for greeting a person one has not seen for a long time). The culture bumps generated by cultural diversity result from disruptions of these patterns and scripts. Familiar behaviors, for instance, can carry different meanings in different cultures. Such behaviors can both confuse and confound, and they can easily be misinterpreted, distrusted, or misjudged.

For example, initiating a task-specific conversation without first establishing rapport through more general conversation can be misinterpreted as an indication of insensitivity in cultural contexts other than those to which this pattern is common. The converse—spending time in general conversation before addressing a specific task—can be misinterpreted as wasting time in cultural contexts that value the first. While serving as director of an early intervention program in South Texas, the first author experienced an example of this dissonance. The social worker for the on-site birth-to-3 program had been born, lived, and worked in South America. Many of the families with whom she worked were monolingual Spanish-speaking Mexican Americans who shared similar values and beliefs with her. In addition, several parents had little or no formal schooling, and several were recent immigrants from rural areas of Mexico. The early childhood intervention environment was unfamiliar and significantly different from environments that they knew how to negotiate. The program's social worker started a morning crochet class to get the parents involved and exchange critical information about their children, which was an immediate success. She established a strong rapport with these parents, and both obtained and shared needed information through easy conversation while crocheting. After a few classes, however, the principal asked the social worker why she was wasting time on crocheting during school hours. The social worker explained that the behavior carried a different meaning in the Hispanic culture. It was perceived as a social context that did not make the parents uncomfortable, which would have been perceived as disrespectful and shaming. As such, the classes were a highly efficient way for the social worker to accomplish the goals for which she had been hired.

This example illustrates the challenge of judgment and interpretation of behaviors across cultural contexts. Eliminating or at least minimizing incorrect behavioral interpretations as well as the negative judgments and miscommunications that occur as a result of those interpretations lies at the core of this challenge.

Stated positively, cultural diversity challenges us to interpret unfamiliar behaviors from the perspective of the culture associated with them and, in doing so, honor those who exhibit them. Understanding and anticipating culture bumps is relatively easy. Compassionately responding to them, however, can be difficult, especially when differences challenge strongly held values or beliefs. For example, if a speech-language pathologist (SLP) encountered a family that valued nonverbal communication over verbal communication, then how could he or she respond to the needs of their child, who demonstrates a significant language delay according to both the practitioner's and the parents' assessments? As another example, how might a practitioner react to a mother who continued to dress and feed her 3-year-old child in many situations?

Challenges of Relationship

Challenges of relationship are rooted in the issues of power and social positioning that accompany all interactions, especially those within the human services professions. These issues have received less attention within ECSE than within other related disciplines, such as bilingual special education and multicultural education (Cushner & Brislin, 1996; Delpit, 1995; Gollnick & Chinn, 1990). Yet, it is ultimately the challenge of recognizing issues of relationship and becoming responsive to them that determines whether one's interactions will yield successful (i.e., culturally responsive) outcomes.

Darder said, "In order to understand the relationship between culture and power we must also comprehend the dynamics that exist between what is considered truth (or knowledge) and power" (1991, p. 27). All cultures judge certain behaviors, values, and beliefs as more powerful or more desirable than others. These are consequently associated with higher social status than other behaviors, values, and beliefs. Some cultures, for example, value being highly articulate over being a quiet observer. These cultures "privilege" verbal skills over observational ones (e.g., would consider a highly articulate person more competent than a quiet one).

Beliefs and behaviors are always value laden. Therefore, one cannot competently respond to cultural diversity without also examining issues of power and social positioning. Using the term *minority* is one example that reflects these issues. A notion (and reality) of privilege underlies the classification of certain populations as minorities,[3] even when this is not the case numerically. Populations identified as culturally linguistically diverse are typically those considered to hold minority status. This is not a coincidence. When compared with the culture that sets institutionalized norms, these populations typically experience reduced voice and participation (Darder, 1991; Delpit, 1995; Gollnick & Chinn, 1990). This is most often attributed to lack of familiarity with those norms. An even stronger reason, however, is the privileging of certain behaviors and attributes over others and the consequent status and power accorded to only those who exhibit these behaviors and attributes. Authors such as Cummins (2000), Skutnabb-Kangas and Cummins (1988), and Wildman (1996) have addressed this issue.

It is important to recognize the degree to which cultural diversity challenges EC/ECSE practitioners to examine the role that privileging certain behaviors plays in their perceptions of and interactions with the children and families they serve. The short vignette that opened this chapter is one example. It is critical to ask questions such as the following in such situations and other similar ones.

- How do practitioners perceive families' behaviors as being different from their own? As of similar or more or less value?

- How do practitioners respond to these diverse behaviors when children or families exhibit behaviors that they personally do not consider desirable or that are not considered desirable within ENC?

- To what degree do early childhood practitioners acknowledge the power that they hold in relation to the families/children with whom they work?

---

[3]As noted in the Introduction, the term *minority* is used throughout this book to denote social and political realities, which may remain in place even when groups attain majority status numerically.

- When offering an assessment of families' behaviors, do practitioners communicate that certain behaviors differ from what they consider most effective? Do they communicate that families' behaviors are wrong without questioning the validity of such judgments?

These are not comfortable questions to ask. They are, nevertheless, essential questions to ask in crafting respectful, reciprocal, and responsive interactions with children and families different from ourselves.

It is also important to recognize the degree to which families' and children's past experiences with power and privilege influence their perceptions of and responses to practitioners' behaviors. The dynamics of power and social positioning are instrumental in shaping the experiences of cultural uprooting, disruption, and shaming, which are unfortunately familiar to many families and children from minority populations. Igoa spoke to this in relation to immigrant children:

> When one engages in a thorough investigation of the child's environment, intellectual and emotional failures often are found to be a result of undercurrents between the child and adult and/or institution wherein the child feels unloved, unchallenged, and disempowered. (1995, p. 8)

In a seminal work, Jalava (1988) addressed this reality through a powerful poem that captures aspects of cultural disruption and the consequent shaming. The words poignantly reflect the feelings of a Finnish mother who has recently immigrated to Sweden and is now finding that she cannot communicate with her 3-year-old child in Swedish—the language that has become the privileged language for that child. Practitioners who are more fluent in English than parents with whom they interact must be careful not to reenact this scenario however unintentionally. Messages about language status are easily sent by who uses which language and the arenas in which each language is used.

The relationship challenge is one that involves issues of power and social positioning. Its affect is sobering. It cannot be neatly split from the other challenges posed by cultural diversity, regardless of how uncomfortable it may be to address.

RECOGNIZING AND ATTENDING TO THE CHALLENGES OF CULTURAL DIVERSITY IN INCLUSIVE EC SETTINGS

It is important to examine why there is a need to recognize and attend to the challenges posed by cultural diversity to practitioners in early childhood environments. Is such recognition and response necessary only when significant numbers of certain cultural groups are present? Is it important for all children or only for some? Three reasons for recognizing and responding to cultural diversity are discussed next.

Responding to Shifting Demographics

Demographics is the most common reason given for recognizing and attending to the challenges to practitioners posed by cultural diversity. Increasing numbers of children and families who are culturally linguistically diverse are present in all communities (Federal Interagency Forum on Child and Family Statistics, 2011; Garcia, 2001).

It was once possible to live out one's life in a community where everyone spoke the same language, held similar values and beliefs, and followed similar practices. That scenario has almost disappeared in every area of the United States. In the 21st century, children from groups currently considered culturally diverse constitute a significant presence in U.S. schools (Brice, 2002; National Center for Education Statistics, 2007). It is believed[4] that there are a greater number than ever of children and families in early childhood environments with limited English proficiency and/or limited familiarity with the values, expectations, and behavioral norms common to institutionalized aspects of these settings. As a consequence, there is an ever increasing probability that early childhood practitioners will serve children and families whose language(s) and culture(s) differ from their own. The probability that practitioners' familiar ways of communicating and interacting will no longer be sufficient to respond competently to these children and families is ever rising.

Unfortunately, there can be an implicit (and sometimes explicit) "we need to pay attention to cultural diversity to meet their needs" dimension to this reason. Certainly, the ability to respond to shifting demographics more appropriately and competently is one of the benefits of recognizing and responding to cultural diversity. Nevertheless, recognizing and attending to cultural diversity in early childhood environments is important mainly because it is critical to meeting the needs of all children, not only those identified as being culturally linguistically diverse. Similar to the arguments used to support inclusive services for children with exceptionalities, the benefits to students who are not culturally linguistically diverse can be as important if not more so. Learning to interact respectfully, reciprocally, and responsively across diverse cultural parameters is an essential skill in a world that is growing ever smaller.

The number of children and families with languages and worldviews diverse from those reflected in early childhood curriculum and environments, though important, should not be primary in determining the need for paying attention to cultural linguistic diversity. Supporting the developmental needs of all children and implementing appropriate and responsive curricula for all children are equally if not more compelling reasons for attending to the challenges of cultural diversity. Diversity is, after all, only the inverse of uniqueness.

---

[4]Current numbers tend to be compared with statistics without reference to data from the late 1800s and early 1900s, when it was common to find significant percentages of families that spoke languages other than English in many parts of the United States (Takaki, 1993).

Supporting Children's Developmental Needs

The earliest essential condition for continued development following birth is that the child and those who care for him or her must become coordinated in such a manner that the adults are able to accumulate enough resources to accommodate the newcomer (Cole, 1998).

The key phrase in this quote is "become coordinated." Becoming coordinated with an infant's rhythms of moving and talking, for example, requires a common fund of knowledge about those rhythms. An example of culture's role in such coordination comes from an early intervention practitioner working with a Korean infant. This practitioner described her frustration in trying to soothe the infant when he became fussy. She would hold him and rock him, but the infant would only become more agitated. One such time, the infant's aunt observed the interaction. She quickly reached for the child and began to jiggle him up and down rapidly. He quickly quieted. The aunt explained that rocking a child gently from side to side was done only prior to nursing or feeding from a bottle. The practitioner had unknowingly added to the infant's frustration by signaling that food was forthcoming when it was not. She could not coordinate her movements with the infant's needs.

Having behaviors and beliefs mirrored and valued by significant adults is one of the core needs of all children. As Brazelton and Cramer noted, "Mirroring is a fundamental dimension of the development and maintenance of a healthy self-image" (1990, p. 12). More research into actual neurological phenomena (Jaffe, 2007; Rizzolatti, Fogassi, & Gallese, 2006) only emphasizes the affect of such mirroring on the development of a sense of identity as well as to optimum cognitive and emotional development. Josselson (1994) referred to "eye to eye validation," the heart of which is being known and recognized for who one truly is. Recognizing cultural parameters (e.g., language, values) is a key component of such validation. Children's needs and strengths can only be appropriately identified relative to cultural and social experiences (Kendall, 1996; Rothstein-Fisch, 2003).

Confusion and shame may result, often with concomitant delays or disruptions in learning and development, when children do not find a sufficient degree of culturally responsive mirroring and validation (Donovan & McIntyre, 1990; see Chapter 11). Family members are the main source of such mirroring and validation. They are the most important caregivers and role models in the eyes of their children. External institutions and communities, though, also play a critical role in supporting or inhibiting mirroring and validation. The presence and modeling of practitioners in the home, as well in educational and other settings, can significantly support or inhibit the development of identity and language. This is especially so with children and families from populations who may have already experienced the invalidation or negative mirroring of their language, values, beliefs, and behaviors.

Having one's identity and experiences acknowledged, mirrored, and validated in environments outside of the home is being increasingly recognized as an important factor (Bredekamp & Copple, 1997; Koplow, 1996). Brazelton and Greenspan (2000), for example, identified the importance of cultural continuity and made three critical points, which summarize this discussion. First, they stated, "Communities and cultures provide the context or framework for the other irreducible needs that we have discussed" (p. 159). They then pointed out that "the reference points for subtle emotional meanings are always stronger in one's basic language" (p. 161), thus encouraging the use of home language in interactions with young children. Finally, they concluded that programs "succeed or fail to the degree to which they are sensitive to cultural needs and the degree to which people who are a part of the [children's] culture shape them" (p. 171).

This is not to say that children should see only their own cultural values, practices, and home language mirrored. It is in fact to advocate for the opposite for all children. The witnessing of a variety of "mirrors" is beneficial as children begin to develop their emotional intelligence in relation to those different from themselves. Although there is little to no literature on this point as yet, it is a logical inference from the more general literature on emotional and social intelligence. Welcoming differences as resources begins in early childhood. In addition, the ability to hold more than one perspective in one's mind at the same time is a critical aspect of cognitive flexibility and mental health.

Developing Appropriate and Responsive Curriculum

As early as 1994, Bowman and Stott remarked, "Cultural differences can lead teachers to misunderstand children, to misassess [sic] their developmental competence, and to plan incorrectly for their educational achievement" (p. 121). It is clear that a sound and developmentally appropriate curriculum cannot be developed without first understanding and attending to children's unique (i.e., diverse) characteristics as well as to the unique (i.e., diverse) funds of knowledge that they bring with them to educational interactions.

Developing appropriate and responsive curriculum for all children does not require learning a new set of pedagogical principles. Rather, it requires a deeper understanding of existing principles. A key pedagogical principle, for example, advocates "beginning where the child is." Only through understanding developmental expectations and experiences associated with specific cultures can one truly determine a child's status in relation to particular goals and interventions. For example, what is the best curricular response when an Inuit child does not demonstrate age-appropriate understanding of the rules of participating in small-group activities (from an ENC perspective)? Is it developing activities to teach small-group participation? Is it simply allowing the child's current behaviors? Is it developing activities that both honor current behaviors and expand the child's existing funds of knowledge to include rules for this setting? The answer selected by a practitioner will depend on the degree to which that practitioner acknowledges and understands cultural diversity (see Section III).

Other pedagogical principles espouse attention to varying teaching and learning formats according to variations in children's learning and development (Bearne, 2002; Edwards, Gandini, & Forman, 1995; Forsten, 2002). This can be done most competently when the range of teaching formats and learning styles valued in various cultures is understood and appreciated. On one hand, for example, a Hispanic child whose attention regularly wanders during reading circle may, in fact, have attention problems and need specific strategies that attend to such problems. On the other hand, it may simply be that the practitioner is not physically close enough to the child, unaware that interpersonal distance in Hispanic culture signals when it is or is not acceptable to pay attention.

Practitioners' understanding and application of pedagogical principles all too often reflect only their own cultural context (Bowers & Flinders, 1990). Understanding and adjusting multiple cultural contexts clarifies the relevance of these principles for all children, including those identified as culturally linguistically diverse. Familiarity with the range and complexity of cultural contexts is an invaluable aid to competently answering questions such as the following:

- What books should I include in my early childhood library?

- To what degree should I use one-to-one activities as compared with small-group activities?

- To what degree should I support reliance on following a mother's lead as compared with promoting independent problem solving?

- Should I organize my activities around relatively formal schedules?

- To what degree should I rely on verbal response formats in activities?

Unfortunately, there are relatively few resources that discuss cultural contexts from this perspective. Rothstein-Fisch (1998) gave several cogent illustrations of how understanding cultural diversity affects curriculum and pedagogy. One involves two children who perceived a discussion about eggs from two different perspectives. One child shared "the teacher's value orientation," which dictated that eggs be described as isolated physical entities (e.g., white, oval, breakable). The second child, from a different culture, assumed that the teacher "was interested in the object as a mediator of social relationships," as would be true in her home culture. This child wanted to "talk about how she cooked eggs with her grandmother" (p. 30). Without recognizing and attending to the cultural diversity that generated such distinct perceptions, it would be easy to simply label one response as right and the other as wrong. Doing so, however, would prevent the expansion of existing skills and perceptions not only for the child from the dissimilar culture, but also for the child who shared the teacher's culture.

Of course, there are risks to making cultural diversity the primary lens for assigning meaning to behaviors and events as well as to discounting culture and cultural diversity as variables that significantly influence behaviors and events. The former perspective can result in stereotyping when not nuanced; the latter results in cultural "melting," which also obliterates individuals' identities. As stated in earlier discussions, people cannot be defined solely by their cultural identities, yet neither can they be adequately defined without some degree of reference to these identities.

Chapters 3 and 4 address the tension between cultural and individual identities and introduce the qualities of dialogue—respect, reciprocity, and responsiveness—that enhance practitioners' responses to diversity by promoting the honoring of diverse voices and identities as well as the connection that unites them.

A LOOK AHEAD

This chapter initiated a discussion of cultural diversity, which continues in the next chapter as the initial elements of responding to such diversity are presented. Chapters 4, 5, and 6 discuss the Skilled Dialogue framework as it has grown out of these elements. These latter chapters also discuss the link between the skills identified in our 2003 text—Anchored Understanding of Diversity (AUD) and 3rd Space—and the dispositions given in our 2009 text—Choosing Relationship over Control and Setting the Stage for Miracles.

Chapter 3

Honoring Identity, Voice, and Connection

THE RESPONSE

Mrs. Tahiti went to her daughter Rachel's early childhood program to meet with Ms. Clemson, the program's SLP. With the assistance of an interpreter, Mrs. Tahiti told Ms. Clemson that she had a question about advice she had received the previous year. "I was told to speak to Rachel in English more often at home. That's very hard for me because I am not as comfortable speaking in English as in Tagalog, my own language. Should I stop using Tagalog? How can I best help my daughter develop strong communication skills?"

This anecdote illustrates in concrete terms three key questions posed to practitioners by cultural linguistic diversity.

1. How can diverse identities be honored? That is, how can respect for what others believe, think, and value be communicated when it seems that it is these very things that are at the root of what it seems needs to be changed?

2. How can diverse voices (i.e., expressions of those diverse identities) be honored? That is, how can practitioners establish interactions across differences where there is no explicit or implicit communication that one way is better or more competent that another (e.g., in which all participants feel valued and experience reciprocity)?

3. How can connection be honored across differences? That is, how can differences be understood as complementary (i.e., positively connected) and as a resource rather than as contradictory (i.e., polarized) and, therefore, as something that must be minimized or eliminated?

These are neither simple nor easy questions. They are, however, critical questions if we are to respond optimally and fully to diversity in early childhood settings. The response in this book centers on the concept of dialogue rather than on the acquisition of knowledge. Although the latter remains important, it is our belief that it is how we interact rather than what we know that ultimately determines the outcomes of our interactions with those who hold diverse values and beliefs and who speak and behave differently from ourselves. This provides the context for accepting or rejecting the knowledge we wish to share.

Yankelovich noted that, when left unexamined, a view that considers knowledge the most important component of cultural competency subtly privileges the ENC perspective that "knowledge and understanding of issues [is gained] primarily through factual information" (1999, p. 24). Such a view consequently places people at risk for "interpose[ing] a vast social distance" (p. 151) between themselves and those with whom they interact. This distance, in turn, limits practitioners' abilities to establish respectful relationships with families, especially when they have different cultural perspectives on gaining knowledge and understanding. It is possible to learn all about others and not really know them in all their complexity and individuality (see also Chapter 5).

CURRENT APPROACHES TO INTERACTIONS ACROSS CULTURALLY LINGUISTICALLY DIVERSE PARAMETERS

The ability to recognize and attend to the challenges posed to practitioners by cultural diversity is commonly referred to as *cultural competence, cultural responsiveness,* or *cultural competency.* These terms are used somewhat interchangeably to describe the set of knowledge, skills, and practices necessary for optimum communication and interaction across cultures, and the terms have varying connotations and perceptions. The term *cultural competency,* for example, is not always positively received in that it de-emphasizes the fact that such competency is a process to be learned rather than a fixed set of skills to be mastered. It is also a term that is typically understood as applying only to interactions with members of certain populations (e.g., American Indian but not Amish).

All three terms tend to be used only in reference to cultural linguistic diversity, making it a special case and neglecting the fact that all interactions involve some degree of diversity. The skill set involved in honoring voice, identity, and connection, though it is perhaps more needed in situations that involve cultural linguistic diversity, is necessary in all interactions. Interacting with those whose culture and/or language differ from our own is not about some unique or different set of skills. Just as diversity is not something unique to only certain people, respectful, reciprocal, and responsive interactions are also not unique only to interactions with certain people. The term the authors have chosen, therefore, is one that is not in current usage: *interactional competency.* There is a book titled *How You Do Anything Is How You Do Everything* (Huber, 1988). That title aptly describes what we are trying to say. If we cannot honor identity, voice, and connection in interactions with those who share our culture and language, then we will not be able to honor those who do not share our culture and language. Paying attention to interactional competency only when in interactions with "them" will not work if we do not also pay attention to it in interactions with "us."

Before discussing interactional competency, however, a discussion of current approaches to diverse cultural linguistic parameters is pertinent. Special education's approach to the competent negotiation of diverse cultural parameters has had a significant influence on ECSE's approach. Although both early childhood and ECSE are beginning to evidence a shift (Artiles, Kozleski, Trent, Osher, & Ortiz, 2010; McDermott, Goldman, & Varenne, 2006), a strong emphasis on narrow group-specific funds of knowledge still remains. Such group-specific knowledge has much to offer and has been effective in many ways. It offers significant insights and supports the development of what Nakkula and Ravitch (1998) termed *forestructure:* "what one has already learned and internalized in life, and the manner in which the learning has been organized in preparation for the future assimilation of anything new" (1998, p. 5). Such forestructure is invaluable in setting up probabilities, just like knowing about trees in general can help anticipate what might be encountered when seeing a specific tree. It is important, though, to remember that that is all group-specific knowledge can do—help anticipate what an individual reality might be like (Barrera, 2000).

Objective knowledge about cultural groups can only approximate the more subjective and dynamic knowledge gained from extended interaction with individual members of those cultures. In addition, conveying the message, however implicitly, that practitioners need to learn cultural parameters for all of the families with whom they interact is overwhelming, especially given the increasingly multifaceted nature of cultural identity itself (Seelye & Wasilewski, 1996). In addition to freezing what is naturally a dynamic reality, static knowledge all too often also leads to remedial or stereotypical responses to diversity. Even armed with such knowledge, practitioners may remain unable to respond to the question, "What do we do now, in this specific and concrete situation with this particular family/child, who does not quite fit this or that category?" It is a question often posed to the authors in requests for workshops and professional development activities.

The familiar two-column approach that clusters cultural characteristics into implicit either-or choices (e.g., behavior that characterizes this group in one column side by side with those that characterize another group in a parallel column) is a second factor about a group-specific approach that can be problematic. Polarization of perspectives, however implicit and unintended, is supported when literature on cultural diversity contrasts the cultural characteristics of ENC with those of other groups. Inadvertently and unintentionally, this format promotes an either-or perspective. The implicit message is that a culture values only this or that (e.g., individualism or collectivism). The idea of a culture that values both or values something else entirely is rarely communicated when this format is used.

Such polarization can be troublesome in at least two ways. The first is the exclusivity implicit in all either-or dichotomies—that is, the idea that moving toward one pole necessitates distancing from the other pole. For instance, when placed on a continuum, the closer one culture is to being individualistic (however defined), the more distant it is from being collectivistic. This aspect of dichotomies by its very nature increases the challenge of deep collaboration necessary to honoring differences and working toward leveraging their complementarity.

Although polarized listings seem to present two perspectives, they actually describe behavior only from a single perspective, which is the second problematic aspect of a side-by-side either-or approach. Typically, behaviors in the first column are defined in contrast to those in the second column (i.e., from the perspective of the culture represented in the first column). Behaviors are thus defined from only one perspective, typically that of ENC, the observing culture. An observed culture's social behavior (e.g., not making decisions without consulting with an elder) may be described as "dependent" based on the degree to which it contrasts with ENC's concept of "independent" (i.e., making decisions autonomously). That behavior might be more accurately described as "interdependent" or "socially responsive," however, from the observed culture's perspective.

This tendency toward exclusive polarization itself reflects an unexamined ENC perspective (Stewart & Bennett, 1991). Polarization's exclusivity is sometimes so strong that the term *exclusive polarization* seems redundant. Although human beings seem to be genetically wired to perceive reality in binary pairs (Newberg, D'Aquili, & Rause, 2001), the tendency to perceive these pairs as exclusive opposites is strongly influenced by cultural contexts (Stewart & Bennett, 1991). Some Asian cultures, for example, tend to perceive pairs as complementary aspects of a single paradoxical reality, as reflected in the familiar symbol for yin and yang (see Figure 3.1). Binary perception, therefore, is not necessarily tied to polarizing what is perceived.

In summary, the ability to honor identity, voice, and connection across diverse cultural parameters can be limited by the tendency to rely on objective knowledge as its key component and to polarize perspectives into exclusive pairs, tendencies which themselves seem to be cultural artifacts of ENC (Stewart & Bennett, 1991). Relying too strongly on objective knowledge distances

Figure 3.1.   Yin and yang symbol.

one from the rich complexity of lived cultures and, consequently, reduces one's ability to understand and respect families as both individually unique and culturally similar. Exclusive polarization obscures the complementary nature of diverse behaviors and the rich resources that they can generate both separately and together. The Skilled Dialogue approach is one that tends to minimize both tendencies.

QUALITIES OF SKILLED DIALOGUE

The concept of dialogue is one that emphasizes the qualities of interaction rather than only the knowledge that guides them. It is a concept that lends itself easily to honoring identity, voice, and connection, which are the key goals of Skilled Dialogue. Yankelovich defined *dialogue* as "the process of successful relationship building" (1999, p. 15). Shelton elaborated on that by adding that a particular kind of listening is the heart of dialogue, a listening in which "one's position is temporarily suspended rather than defended" (1999, p. 151). Buber (1958), perhaps one of the earliest to address dialogue, differentiates it as "I-Thou" rather than "I-It." Similarly, Isaacs stated, "Dialogue is a process by which we can create containers that are capable of holding our [diverse] experience in ever more rich and complex ways" (1999, p. 256).

Skilled Dialogue addresses dialogue from a relational worldview grounded in three qualities that acknowledge and honor both individual uniqueness and cultural similarity: 1) respect, defined as honoring identity; 2) reciprocity, defined as honoring voice; and 3) responsiveness, defined as honoring connection, that which unites perspectives across diverse cultural parameters. Bush and Folger identified the most important value of this relational worldview as "transformation, the achievement of human conduct that integrates the strength of self and compassion toward others" (1994, p. 242).

The following vignette provides a starting point for exploring respect (i.e., honoring identity), reciprocity (i.e., honoring voice), and responsiveness (i.e., honoring connection).

Betsy, an early childhood interventionist, poses the following question: "How can I be culturally responsive when I go into the homes of families from cultures that make sharp distinctions between parents and 'experts?' Karen is a single mother from Puerto Rico whom I visit weekly. When I ask her to tell me what she'd like for her child Maya or when I ask her to work with Maya, she says that I am the expert and that I should tell her what needs to be done. Sometimes she'll even leave me alone with Maya. I know that Karen cares about Maya and is just expressing her respect for me, but how can I get Karen more involved in Maya's activities while I am visiting?"

Respect: Honoring Identity

> Making oneself vulnerable is an act of trust and respect, as is receiving and honoring the vulnerability of another. Such an offering of oneself aligns with Martin Buber's idea that a person who says "you" does not "have" something, but [rather] "stands in relation [to someone]." Dreams, when "offered," do not become the possession of the other. They represent the trust and respect that forges a connection. (Lawrence-Lightfoot, 1999, p. 93)

Respect is a hallmark quality of Skilled Dialogue. Used in this context, *respect* refers to an acknowledgment and acceptance of the validity of boundaries that exist between people and that define each person's identity in relation to the other. Even though other's boundaries differ or perhaps even seem to contradict our own, it is essential to acknowledge that they are as evidence-based as our own; that is, they have been developed and validated based on life experiences, as have our own. This does not mean that they are the most life-enhancing choices in all cases; it does mean that they have worked within the context of those experiences (e.g., lessened pain, protected, gained desired results) and, thus, are proven.

Boundaries are markers that simultaneously connect and distinguish one person from another. They identify the parameters of the spaces that one occupies. Physical boundaries, for example, delineate the physical space around a person. A person feels disturbed or even violated when these boundaries are crossed without permission. Trust and connection are supported when they are acknowledged and crossed with permission.

Similarly, emotional boundaries define parameters of relatedness. They identify when words and actions convey insult or praise. A sense of confidence and esteem is fostered when these are validated. A sense of shame often arises when they are not acknowledged or validated.

Cognitive boundaries outline what one believes to be true; misunderstanding, confusion, or anger may result when these are crossed. A greater sense of confidence and competence tends to emerge when these boundaries are validated.

Spiritual boundaries relate to one's connection with the larger aspects of the universe (e.g., God, spirit, energy, self). One may feel lost or somehow less well defined when these are crossed. A sense of safety and right order is present when these boundaries are affirmed.

Boundaries thus reflect basic assumptions about oneself, others, and the surrounding world. These assumptions are the core of the meanings that individuals attach to their actions and words (Janoff-Bulman, 1992). Boundaries and their underlying assumptions are shaped and supported by the cultural contexts in which people are raised and later choose to live.

Acknowledging and accepting another's boundaries communicates that he or she is competent to craft his or her life based on the experiences and other data he or she has encountered. Such acknowledgment and acceptance becomes challenging, however, when differences between boundaries challenge fixed assumptions about what should be (e.g., someone stands too close as they speak and challenges our assumptions about correct social behavior or interpersonal safety).

Boundaries both separate and connect. At times, ENC seems to convey the idea that acknowledging or identifying distinctions or differences somehow makes connections less sustainable (Althen, 1988; Stewart & Bennett, 1991). This idea reflects a lack of recognition that it is not the distinctions but the meanings attached to them that divide or connect. The Rio Grande River, for example, is a physical boundary that marks both where two countries connect and where they separate one from the other. It may be thought of as dividing the two countries of Mexico and the United States. Yet, the first author grew up alongside this river and learned to recognize how it also connects these two countries. The river is a common source of water and recreation for people on both sides of the border; everyone talks of "our" river and "our" bridge. The Rio Grande, like all boundaries, both joins and distinguishes. Being aware of and acknowledging the boundary that it sets distinguishes one country from the other while simultaneously providing a common point of contact.

The vignette about Betsy and Karen describes the different boundaries that each has around their respective roles with Maya. Is it possible to honor both Betsy's and Karen's identities as expressed through the boundaries each seeks to set or maintain? Respectful communication would require just that. Practitioners such as Betsy would need to recognize that Karen's truths, or boundaries, are as valid (i.e., true to her cultural and life experiences) as her own are within her cultural and life experiences. This would mean accepting that parents such as Karen, who perceive practitioners as the experts, have a right to their perception of reality, even when that perception differs from what practitioners might prefer or believe to be correct, and even when there is a perceived or actual need to promote new perceptions.

It is important to remember that one person's boundaries neither define nor depend on another's. Karen's perception of Betsy's role as the expert in charge, for example, does not actually define Betsy's role in an absolute sense; it only describes Karen's perception of Betsy. Similarly, Betsy's perception of Karen as passive recipient does not actually define Karen; it only describes Betsy's perception of her. Neither Betsy's nor Karen's truths define the whole of reality. There are more aspects to who they each are and to the roles they play in relation to Maya.

Respecting parents such as Karen, who leave the practitioner alone with their child, requires acknowledging the validity (i.e., evidence base) of the boundaries that they set and the fact that these may cast practitioners in the roles other than those they wish. It also requires accepting that they have the same right to those boundaries as practitioners have to theirs. This acknowledgment and acceptance establishes the foundation for Skilled Dialogue and is concretely expressed through the strategies of Welcoming and Allowing, which are discussed in Chapter 7 and further illustrated in Section III. Such acknowledgment and acceptance does not, however, mean that practitioners or families have to accept the status quo and abandon seeking further change. It only means that there is a willingness to acknowledge differing perceptions and boundaries as well as to suspend the need to make them match.

Reciprocity: Honoring Voice

> Great artists are not first problem solvers; they are first creators, who solve problems secondarily as a necessary and inevitable result of their commitment to producing a remarkable artistic result. (Childs, 1998, p. 34)

Reciprocity builds on respect. It seeks to balance power between people in dialogue through the explicit recognition that each person in an interaction is equally capable. In other words, reciprocity erases the "one-up" perspective that is implicitly communicated in many family–practitioner interactions. It does not require denying that one person has more expertise, knowledge, or authority than another in particular areas (e.g., a social worker who has the authority to remove children from their home). It does require acknowledging and trusting families' expertise, knowledge, and authority (i.e., communicating that every person involved brings experience and perceptions of value to the table). To understand reciprocity in this sense is to distinguish the more common understanding of power as expertise or authority from the less common understanding of power as capacity or capability. The Spanish word *poder* reflects this latter understanding. It can be used both as a noun meaning "power" and as a verb meaning "to be able," as in "*Yo puedo*" (i.e., "I can").

Reciprocal interactions provide equal opportunity to all participants in an interaction to contribute and make choices. Recognizing that one point of view should not dominate or exclude diverse points of view, as well as the resulting support of open or free choice over forced either-or choice, are important aspects of reciprocal interactions.

A reciprocal perspective changes how one thinks when encountering differences. Without a reciprocal perspective, one may think, "Oh, here's someone who doesn't have what I have or what I believe they need (and is somehow deficient as a result)." The parenthetical phrase is unspoken yet clearly communicated. From a reciprocal perspective, however, one is more likely to think, "Oh, here's someone who does not have the knowledge/skill I have and may benefit from what I have to offer and who, at the same time, has knowledge/skill I don't have and is someone from whom I can benefit because he or she has something new or different that can add to or extend available resources." This latter sentiment is always clear regardless of whether it is verbalized. One of the few references to this type of reciprocity comes from Dunst, Trivette, and Deal: "Help is more likely to be favorably received if it can be reciprocated and the possibility of 'repaying' the help-giver is sanctioned and approved but not expected" (1988, p. 95). Gernsbacher (2006) references reciprocity in a similar fashion.

The distinction between givers and receivers is erased when differences are acknowledged as potential contributions, and no sense of debt is incurred by any of the people involved. The unique contributions of others cannot be acknowledged or accessed when one enters interactions only to give—whether knowledge, support, direction, or something else. This lack of reciprocity inhibits not only what might be received, but also the full potential of what is given.

Everyone has something to offer in reciprocal relationships. Reciprocity enriches not only the people involved, but also the outcome of their interactions.

Returning once more to Betsy, who wants more involvement (as she defines it) on Karen's part: How might reciprocity be established in their interactions with each other? Nonjudgmental acknowledgment that diverse perspectives are present is the first step. Suspending the need to impose one experience of reality on another (i.e., to push Karen to become engaged in the ways that Betsy values or, conversely, to acquiesce and offer no options for change) starts the process of reciprocity. A second step is Betsy's acknowledgement of Karen's capacity to contribute in this particular situation—to explore her understanding of participation and how she might in fact already be participating by allowing time and space for Betsy's agenda (e.g., participating in the role of novice vis-à-vis Karen's role of expert). This acknowledgment might lead to recognizing Karen's participation in other similar interactions with her child and in other environments. Eventually, to establish reciprocity, Betsy must understand that Karen is already equally, if not more, involved with Maya in a variety of ways. This understanding then provides a context for responding to the two women's differing perceptions as well as to the specific needs of both Karen and Maya. It could also lead to the expansion of Betsy's and Karen's repertoire of participatory skills. The concrete expression of reciprocity in this fashion is closely tied to Skilled Dialogue's strategies of Sense-Making and Appreciation, which are discussed in Chapter 7.

Responsiveness: Honoring Connection

> So I no longer have theories about people. I don't diagnose them or decide what their problem is. I simply meet with them and listen. As we sit together, I don't even have an agenda, but I know that something will emerge from our conversation over time that is a part of a larger coherent pattern that neither of us can fully see at the moment. So I sit with them and wait. (Remen, 2000, p. 90)

If respect means recognizing the validity of differing boundaries and reciprocity means acknowledging that every person has something of value to contribute, then responsiveness means taking the next step by recognizing and affirming the connection(s) that hold those different boundaries and contributions in place. Recognizing and affirming that there is a single inclusive reality holding and guiding our interactions (e.g., the script of novice and expert in Karen's and Betsy's case), rather than two contradictory realities, is the cornerstone of responsiveness.

Responsiveness starts with turning all fixed assumptions (e.g., saying, "Karen is not participating") into lightly held hypotheses (e.g., saying, "I wonder if Karen is really not participating," or "Maybe Karen is participating, just in ways I'm not recognizing" instead of, "I know she's not participating," or "I'm sure she's not participating"). It is not possible to be responsive to another without first becoming open to the possibility of a reality different from that we assume to be true. To be responsive is to be willing to entertain a mystery and ask, "I wonder if things are different than I think?" a question that leads to other questions such as, "What is it that might be connecting our two distinct and even contradictory perspectives?" "Might each actually be complementary to the other?" We cannot truly be responsive until "you" and "I" become "we"; that is, until I can move from dispassionate and disconnecting thoughts such as, "I'm not you," "I'd never do that," and "I know better" to compassionate and connecting thoughts such as, "I'm part of this situation," and "I am somehow contributing to what is; it is not only your problem."

Forgetting mystery makes it all too easy to believe we already know what we need to know. Forgetting mystery allows us to place both children and families in the tightly bound circles of our own categories and labels. In doing so, we become unresponsive, reducing them to a singular identity (e.g., the child with attention-deficit/hyperactivity disorder, the resistant mother) and consequently becoming engaged with our ideas about them rather than with them. Responsiveness, conversely, requires releasing preconceptions and listening to children and families "with focused attention, patience and curiosity" (Freedman & Combs, 1996, p. 44) in order to discover the single reality in which we participate. Only then can one become truly responsive—that is, become attuned to families' and children's realities as they connect with our own rather than remaining focused just on our own ideas about those realities.

In this sense, responsiveness means being willing to give up certainty, to not know exactly what to do or what to say—at least not until we step outside of our ideas about another and truly meet him or her. Remen stated, "Knowing where we are going encourages us to stop seeing and hearing and allows us to fall asleep. [Such knowing allows] a part of [us] to rush ahead to [our destination] the moment [we] see it" (2000, p. 289). Unfortunately, this is an apt description of what often happens when practitioners present families with their diagnostic findings and intervention recommendations, being responsive only their own interpretations and understandings. Once a child is assessed, or sometimes even before, it is all too easy to press on to conclusions about what needs to be done without paying attention to the child and family sitting before us.

Responding and responsiveness are not necessarily the same. Responsiveness requires leaving room for the unexpected and the unpredictable. Examples of responsiveness include thoughts such as the following, which move us outside of our own culturally slanted reality and invite us into the cultural and personal realities of the children and families who stand before us.

- "Maybe this child will be different from all others I think are just like him or her; maybe he or she will be able to do the task."

- "Maybe this family will be much more resourceful than I can foresee; maybe they will be able to support their child in ways that I cannot anticipate or imagine."

- "Perhaps I have missed truly understanding a particular aspect of this family's concerns and am rushing ahead in a direction unrelated to those concerns."

Being responsive is particularly important in culturally diverse situations because the very diversity of these situations challenges us to recognize that people are always more than (and perhaps even radically different from) others' ideas about who they are. Although preconceived ideas and judgments can never be totally eliminated, it is nevertheless possible to refuse to reduce others' reality to one's limited dimensions. Joining and Harmonizing are the two Skilled Dialogue strategies that can help. These are further discussed in Chapter 7.

As one more brief example in the case of our given scenario, Betsy can refuse to place Karen in a box labeled "inattentive or uninvolved mother," the interpretation that her cultural perspective might give to Karen's behaviors. She can listen to Karen "with focused attention, patience and curiosity" (Freedman & Combs, 1996, p. 44) while reminding herself that she knows little of Karen's cultural perspective, which may attach totally different meanings to her behaviors. Most important, Betsy can continue to act as if cooperation and collaboration are eminent (i.e., join with Karen).

Although they do not use the term *Skilled Dialogue,* Freedman and Combs described a characteristic quality of responsiveness in a way that is particularly relevant to early childhood practitioners:

> *Instead of seeing ourselves as mechanics working to fix a broken machine…we experience ourselves as interested people…skilled at asking questions to bring forth the knowledge and experience…carried in the stories of the people we work with….This means turning our backs on "expert" filters:* [emphasis added]…not comparing the selves they portray in their stories to [what we believe to be] normative standards. (1996, p. 18)

Returning once more to Betsy and Karen, in what other ways might Betsy be responsive Karen (i.e., take her perspective into account in a way that would allow them to harmonize their diverse behaviors)? The answer, of course, lies in the situation's specifics, so only possibilities can be listed here.

Betsy might be responsive to Karen through one or more of the following, each of which focus on stepping into Karen's reality (i.e., seeing it from a compassionate perspective).

- Avoid "freezing" her idea of Karen as a passive parent, unwilling or unable to change (i.e., understand that her cultural understanding of Karen's behavior is just that, *her* cultural understanding and not reality itself).

- Understand that some cultures believe that necessary knowledge is interpersonally distributed; that is, that everyone does not need to know the same thing; that knowledge need not be personally possessed because it can be obtained though social connections (Moll & Greenberg, 1990). People from these cultures consequently feel no need to "duplicate" someone else's expertise and that doing so would be disrespectful. (This point is further discussed in Chapter 8.)

- Accept that Karen may desperately need respite time and lessened demands for her involvement until Betsy can identify means of helping Karen find that time in ways that support working with Maya during Betsy's sessions

- Respect Karen's perception of Betsy as an expert and explore what this means. Does Karen truly believe that she has nothing to offer (i.e., that only experts' opinions matter)? Or, is it that she believes what she has to offer would not be accepted or would not be appropriate? What specific responsibilities is she assigning to Betsy with this perception? What have Karen's experiences with other experts been like? In what areas does she feel confident of her expertise? Is her withdrawal an expression of fear over doing the wrong thing and harming her child? Is Betsy somehow unconsciously communicating her own need to be the expert?

- Invite Karen to share what she has to offer in this situation and structure sessions so that Karen can contribute her knowledge (e.g., give instructions on cooking Maya's favorite food, which can be used in planned activities to elicit specific language); that is, create opportunities to join with Karen as partners.

- Use materials and routines familiar and meaningful to Karen.

These possibilities and other similar ones may not necessarily solve the problem. They will, however, gradually redefine it and change the tenor of interactions between Betsy and Karen, thereby increasing the possibility of arriving at more satisfactory and competent interactions between them.

A LOOK AHEAD

Section II continues the discussion of the Skilled Dialogue framework in more detail, starting with Chapter 4, which focuses on its definition, key beliefs and skills, and dispositions. Chapters 5 and 6 discuss the two original skills presented in our 2003 text—AUD and 3rd Space—as these relate to the two dispositions subsequently developed and presented in our 2009 text—Choosing

Relationship over Control and Setting the Stage for Miracles. The last chapter in this section presents the Skilled Dialogue strategies that have been developed since the 2003 text, in which strategies were discussed only in general terms.

Section III follows with a discussion of the application of this framework to the assessment and instruction of young children and their families when cultural contexts differ significantly from those of early childhood practitioners as well as those reflected in typical ECSE practices. Finally, Chapter 11 reprises the discussion of culture and trauma formerly contained in Appendix A of the first edition.

Dialogue Across Culturally Linguistically Based Differences

The chapters in this section introduce the various components of Skilled Dialogue. Chapter 4 presents the framework for Skilled Dialogue—its dispositions and qualities. Chapters 5–7 focus on the additional elements that fill out this framework, with particular attention to bridging the information originally presented in the first edition with the later information developed in our 2009 text. Chapters 5 and 6 focus on the transition from skills to dispositions as the primary elements that define and guide the strategies, which are discussed in Chapter 7. The goal of this section is to give readers the various parts of Skilled Dialogue as a context for the material in Section III.

Skilled Dialogue

THE FRAMEWORK

The previous chapters discussed the qualities associated with Skilled Dialogue. This chapter introduces the main elements of Skilled Dialogue. These elements are specifically designed to honor identity, voice, and connection in interactions in which there exist significantly diverse perspectives, especially those that are culturally based. The evolution of these elements is briefly described in the Introduction to this text and referred to again in this chapter.

DEFINITION

Skilled Dialogue is an approach to communication and interaction that was developed in response to the need to meet the challenges posed to practitioners by cultural diversity. It seeks to respond to these challenges in ways that explicitly craft interactions that are respectful, reciprocal, and responsive. The Skilled Dialogue approach takes the perspective that all interactions, including those involved in assessment and instruction, are in fact dialogic and that the success of the behaviors involved in these interactions is largely determined by the quality of that dialogue.

Differences are perceived as resources rather than limitations in Skilled Dialogue. Seemingly paradoxical viewpoints are reconciled as coherence is achieved. Eventually, solutions arise that are inclusive of all points of view. The final outcome is always greater than the sum of the individual perspectives (Shelton, 1999).

KEY BELIEFS

The key beliefs that underlie Skilled Dialogue are addressed in the chapters in the preceding section. Chapter 1 discusses the belief that it is necessary to define culture before addressing cultural diversity. An understanding of culture as a dynamic that shapes the behaviors and beliefs of all people is essential to truly understanding elements that are considered diverse. The statement, "I have no culture"—uttered by numerous practitioners at various workshops conducted by the authors—points to the pitfalls of not understanding culture.

Chapter 2 notes that diversity is a relational reality that exists between rather than within people. The process of Skilled Dialogue understands diversity as a reality that emerges only as people or communities are compared one to the other, not as a characteristic of individuals or communities.

These two beliefs frame the third one, introduced in Chapter 3—the belief that the degree of interactional competency achieved is based more on the ability to craft respectful, reciprocal, and responsive relationships than on the extent of information possessed about particular cultures. The belief that one must have information about others before one can be culturally competent is itself a cultural artifact. To adhere to it is to privilege some cultures over others and, in so doing, to undermine the very competency that is sought.

The overall framework based on these beliefs is shown in Figure 4.1. This framework is summarized next, and then each section is discussed in more detail in the following chapters in this section.

SKILLS AND DISPOSITIONS

Taken together, the three beliefs set a context for Skilled Dialogue's skills and dispositions. The qualities of respect, responsiveness, and reciprocity discussed

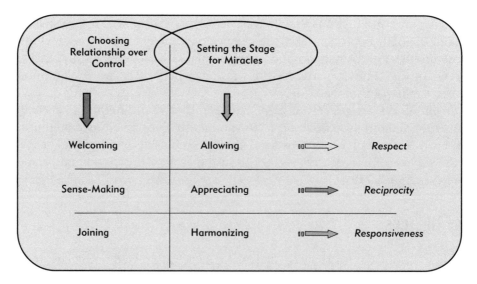

Figure 4.1. Skilled Dialogue framework.

in Chapter 3 require concrete expression if identity, voice, and connection are to be truly honored. Skilled Dialogue initially proposed two skills as key to these qualities: AUD and 3rd Space.[1] These two skills have subsequently evolved into two dispositions based on the authors' research and feedback from practitioners who have participated in Skilled Dialogue workshops. This chapter retains all the material in the prior edition on the two skills and adds new material on the linkages between them and the new dispositions.

AUD and its correlate disposition—Choosing Relationship over Control—address the need to move from knowing about diversity to knowing diversity as it manifests in specific interactions (i.e., to place general cultural knowledge into concrete and compassionate contexts).

3rd Space and its correlate disposition—Setting the Stage for Miracles—address the need to move from exclusive either-or perspectives to inclusive 3rd Space perspectives (i.e., to focus on the complementary nature of differences and develop creative and inclusive choices that connect rather than divide diverse perspectives).

Both skills and dispositions reflect the importance of authentic relationships rooted in compassionate knowledge and creative choices. The skills emerged as key as the authors observed, discussed, and studied competent interactions across a range of cultural backgrounds and experiences (Barrera & Kramer, 1997; Kramer, 1997). The dispositions shift them from behaviors to be achieved to attitudes that must be adopted prior to exercising the skills.

Anchored Understanding of Diversity/Choosing Relationship over Control

The authors' observed interactions of culturally responsive practitioners[2] made clear the contrast between having information about something or someone (i.e., knowing about) and knowing on a compassionate, deeper, more experiential level. Such knowing occurs when people interact on a personal, face-to-face basis and learn each other's stories. Talking generally about American Indians, for example, is entirely different from having that same discussion over time with individual American Indians. Previously held knowledge becomes personalized in such extended face-to-face interactions. Its boundaries are tested and stretched. The following statements by practitioners at a workshop reflect how previously held categories and assumptions are both challenged and deepened: "I thought that religion was only a one-day-a-week

---

[1]Other authors have used the term *third space*, though it is still infrequent. Its meaning here, however, is distinct and specific to Skilled Dialogue. The numeric format is used to emphasize this unique usage. Its focus on both paradox and integration is one of its distinguishing aspects.

[2]Colleen Alivado and Elaine Costello are gratefully acknowledged for all their contributions to the authors' conceptualization of Skilled Dialogue.

thing for whites," and "Oh, so that's what it means that Navajos have differ-ing perceptions of time." As Clandinin and Connelly stated, "When [people] are known intimately as people, not merely as categorical representatives, categories tend to fragment" (2000, p. 141). Categories can only serve a useful purpose when they are held loosely, like puzzle pieces that reflect only part of a larger picture.

Experiential knowing helps to better navigate the tension between cat-egories and individuality. On the one hand, identities are not crafted single handedly by individuals or even by individual families. Identities are drawn from and embedded in the communities and cultures in which people partici-pate and within which they grew up. Methods of negotiating development as individuals and skill repertoires are significantly influenced in both pro-cess and content by the cultural templates into which people are acculturated within their families. On the other hand, everyone is unique. No one person reflects a single culture 100% (see Figure 1.1 in Chapter 1).

This tension between recognizing individuals' participation in common cultural frameworks while acknowledging their unique individuality underlies AUD, the first Skilled Dialogue skill identified by the authors. As we worked with this skill, however, we realized that something was missing. AUD was in fact a skill that itself needed to be grounded. It needed to be understood as more than just a means to an end. This realization led to the identification of the disposition of Choosing Relationship over Control (see Chapter 5 for more detail). Without this underlying disposition, knowledge remains only a means to achieving a preidentified goal/change.

We realized that was the message we had been trying to communicate all along through our use of the term "anchored understanding"—that relation-ship was a more important focus than achieving a desired change. Although such change could still be desired, the qualities of respect, reciprocity, and responsiveness could never be authentically established as long as change re-mained the primary intention. Identities and voices can only be truly honored when change is chosen by the person changing rather than imposed by the person desiring the change.

I cannot, after all, honor another's identity if I am implementing a behav-ioral change program that defines particular behaviors from the perspective of only a single culture and does not take into account their meaning, value, or function in another. I cannot honor another's voice if that same program is simply given to a child/family and does not allow for true collaboration or part-nership. Equally, I cannot honor connection if I do not also seek to change but only see the need for change in another. To honor connection requires being in relationship, and being in relationship requires mindful allowing of diverse voices other than my own, and allowing diverse voices other than my own must emerge from a respect for another's identity, however diverse from my own.

AUD's emphasis on relationship thus gradually crystallized into the more explicit disposition of Choosing Relationship over Control. Both are discussed in more detail in Chapter 5.

3rd Space/Setting the Stage for Miracles

Stewart and Bennett (1991) noted a tendency within ENC to polarize reality into exclusive either-or dichotomies with one positive pole and one negative pole. They also identified a tendency to judge disagreement as the negative pole on an agree-disagree dichotomy. Given these tendencies, it is easy to see why differences can generate substantial discomfort. At workshops conducted by the authors, practitioners and family members commonly expressed significant discomfort in the presence of dichotomous cultural perspectives. Typically, there was an urgency to act in ways that would dissolve or remove that discomfort. Comments such as, "We'll just agree to disagree," "Let's find a compromise," and "Why can't we all be alike?" were common. Such discomfort brings to the fore the need to hold diverse perspectives in one's mind without excluding one in order to accept the other. The authors thus identified a second skill key to intercultural competency—the ability to address the tension generated by contradictions in behaviors and perceptions. Skilled Dialogue's second skill—3rd Space—was identified to address this ability.

A dualistic either-or mindset is largely common to ENC and, thus, to most early childhood service settings and curricula. This mindset, although useful, has significant disadvantages in working across diverse cultural linguistic parameters. 3rd Space describes both that skill and its requisite mindset that promotes an alternate inclusive perspective that simultaneously encompasses and integrates dichotomous perspectives so as to mine their strengths and resources.

As with AUD, however, it soon became apparent that something was missing. Two findings emerged as we conducted Skilled Dialogue workshops: 1) the depth of unfamiliarity with the idea of 3rd Space and 2) the tendency to understand the idea of 3rd Space as a purely cognitive exercise. Its most basic sense as an exercise in setting the stage for unanticipated and inclusive options was all too often lost as it dissolved into more familiar concepts such as compromise. As a concept, it lacked grounding in an explicit disposition. We chose the title of this disposition to make the purpose of 3rd Space explicit: setting the stage for miracles. This in fact became the title of Skilled Dialogue's second disposition (see Chapter 6 for a full description). The skill and mindset of 3rd Space remain essential in expressing this disposition but now have a broader context for their development and application.

STRATEGIES

The fourth and final piece of the Skilled Dialogue framework is composed of its strategies. Each disposition is expressed through three strategies. These serve as the concrete expression of both beliefs and skills/dispositions. Initially conceptualized as general guidelines, these strategies have now become more defined and replace the three clusters of guidelines given for each skill in the first edition of this text. The relationship between these is discussed in Chapter 7, which focuses on both the original strategies (2003 original edition) and newer, more defined strategies (2009 text).

A LOOK AHEAD

Chapters 5 and 6 discuss Skilled Dialogue's skills/dispositions in more detail. Chapter 7 briefly overviews the newer, more concrete strategies associated with the expression of each skill/disposition as these seek to honor identity, voice, and connection. A much fuller discussion of these strategies is provided in our 2009 text and so will not be duplicated here.

Section III focuses on the interface between cultural linguistic diversity and Skilled Dialogue in the assessment and instruction of young children from backgrounds that are significantly culturally or linguistically diverse from the backgrounds of their practitioners and/or the cultural context reflected in their early childhood service settings.

Chapter 5

Anchored Understanding of Diversity/Choosing Relationship over Control

THE CONTEXT, PART I

> When we do not agree, perhaps it is because none of us see
> far enough. People living on opposite sides of a mountain
> rarely see the land the same way until they meet at the top.
> (Navajo saying quoted in Shem & Surrey, 1998, p. 11)

This chapter reprises the discussion of AUD contained in the first edition. Following that is a discussion about Choosing Relationship over Control, the disposition that now encompasses this skill, focusing on the linkages between the two. The latter overview is not intended to replace the extensive discussion of that disposition contained in Barrera and Kramer (2009). It is intended rather to show how AUD is connected to and supports Choosing Relationship over Control. Readers wishing more information on Choosing Relationship over Control are referred to Barrera and Kramer.

AUD was one of the first Skilled Dialogue elements developed by the authors. It refers to an understanding of differences that is anchored both experientially and cognitively. It is anchored in experiences that stem from personal interactions and hands-on experiences and the knowing that these yield. It is anchored cognitively in understanding that others' behaviors make as much sense as one's own. This latter understanding yields the corollary understanding that differences are just that—differences—and, thus, allows one to suspend or release judgment. Wilson gave an excellent example of these two anchors in practice, describing an encounter in which one group came to conclusions about a woman based on their experiences with others like her, rather than on interactions with her. His conclusion is particularly relevant to the current discussion of AUD:

And as I think about how easy it is, even for those of intelligence and heart, to pre-conceive and presuppose based on the apparent rather than the true, I want to cry out to all of us—but mostly to myself—to slow down; to look more closely and listen more carefully. For those of us in search of real possibilities in our encounters, we'll surely find them when we ditch our assumptions and listen with our hearts. (2001, p. 64)

Knowing about diversity (i.e., unanchored understanding) is important but not sufficient for interactional competency (i.e., behavior toward and with another that honors identity, voice, and connection), no matter how detailed or thorough the information. "Knowing about" is based on external informa-tion (i.e., public knowledge) to which anyone can gain access. One can, for example, know all about skiing without ever having set foot on snow. One can garner information in a fairly comprehensive fashion from books, DVDs, interviews, and other materials. Certainly, this type of knowing makes signifi-cant contributions to negotiating a variety of situations and interactions. One typically learns about diverse cultures using strategies similar to those just cited. Such "knowing about," however, tends to leave one detached, stand-ing outside (Yankelovich, 1999), with a relatively general and perhaps even stereotypical picture.

AUD, however, is intentionally particular and reciprocal. It is designed to generate knowledge that "arises not from standing back in order to look at, but by active and intentional engagement in lived experience" (Groome, 1980, p. 141).[1] Such knowledge is personal and idiosyncratic. AUD is specifi-cally designed to capture the characteristics and experiences that are specific to individuals rather than those that remain at the level of general descrip-tions of whole populations.

AUD is akin to Lave and Wenger's concept of situated learning: "In con-trast to learning as internalization, learning as increasing participation in communities of practice concerns the whole person acting in the world" (1991, p. 49). Similarly, AUD emphasizes the centrality of direct experien-tial knowing—knowing that is anchored in shared or relational experiences with individual children and families (e.g., having skied as compared with just knowing about skiing). Such knowing is not public information; it can be obtained only through personal and particular face-to-face relationships. This relational aspect of knowing, with all its particularity and subjectivity, keeps generalizations in check that stem from knowing about something in a more abstract fashion.

Remen (2000) illustrated the distinction between experientially anchored knowing and unanchored knowing. For more than 2 years, she recounted, a young physician provided medical care for an older Navajo woman. During

---

[1]Interestingly, a more recent citation could not be found, perhaps because of the increasing em-phasis on non–face-to-face interactions in today's society.

this time, the woman's daughter did all of the talking. The physician treated the elderly woman for a variety of diseases and helped mobilize "social services to help the daughter in caring for her mother and enabled her to find financial support from a government grant" (2000, p. 68). After the Navajo woman died at the age of 96, the physician received a call from a researcher who was writing a book about American Indian medicine traditions. When he contacted the family of a great medicine woman, the researcher was told that this physician had given their mother medical attention on many occasions and would be able to provide the needed answers because "she knew their mother well" (Remen, 2000, p. 69). Remen recounted the physician's reflections on this experience many years later.

> I think of her sitting there all those months, watching me shuffling my papers and tracking my lab data and knowing what she knew....What I would give for even one hour with her now, to ask her any of my unanswered questions, to have her perspective on suffering or loss or illness or death. Or simply to ask for her blessing. (2000, p. 69)

This poignant story reveals that the truth of someone's reality, no matter how similar to or diverse from one's own, lies in the delicate balance between the particular and the general. Although this story does not reference an ECSE situation, its application to such a scenario is not a difficult leap. Practitioners are both recipients and generators of a large volume of information about young children and families with whom they work. Similarly to the physician in Remen's (2000) story, practitioners can name the particular type of delay or syndrome that a child exhibits, describe family dynamics in clinical terms, and describe developmental concerns in detail. They can, perhaps, even describe the values associated with the family's culture. Yet, when asked to describe a particular child, would the practitioners' answers match the family's? Could they talk about the family's hopes and dreams? Could they tell someone about that child without referencing developmental status or disabilities? Could they define what success or family means to that particular child and family? The ability to answer these questions reflects the degree to which AUD is present in relation to any family.

It is not, however, sufficient to simply interact with a child or family as Remen's (2000) story so eloquently illustrated. There is also the need to anchor one's understanding of diversity cognitively. The beliefs and understandings that guide and shape our interactions are critical. Believing that only his or her behaviors have a positive intent makes a person less curious about diverse behaviors and certainly less able to respond to them respectfully. How can he or she respect someone whose behavior is believed to have no positive intent (e.g., sitting quietly and asking no questions)? How can curiosity about that person's point of view even exist? This need for cognitively anchoring is one of the factors that resulted in the shift from this skill to the broader disposition of Choosing Relationship over Control (see discussion at the end of this chapter).

ANCHORED UNDERSTANDING OF DIVERSITY IN PRACTICE

Anchored understanding of others does not require admiring their behaviors but rather requires coming to an understanding of how they make sense from their cultural or personal perspective as much as others' do from their perspectives. Not understanding and acknowledging the sense of diverse behaviors risks missing what they have to contribute (i.e., their strengths). For example, a practitioner may not admire the behavior of a mother who sets no firm bedtime for her 4-year-old child. Yet, cognitively anchoring his or her understanding of that behavior requires the practitioner to ask why the mother's behavior makes sense to her. What is the mother's intent? Why does the mother think this particular option more appropriate than the option the practitioner values (e.g., a consistent bedtime)? What does the mother believe would happen if she changed her behavior?

Facts about diversity can be learned relatively easily. Anchoring these facts in experiential contexts, however, is more difficult. Translating them in response to concrete situations is an even more complex process. One can read, for instance, about child-rearing practices common in Italian families and yet not be able to answer questions such as, "How does the particular Italian family with whom I work incorporate into their daily lives the practices that I read about?" and "What do these practices look like in this particular Italian family, which has a high degree of acculturation into ENC?" Only an open mind and extended relationships with particular families can yield answers to those questions. Anchoring understanding can change the tone of one's interactions with parents and open the door to collaborative rather than polarized interactions.

Certain culturally sanctioned behaviors may be perceived as abusive or neglectful; in fact, sometimes they may be so. Cultures, like individuals, are not always fully healthy. What happens then? There are no easy or simple answers. Nevertheless, anchoring one's understanding of families' behaviors in these as in all situations entails understanding the positive intent underlying particular behaviors (e.g., to heal a child, to eliminate behaviors believed to be harmful) while also taking necessary action to protect children's well-being. Respect requires an honest communication of boundaries, and reciprocity requires believing that everyone can grow. Behaviors that are responsive only to adult family members and not to children are neither respectful nor competent. Behaviors that are responsive only to children and not to their families likewise diminish respect and competence. Being responsive to parents who, for example, feel compelled to follow practices that harm children simultaneously necessitates being responsive to the emotional and physical safety needs of those children.

Initial attempts to understand diversity typically define differences by contrasting them with that which is familiar. For example, for many years, the first author's understanding of nuclear family was mostly defined by what it was not. She explained,

Being Hispanic, my experiences were rooted in extended family. I had "aunts" who were not biological kin; I knew my second and even fifth cousins; relatives routinely moved in and lived with us—and even had something to say about how we were raised. An answer to the question "Who are you?" could involve a one- to two-generation genealogy. I did, of course, know that others (e.g., Dick and Jane) lived differently in what were called nuclear families. I could even define the term—families limited only to parents and children. I understood that a nuclear family was different from us—that is, it was what we were not. Yet, I had little personal experience with nuclear families to anchor my understanding. I could not truly say that I knew what it was like to live in a nuclear family.

That anchored level of understanding came only as I established close friend-ships with others raised in such families or currently living within them. At that point, my understanding became much richer. I realized that nuclear families were rooted in an overall cultural perspective that addressed far more than just how many people lived in a house. Only then did my understanding become anchored; only then could I begin to understand nuclear families for what they are, not simply for what they are not.

The intention or disposition underlying practitioners' search for anchored un-derstanding ultimately determines if they will be able to authentically honor identity, voice, and connection. If understanding is sought only to better ac-complish their goals (e.g., changing family behaviors), their understanding may be more accurate but their interactions will still not communicate the levels of respect, reciprocity, and responsiveness that result in full collabora-tion. The current disposition of Choosing Relationship over Control was iden-tified to reflect the underlying intention more concretely.

CHOOSING RELATIONSHIP OVER CONTROL

As the authors talked about and taught AUD to practitioners in their classes and in workshops, it became clear that its underlying intent was relational. The importance of relationships as a context for supporting diverse identities and voices and the connections that united them was, however, often obscured as the mechanics of gathering information were discussed. Time lines and the variety and range of information needing to be gathered tended to override attention to the relationships within which it needed to be gathered. Some practitioners, for example, reported that their performance was measured in terms of how many families they could measure change in within 30 days. How can one experience another as someone to respect when outcomes are framed in terms of such rapid change and are reflective only of the perspec-tives of those desiring that change? How can rapport be established if I only have one or perhaps two visits to get to know you? If I need to document that you now have established a set routine, which may or may not be culturally respectful or responsive, with your child? How can your identity and voice be honored within your cultural framework—a framework that may support a different routine or no routine at all?

The disposition of Choosing Relationship over Control makes explicit the intent of AUD—to place knowledge within an experiential and cognitive context defined by our relationship with those diverse from ourselves. To use knowledge respectfully requires connecting with the person we hold that knowledge about. It takes time and a curious yet respectful mind. It emphasizes first establishing ongoing relationships with people from different cultures and asking questions grounded in those relationships before making decisions about what or who needs to change. Otherwise, we relate not to the person with whom we are interacting but only to our idea of that person and what he or she needs.

Barrera and Kramer (2009) discussed the disposition of Choosing Relationship over Control extensively and defined it as "an energetic intention that focuses on creating a relationship space" (2009, p. 51) within which disparate identities and voices can make sense and reveal connections rather than divisions. This disposition does not refer to establishing personal relationships. Rather, it refers to the willingness to craft interactions within which identity and voice are recognized and acknowledged as complementary (i.e., related one to the other as parts of one whole) rather than as separate—and "subjective knowledge is valued" (p. 51) as that adds to rather than detracts from the truth. "Alone, I have seen many marvelous things, none of which were true" (African proverb cited in Wheatley, 2005, p. 25). It is relationship that transforms interactions from I-It interactions to I-Thou interactions; that is, that transforms side-by-side monologues into true dialogues in which information becomes knowing rather than remaining merely factual. Looking back at Karen and Betsy, for example (see Chapter 3), Betsy's seeking of AUD would now be guided by the explicit intention to Choose Relationship over Control rather than by only her desire to better understand Karen's motives and behaviors, not only so that she could gain access to and leverage their strengths and bring Karen into a mutual partnership, but also so that she could more efficiently and effectively accomplish her (Betsy's) goals. Choosing Relationship over Control is about no single person making decisions for another. (See Chapter 7 for a more detailed description of how Betsy would approach the situation.)

The linkage between AUD and Choosing Relationship over Control is therefore strong. The first speaks to the shift from mere information (i.e., knowing about) to full knowledge (i.e., knowing); the second to the intentionality that guides that transition. When seen as complementary, the material written about AUD in this text and that written about Choosing Relationship over Control in the 2009 text should only enrich readers' understanding of the full scope of Skilled Dialogue. Strategies associated with both AUD and Choosing Relationship over Control are presented and discussed in Chapter 7.

3ʳᵈ Space/Setting the Stage for Miracles

THE CONTEXT, PART II

> We split paradoxes so reflexively that we do not understand the price we pay for our habit. The poles of a paradox are like the poles of a battery: hold them together, and they generate the energy of life; pull them apart, and the current stops flowing. When we separate any of the profound paired truths of our lives, both poles become lifeless as well. Dissecting a living paradox has the same impact on our intellectual, emotional, and spiritual well-being as the decision to breathe in without ever breathing out would have on our physical health. (Palmer, 1997, p. 64)

This chapter is organized in the same manner as the previous one. First, the discussion of 3ʳᵈ Space contained in the first edition is reprised. Second, Setting the Stage for Miracles, the disposition that now encompasses the skill of 3ʳᵈ Space, is presented, focusing on the linkages between the two. This latter overview is not intended to replace the extensive discussion of that disposition contained in Barrera and Kramer (2009). It is intended only to show how 3ʳᵈ Space is connected to and supports Setting the Stage for Miracles.

The skill of 3ʳᵈ Space builds on and grows out of AUD. AUD leads to a "both-and" perspective, and sometimes that is enough. Many times, however, this perspective does not go far enough. In the vignette about Betsy and Karen introduced in Chapter 3, Betsy has a truer understanding of Karen's perspective once she anchors her understanding experientially and cognitively. Yet, she may still be left wanting one set of behaviors while Karen exhibits a contradictory set. The skill of 3ʳᵈ Space goes one step further to ask: How can both working with Maya (Betsy's perspective) and not working with Maya (Karen's perspective) be integrated so that one perspective does not have to be excluded or chosen over the other? 3rd Space becomes essential when apparently contradictory or irreconcilable perspectives need to be honored simultaneously.

3RD SPACE

3rd Space focuses on creatively reframing contradictions, which are exclusive, into paradoxes, which are inclusive. It invites practitioners to make a fundamental shift from dualistic perceptions of reality to a mindset that integrates the complementary aspects of diverse values, behaviors, and beliefs into a new whole within which each contributes something. 3rd Space thus mines the riches of multiple perspectives while simultaneously promoting respect and reciprocity by not excluding one perspective to privilege another. For example, how can Karen's present behavior (i.e., not staying to work with Maya) complement Betsy's goal (i.e., increasing parent–child interactions)? The answer to that question is explored following the chapter's initial discussion of 3rd Space. As both a skill and a mindset, a 3rd Space perspective capitalizes on the potential of diversity to enrich and expand rather than reduce and separate. The following three characteristics give an indication of how this is possible.

1. From a 3rd Space perspective reality is not dichotomous.

Differences between views are better described as on a spectrum than on a continuum. A continuum is directional and exclusive by definition. Its two ends remain opposed to each other—as one draws nearer to one end, the other grows further away. A spectrum, however, is inclusive—it does not contain a directional perspective. This aspect of 3rd Space introduces the possibility of conceptualizing each person's perspective in nonpolarized ways—that is, in ways in which choosing one perspective does not necessitate moving away from or excluding the other.

2. From a 3rd Space perspective, there are always at least three (or more) choices.

There is never a need for a forced choice (i.e., either-or) because reality is not dichotomous in 3rd Space. Rather than splitting reality into dualistic sets of exclusive choices (e.g., Karen is involved or uninvolved; Betsy must go along with Karen's perspective or insist on her own), a 3rd Space perspectives always posits the availability of three or more choices (e.g., Karen's noninvolvement can be reframed as involvement, though of a different sort than expected by Betsy; Betsy can integrate both perspectives into one). This characteristic of 3rd Space allows for creatively generating alternatives beyond the obvious ones. For example, Betsy could reframe Karen's noninvolvement as a type of engagement. Paradise gave an interesting example of this in an article on Mazahua mothers and children, in which she described a "separate-but-together" interaction: "[Mothers and children] are together [i.e., engaged] while each at the same time is involved in his or her own separate activity" (1994, p. 160). This type of interaction is similar to, yet different from, parallel play in young children; it is actually a type of cooperative interaction, but is different from that with which practitioners are familiar. This type of reframing involves learning about multiple perspectives, one of the treasures offered by diversity.

Even more radically, Betsy could choose to set the perceived problem aside for a while and "waste time" talking with Karen over a cup of coffee while they both watch Maya play with her toys, thus redefining the level of involvement for both. Who knows what that could lead to?

3. From a 3rd Space perspective, differences are understood to be complementary rather than divisive.

This characteristic of 3rd Space is a hallmark of Skilled Dialogue. It comes from the understanding the nature of boundaries, which serve both as distinctions and as points of contact that, like the poles of a battery (Palmer, 1997), generate constructive tension when connected. Third, fourth, and even fifth choices are generated not only to expand behavioral repertoires, but also to explore connections between apparently polarized perspectives.

The idea that two or more diverse perspectives are complementary (i.e., can be somehow integrated to form a greater whole) is the core of 3rd Space. A classic example of this "the whole is greater than the sum of the parts" perspective is the story of the men who met an elephant in the dark (Perkins, 2001). All of them believed that they could describe this strange animal. "He is like a tree trunk," said the man who bumped into the elephant's leg. "No, he is like a rope," said the one who touched his trunk—and so forth. In this story each person was correct, given his limited scope of experience, and also incorrect, given the reality of the elephant. Each man's experience yielded only one part of the total picture. Yet, the full picture was not just the sum of each man's impressions—a bizarre creature that is part tree, part rope, and so forth. The full and truest picture could not be known until all perspectives were integrated. Only then could the whole elephant emerge, something more than the simple sum of their individual impressions.

The skill of 3rd Space requires that practitioners jointly explore the "elephant" and not just their individual perspectives. What might the elephant be in Betsy's and Karen's case? (Clue: The three parts are Maya alone with

Betsy, Maya alone with Karen, and Maya with both Betsy and Karen.) (See the following section for further discussion of 3rd Space options and a hint as to how to answer the question just posed.)

A more concrete description of 3rd Space emerges when we imagine that our perspectives are actual rooms in physical space. From a singular space perspective, there is literally only one room: the one that I am in. From this perspective, I believe that my room (e.g., view, value, belief, language) is the only one that exists. I can neither seen nor imagine anything different—or if I can, I judge those things to be nonexistent or without value. If I am told about them, I do not accept them as real. Real events and interactions only take place in my room. From a singular space perspective, Betsy would be absolutely certain that only her beliefs and values are true and/or valid. She would have difficulty perceiving that others could hold diverse beliefs and values and even greater difficulty believing those beliefs and values to be equally valid and true.

But there can also be a dualistic space perspective. From this perspective, I realize that mine is not the only room. I accept other views as real but place them outside of my space (i.e., exclude them from my room). I am, so to speak, in one room and people different from me are in a different room(s). Events and interactions take place in one room or the other (e.g., my way or your way, this or that, right or wrong). In dualistic space, there is no common ground. I cannot meet you unless one or both of us move: I must leave my room (i.e., comfortable space), you must leave your room, or we must both leave our rooms and go to another neutral room. If I hold a both-and perspective (a variation of a dualistic perspective), then we each remain in our separate rooms, side by side yet unable to connect or integrate our respective rooms (i.e., perspectives).

From a dualistic space perspective, Betsy would understand that Karen's values and beliefs are different from her own and are perhaps even equally valid. Yet, she would have only two ways of responding. If she felt strongly that the differences needed to be resolved, then she would try to reach agreement. That is, one or the other would concede her beliefs/values or each would compromise those beliefs/values to a certain degree. If Betsy felt less strongly about the need to reach agreement, then she could simply let both sets of beliefs remain side by side, separate but equal.

In contrast to mindsets associated with both singular and dualistic space, a 3rd Space perspective accepts the possibility that our diverse perspectives could be integrated. It asks the question, "If we are in separate rooms, how can we both end up in the same space without moving?" Through this question, 3rd Space challenges us to realize that it is not our respective positions that keep us from occupying common space. Rather, it is the wall that we have erected between our positions that divides us.

Walls are different from boundaries. Boundaries are markers of space and identity. They may generate diversity bumps, but they do not obstruct one's view and are permeable. Conversely, walls are opaque and impenetrable. Depending on their size and thickness, walls can exclude and result in diversity clashes or sometimes outright crashes. It is important to recognize that a wall is often boundary that has fossilized over time, becoming hard and dense in response to repeated assaults. For example, if a person's language is repeatedly perceived to have low status or to be inadequate, he or she is then likely to form strong walls around it, perhaps refusing to speak it outside of the home or even refusing to speak it entirely.

With a 3ʳᵈ Space perspective, lowering or removing the wall between rooms allows people to be in the same room without having to move (e.g., realizing that both languages are equally valid no matter how others perceive them). In 3ʳᵈ Space, for example, Betsy would be able to ask herself, "What walls (e.g., judgments about her intent) have I erected between Karen's perspective and my own?" "Am I not communicating the value of what she brings to this situation?" "For Maya's best interests, how I can integrate my beliefs and values with Karen's to extract their strengths and diminish their limitations?" (*Note:* the strategies of Sense-Making and Appreciation discussed in Chapter 7 facilitate the lowering of walls.)

The skill of 3ʳᵈ Space invites practitioners into a conceptual space in which reality is not dichotomous, three or more choices always exist, and differences are complementary. It challenges people to lower or dissolve their walls and adopt an inclusive mindset that can integrate two or more diverse perspectives into a whole and mine the strengths of both.

3ᴿᴰ SPACE IN EARLY CHILDHOOD ENVIRONMENTS

Early childhood practitioners are trained to seek solutions, which is a natural tendency. Some readers, for example, will be impatient with these first chapters and turn to Section III first. Similarly, our current ENC culture tends to emphasize answers rather than the process of how we can arrive at those answers.

When the authors present scenarios at workshops, participants often start to propose solutions without first focusing on shifting into a 3ʳᵈ Space perspective. Immediate attention is given to what should or could be done. When for example a scenario such as that of Betsy and Karen is given, participants often start brainstorming solutions rather than first carefully reflecting on all aspects of the situation. This is natural but can be counterproductive, especially when dealing with culturally linguistically diverse behaviors and perspectives with which we may be less familiar. ENC values and beliefs tend to reinforce moving to resolution or reconciliation before tension is sufficiently experienced (Stewart & Bennett, 1991). As Perkins noted: "People have a strong tendency to generate a quick vision of the nature of a solution and set off from there" (2001, p. 150). The problem being that such a vision has no room for new information; it can only come from what is already known.

The purpose of conceptualizing and creating 3ʳᵈ Space is not to make decisions or resolve differences. Rather, it is to first create a common shared space within which the strengths of those differences can be leveraged and the probability of making optimum decisions increased, even when others' identities and voices result in practices different from those desired by practitioners. Fritz commented on the differences between a problem-solving orientation and a creative one:

> When you are solving a problem, you are taking action to have something go away: the problem. [How can persons honor a difference if they are trying to make it go away?] When you are creating, you are taking action to have something come into being: the creation [of something different and richer]. (Fritz, 1989, p. 11)

Skilled Dialogue invites people to use the skill of 3ʳᵈ Space for the purpose of having "something come into being." In this sense, they become creators "who solve problems secondarily as a necessary and inevitable result of [their] commitment to producing a remarkable artistic result" (Childs, 1998, p. 34). Decisions are made and problems are solved, but only secondarily, as a result of practitioners' commitment to creatively crafting interactions that are respectful, reciprocal, and responsive.

As the mindset of 3ʳᵈ Space is developed and its skill practiced, the options that arise cannot be predetermined. They can emerge only from and through respectful, responsive, and reciprocal interactions between people holding diverse perspectives. The following examples are therefore not answers but only illustrations of how 3ʳᵈ Space options emerge in particular situations. They may or (more likely) may not be applicable to other particular situations.

A group of Head Start staff was asked to select a situation to which they would like to apply the idea and skill of 3ʳᵈ Space. They immediately chose their recent experiences with Martha, a mother whose 4-year-old son was exhibiting aggressive and hyperactive behavior (e.g., throwing chairs, hitting students, running around the room). The staff had developed a behavior management program that was somewhat successful on site, but Martha would not agree to use it at home. Her response was, "As long as he doesn't burn the house down, I'm okay with his behavior." They added that Martha was an older single mother who worked two jobs, one of which was working the night shift at a juvenile detention facility. The first step was for the practitioners to achieve AUD in this situation. They asked themselves many of the questions referenced in the next chapter. They especially focused on identifying possible positive intents underlying Martha's behavior. After extended discussion, they decided that they could accept Martha's perspective as valid (although still undesirable) if Martha perceived her choices as either ignoring her son's behavior or end up hitting him out of frustration and exhaustion. For the first time, the group felt that they could respect this mother's decision. Even though they disagreed with her perceived choices, they could now respect her need to avoid physical violence.

But how could they begin to create 3ʳᵈ Space? The two existing spaces—the space where the mother was inattentive to her son and the space in which the staff felt compelled to force compliance—had significant drawbacks. The ensuing discussion was even more prolonged than the previous one. Although the staff could respect Martha's choice, their negative judgment of her behavior seemed to preclude the possibility of creating inclusive 3rd Space options. When the question, "How could you compliment this mom in this situation?" was raised, no one had an immediate answer. Finally, one staff member said, "We could compliment her on how well she has encouraged her son to become self-reliant because she expects him to fix his own dinner and entertain himself until she gets home."

The change in staff energy after this statement was palpable. A 3rd Space perspective in which Martha's behavior (reframed as supporting self-reliance) could be integrated with the staff's desired behavior (nurturing relational and social skills) began to develop. The staff could approach Martha as an equal partner who provided one part of the whole. The staff reformulated their interactions as "adding to that part" rather than trying to erase it. As a result, they reported that they no longer felt the need to approach Martha from a "we need to fix this" approach and, instead, could approach her from a sincere "How can we work together?" position. The final outcome remained uncertain, but the staff's shift in perspective promised a more positive outcome than their initial position of "Implement our behavior management program at home or we will no longer be able to serve your child."

Reconciling Differences (Gonzalez-Mena, Herzog, & Herzog, 2000), a video based on the Skilled Dialogue concept of 3rd Space, provides a second example of finding 3rd Space options. In this example, two early childhood practitioners role-play a discussion of children's drawing activities.

Dora, a program administrator, observed Lisa, a teacher, help a child to complete a drawing. Dora expressed both developmental and administrative concerns about this behavior. She told Lisa that early education values support independent exploration of skills over the imposition of patterns deemed desirable by adults. She also expressed concern regarding what might happen if teachers helped children to draw during an accreditation visit. The two practitioners discussed their different perspectives for a while, realizing that a deep disagreement as well as some disapproval existed between them. Their discussion did, however, evidence their respect for each other and their desire to reach a mutual understanding. Finally, Lisa began talking about the meaning she associated with helping a child to draw. She recalled her parents drawing with her and the closeness that she experienced during this activity. Dora acknowledged that she has had similar experiences. Lisa's comment, "Then, why can't we have both?" opened the door to the creation of an inclusive 3rd Space option that would integrate their diverse perspectives. When the goal was to teach fine motor skills, Lisa agreed on the need for more independent functioning. When, however, the goal was to relate with the child to establish stronger rapport or elicit a wider range of behaviors, Dora agreed that it was okay to help the child to draw. Although they did not fully develop this option, the tone of their interaction clearly shifted as they discussed it. Their postures and their voices changed from adversarial to collaborative.

These examples illustrate the function of 3rd Space as both a skill and a mindset. A 3rd Space perspective does not solve the problem. Rather, it changes the arena within which that problem is addressed, thereby increasing the probability of respectful, responsive, and reciprocal interactions. In so doing, an optimal response to the situation becomes more likely.

PRACTICING 3RD SPACE

The following discussion of various strategies[1] associated with learning and using 3rd Space will help to further describe its character. Therefore, it is retained in this chapter even though the following chapter also discusses these strategies as well as those for its correlate disposition: Setting the Stage for Miracles.

The first step is to acquire the mindset—that is, to entertain the possibility of a shift from perceiving two (or more) perspectives as contradictory to perceiving them as complementary. Some practitioners have experience with such inclusive mindsets, and, therefore, can develop 3rd Space options more easily. Other practitioners may have more difficulty shifting out of habitual either-or thinking. For these practitioners, the books, activities, and games referenced within this chapter, as well as in Barrera and Kramer (2009), may be of help in anchoring their understanding of 3rd Space.

Appropriate 3rd Space options can emerge only when practitioners can pause respectfully before trying to change something. This pause helps practitioners to listen and observe without judgment (or giving advice). Both judgment and advice, when given too soon, communicate that a person already knows everything and, consequently, close out 3rd Space options.

Paradoxically, identifying specific tension points (i.e., contradictions) is as important to creating 3rd Space as is withholding judgment. Identifying contradictions helps people to explore and question why they want to change, contradict, or even oppose another's perspective. What is it about that perspective that is threatening or uncomfortable?

Identifying contradictions and staying with the tension send a strong message of respect. They say, "I recognize that you believe/behave differently from me and I do not judge you as wrong or somehow less than me for that reason." It should be noted, however, that this message does not preclude continuing to invite others to change or take action to protect a child. It does preclude doing so in ways that dishonor or shame families.

Developing the skill of 3rd Space requires creating opportunities for equalizing power across interactions. Power cannot be equalized as long as one perspective must be excluded or proven wrong to justify change to another.

---

[1]These strategies were developed in pilot research with Dr. Rosalita Mitchell and graduate students at the University of New Mexico.

For example, practitioners do not have to communicate that a family's behavior (e.g., speaking a language other than English with their child) is wrong to communicate that an additional behavior is desirable (e.g., developing English language skills).

Exploring how contradictory behaviors or perspectives can be complementary is a key strategy for establishing 3rd Space. This means recognizing how more than one behavior/perspective is true at the same time (e.g., involvement can be expressed as both engagement and no engagement). The complementary nature of contradictory behaviors also can be understood by asking how one behavior or perspective balances the other. Chaos, for example, balances order to produce creativity. Order without some degree of chaos freezes into rigidity and precludes change. Chaos without some degree of order becomes destructive disorder and precludes growth.

It is also important to explore responses that integrate contradictions. The question at this point is, "What response incorporates both your perspective and mine?" Two metaphors that may be used to communicate this goal are the metaphor of "half empty, half full" and the metaphor of a musical chord (see also Chapter 7).

Setting the Stage for Miracles

As with AUD, the need to shift the skill of 3rd Space into a broader context became apparent as the authors worked with practitioners. The concept of 3rd Space tended to be an unfamiliar one that all too often was understood as only a cognitive exercise. And, in fact, there is a strong cognitive dimension to 3rd Space as it requires a paradigm shift. Skills such as reframing and lateral thinking (DeBono, 1970, 1991) are important to facilitating such a shift. The intent of 3rd Space, however, is not only to exercise these skills but also, more important, to use them in the service of creating options other than those already present. The disposition of Setting the Stage for Miracles makes this intent explicit. *Miracle* is defined by the authors as an outcome that is not predictable from the known variables/conditions; in other words an outcome that is unpredictable and unanticipated.

In general, Setting the Stage for Miracles involves the willingness not to focus on immediate change, but rather to stay with the tension of differing perspectives and identify the strengths of those that seem to contradict our own. In addition, Setting the Stage for Miracles involves reframing and brainstorming to expand current perceptions and transform contradictions into complementarities.

The disposition of Setting the Stage for Miracles asks practitioners to tap into their creativity and focus on creating a cognitive space within which disparate identities are allowed to exist side by side, disparate voices are simultaneously appreciated, and differences are integrated and harmonized. It is the intent to create 3rd Space so as to build mutual partnerships in which the strengths of all parties are accessed and leveraged.

Setting the Stage for Miracles is the intent to move beyond what is known in order to allow something greater to emerge. Wheatley referenced Joel Baker who "stated that when something is impossible to achieve with one worldview, it can be surprisingly easy to accomplish with another" (2005, p. 75). She went on to say, "Where there is diversity [of perspectives] innovative solutions are created all the time, just because different people do things differently" (p. 78). Setting the Stage for Miracles is necessary as a direct acknowledgment of the value of and need for diverse perspectives. It takes practitioners beyond a "you're different and that's nice" perspective to a "you're different and bring beliefs, behaviors, and values that are of value to this situation."

Barrera and Kramer (2009) discussed the disposition of Setting the Stage for Miracles much more extensively. They provided illustrations of its use and suggestions for developing it.

A LOOK AHEAD

The next chapter discusses strategies for both 3rd Space and AUD in relation to Skilled Dialogue's skills and dispositions. It integrates both original strategies and the newer more formalized ones presented in our 2009 text. Section III provides additional guidelines and materials specific to interactions associated with assessment and instruction. Several vignettes drawn from the authors' experiences in culturally diverse early childhood environments are presented and discussed to illustrate the use of these guidelines and materials.

Strategies

THEN AND NOW

Each of Skilled Dialogue's characteristic qualities—respect, reciprocity, and re-sponsiveness—is expressed somewhat differently in relation to each of Skilled Dialogue's two skills/dispositions, resulting in a range of strategies[1] associated with each quality and each skill. These strategies, as presented in the first edition, differ from those presented in Barrera and Kramer (2009). They are reviewed in their original form in the first part of the chapter and are the precursors of those presented in our 2009 text. Linkages to newer strategies are made in the section on current strategies. The original strategies can be thought of as specific examples of the newer ones, which are broader categories (see Tables 7.1 and 7.2, which list the original strategies as well as their newer counterparts).

ESTABLISHING RESPECT

Respect and Anchored Understanding of Diversity

In relation to AUD, respect is best expressed as the willingness to acknowl-edge the validity of diverse perspectives to achieve a particular goal. The first strategy associated with establishing respect thus focuses on mindful listening, which involves widening "the gap of time between perceiving a message and interpreting its content" (Shafir, 2000, p. 42). A first step to listening mind-fully is to ask questions such as the following.

- How much time am I allowing between hearing others' messages and in-terpreting their content?

- Do I assume I know what is meant almost before the other person has finished speaking? Or do I listen and wait to gather additional information from others and from myself?

[1]These strategies were developed as part of field-testing activities done with Dr. Rosalita Mitchell and graduate students at the University of New Mexico. Their support and contributions are gratefully acknowledged.

Table 7.1. Relationship of strategies for Anchored Understanding of Diversity with strategies in current Skilled Dialogue model

Anchored Understanding of Diversity strategies	Corollary strategies in current model
Respect Strategy 1: Listen mindfully to others' comments/ responses. Strategy 2: Get information about others' perspectives. Strategy 3: Examine your own perspective.	*Welcoming* (associated with respect and Choosing Relationship over Control) *Sense-Making* (associated with reciprocity and Choosing Relationship over Control) *Joining* (associated with responsiveness and Choosing Relationship over Control
Reciprocity Strategy 1: Allow yourself to believe that others' contributions are of equal value to yours. Strategy 2: Clarify others' understanding of your perspective. Strategy 3: Recognize the value of others' contributions.[a]	*Appreciating* (associated with reciprocity and Setting the Stage for Miracles) *Sense-Making* (associated with reciprocity and Choosing Relationship over Control) *Appreciating* (associated with reciprocity and Setting the Stage for Miracles)
Responsiveness Strategy 1: Remain mindful and open to mystery (i.e., not knowing). Strategy 2: Keep paying attention. Strategy 3: Reflect an understanding of others' perspectives.	*Allowing* (associated with respect and Setting the Stage for Miracles) *Allowing* (associated with respect and Setting the Stage for Miracles) *Joining* (associated with responsiveness and Choosing Relationship over Control)

[a]This strategy is more aligned with a strategy for Setting the Stage for Miracles (3rd Space) than with Choosing Relationship over Control (Anchored Understanding of Diversity), as these are organized in the current Skilled Dialogue model.

Exploring these questions and other similar ones helps reveal the story that practitioners and families tell themselves about each other or about the situation in which they find themselves. Once determined, the stories themselves can be gently challenged if necessary. Are they, in fact, true (Katie, 2002)? For example, practitioners need to ask whether their story is true. Are they telling themselves and communicating, however inadvertently, something such as, "Here I am; all I am trying to do is help and you don't seem to recognize, much less appreciate, that," or "Your behavior just doesn't communicate any respect for my time and effort." Or, perhaps the practitioner's storyline is more like the following: "I seem to be more interested in working with this child than the parents."

Of course, family members are in all probability telling themselves different stories that they believe to be the truth. They might, for example, be telling themselves, "This teacher seems to know so much about my child; maybe I should just let her work with my child so as not to waste any time," or "I don't understand why this teacher seems so concerned about my child's language; I can understand her and, anyway, that isn't what I'm most concerned about."

Table 7.2. Relationship of strategies for creating 3ʳᵈ Space options with strategies in current Skilled Dialogue model

3ʳᵈ Space strategies	Strategies in current model that reflect original ones
Respect Strategy 1: Release the natural inclination to focus on solutions/resolutions. Strategy 2: Listen/observe without judgment. Strategy 3: Identify specific tension points.	*Allowing* (associated with respect and Setting the Stage for Miracles) *Allowing* (associated with respect and Setting the Stage for Miracles) *Harmonizing* (associated with responsiveness and Setting the Stage for Miracles)
Reciprocity Strategy 1: Recognize that there is no need to make one perspective wrong to justify another as right. Strategy 2: Shift the focus of conversation to equalize participation.ᵃ Strategy 3: Explore how contradictory behaviors/perspectives could be complementary.	*Allowing* (associated with respect and Setting the Stage for Miracles) *Joining* (associated with responsiveness and Choosing Relationship over Control) *Harmonizing* (associated with responsiveness and Setting the Stage for Miracles)
Responsiveness Strategy 1: Trust the possibility of options that honor diversity. Strategy 2: Explore responses that integrate contradictions.	*Appreciating* (associated with reciprocity and Setting the Stage for Miracles) *Harmonizing* (associated with responsiveness and Setting the Stage for Miracles)

ᵃNote that this strategy is more aligned with a strategy for Choosing Relationship over Control (Anchored Understanding of Diversity) than with one for Setting the Stage for Miracles (3ʳᵈ Space), as these are organized in the current Skilled Dialogue model.

Whatever the stories, practitioners must anchor their understanding of both their own stories and those of families. They need to identify these stories and question the assumptions that may underlie them (e.g., assumptions about skills levels or degree of motivation). Katie (2002) presented an interesting framework for challenging stories about ones self and others. She suggested first asking, "Is it true?" whenever assumptions are made about others' behaviors and then examining why those assumptions may have been made.

Respect and 3ʳᵈ Space

In relation to 3ʳᵈ Space, respect is communicated by acknowledging that others' perspectives and behaviors are as evidence based as our own; that is, that they are rooted in lived evidence and are not just willful or ignorant reactions. The stage for 3ʳᵈ Space is set only when practitioners can pause respectfully before trying to change something and thus communicate that there is not just one set of answers and that these are best known only by them.

The first strategy for establishing respect in relation to 3rd Space addresses this need to reflect on and release the natural inclination to focus on solutions and resolutions. This strategy is misleading in that it can seem much more simple than it is. It is simple in that it merely requires a pause before interjecting comments, suggestions, advice, and/or opinions. It is extremely challenging, however, in that it requires that very thing. The authors have often asked participants in workshops to try such a pause after listening to an opinion with which they disagree strongly (e.g., children should be allowed to do what they want). Most report that this can be difficult to accomplish for even 60 seconds. There are no questions to ask in relation to this strategy; there is only the commitment to silent attention.

The next strategy involves not only pausing but also withholding judgment (or giving advice). Verbal and nonverbal indicators of interest and curiosity are important if others are to feel safe enough to lower or remove their walls. Both judgment and advice, especially when given too soon, communicate that a person already knows everything and consequently raises walls. There are no questions associated with this strategy either.

Paradoxically, explicitly identifying specific tension points (i.e., contradictions)—the third strategy—is as important to the creation of 3rd Space as is withholding judgment. Awareness of others' boundaries is communicated when contradictions are identified. Differences cannot be honored if they are not first acknowledged. Not acknowledging differences often does not communicate respect. All too often it just communicates a discomfort with the differences themselves. It is only after people are sure that others recognize them in all of their particularity that they are willing to lower their walls.

Questions that can be asked with this third strategy include the following:

- What aspects of others behavior/perspective am I finding the most difficulty or disagreeable?

- Why? What meaning(s) am I attaching to that behavior/perspective (e.g., the person is unmotivated, the person will sabotage all I am trying to do)?

- What would happen if I did not contradict, oppose, or try to change that behavior/perspective?

Identifying contradictions helps practitioners explore and question why they want to change, contradict, or even oppose another's perspective. What is it about that perspective that is uncomfortable or threatening? For example, as the previously described Head Start staff worked on becoming more skilled in their interactions with Martha, the first author suggested that they ask what would happen if they stopped trying to change Martha's behavior. After some thought, one of them responded, "If we can't change her behavior, Mikey (her son) will continue to be aggressive and hyperactive and will probably grow up to join a gang, drop out of school, and get involved in real violence." This scenario, which was plausible given the populations with whom they worked, gave an important clue to the staff's underlying beliefs. In some sense, they perceived Martha's behavior as a threat to their definition of themselves as teachers who could prevent such outcomes.

The problem with such a scenario was that it focused on future outcomes as a motivation for changing Martha's present behavior. With such a scenario in mind, it was only natural to communicate a high level of judgment and urgency. Neither quality, however, would help Martha feel safe enough to lower her walls and enter into a truly collaborative relationship with the staff. In all likelihood, these qualities would only trigger counterscenarios of her own.

The first author asked the staff about children with similar backgrounds who had previously attended the program. What had happened as these children grew up? The answers varied, but most had not followed the path predicted for Mikey. This recognition allowed the staff to realize that their projected outcome was not inevitable; neither was it solely up to them to "save" Mikey and the others whom he might later harm. This realization allowed the staff to approach Martha from a more mindful perspective, which, in turn, created a greater potential for Skilled Dialogue.

Taken together, the strategies of identifying contradictions and staying with the tension send a strong message of respect. They say, "I recognize that you believe/behave differently from me and I do not judge you as wrong or somehow less than me for that reason." It should be noted, however, that this message does not preclude continuing to invite others to change or taking action to protect a child. It does preclude doing so in ways that dishonor or shame families.

ESTABLISHING RECIPROCITY

Reciprocity and Anchored Understanding of Diversity

In relation to AUD, reciprocity is more strongly established when it is expressed concretely as the intent to support equal voice for those with whom one is interacting. Three strategies actualize this intent and, in so doing, promote AUD. The first strategy is simply to allow oneself to believe that all interactions can, in fact, be reciprocal (i.e., allow for the expression of diverse perspectives without privileging one over another). This strategy requires entering into interactions ready to learn as well as to teach; that is, as ready to receive as to give.

A corollary strategy—clarifying others' understanding of one's own perspective—expresses acknowledgement that there is no single story that yields a universal meaning for behaviors and actions. Questions such as the following are helpful at this point.

- How do you see my actions?

- What do you hear me saying/asking?

- What are your thoughts when I do/say _____?

- What does complying with my request (e.g., to read to your child) mean to you?

These questions may be asked directly of the families or practitioners with whom one is interacting if sufficient rapport has been established. They may also be asked of people from similar experiential, cultural, and linguistic backgrounds (e.g., other practitioners, community members). It is important to acknowledge that reciprocity involves accepting multiple perspectives.

This acknowledgment leads directly to a third strategy—actively recognizing the value of others' contributions. It is only through acknowledging that everyone brings something of value to an interaction that interactions truly become reciprocal. Three questions are suggested. The first two questions can be asked in every situation. The third needs to be asked specifically in situations in which practitioners are seeking behavior changes.

1. What resources does this person bring to our interaction (e.g., daily knowledge of child's behavior, connections with community)?

2. What can I learn from this person (e.g., how to function in unfamiliar environments)?

3. What are the positive aspects of this person's current behavior?

These questions actually address both respect and reciprocity. Unless one can acknowledge what is positive about someone else's behavior or what one can learn from that behavior, one is unlikely to respect that person, much less establish reciprocity with him or her.

The following vignette shows how the third question can be used to establish reciprocity in an early childhood program environment.

Sara's parents, Mr. and Mrs. Flores, identified themselves as Hispanic. Sara had two older sisters, and her entire family spent a lot of time playing with her and attending to her needs. At a team meeting to discuss intervention goals for Sara, several team members expressed concern about Sara's developing motor and verbal skills. Margie, the physical therapist, said, "Her family caters to her needs; she never has to ask for anything verbally, and she is always carried by one family member or another. I've asked them not to carry her so much." Connie, the SLP, added, "We've asked Mr. and Mrs. Flores to encourage Sara to ask for things verbally before giving them to her."

Rose, the meeting coordinator, first discussed the culturally based values and beliefs that seemed to underlie Mr. and Mrs. Flores' behavior and the need to respect these beliefs. She explained that from their cultural perspective, it was important to Mr. and Mrs. Flores to keep Sara from experiencing any additional discomfort. In their eyes, it was important to communicate to Sara that she was acceptable and loved as she was, that her family's love was not contingent on the presence of particular behaviors.

Rose then asked, "What is positive about the family's current behavior? How are they contributing to Sara's development?" After some thought, Margie answered, "Maybe all of that unconditional and consistent attention to Sara has nurtured her trust in adults. I've noticed how willing she is to follow our directions." That statement opened the door to seeing Mr. and Mrs. Flores as collaborators in supporting Sara's development rather than as parents unwilling to follow the team's recommendations. Tension between the family and team members dissolved, and energy that had been tied up in trying to change the family was freed to create ways of working collaboratively.

Reciprocity and 3rd Space

Reciprocity has a twofold goal in relation to 3rd Space: 1) to communicate the recognition that there is no need to make one perspective wrong to justify another as right and 2) to explore how diverse perspectives can bring complementary resources to a given situation. Although reciprocity addresses the equalizing of power across interactions vis-à-vis AUD, it now requires creating space for that to happen.

The first strategy associated with reciprocity in relation to 3rd Space is simply recognizing that it is unnecessary to make one perspective wrong to justify another as right. Power cannot be equalized as long as one perspective must be excluded or proven wrong to justify change to another. For example, practitioners do not have to communicate that a family's behavior (e.g., speaking a language other than English with their child) is wrong to communicate that an additional behavior is desirable (e.g., developing English language skills). As Cummins remarked,

> Educators who see their role as adding a second language and cultural affiliation to students' repertoires are likely to empower students more than those who see their role as replacing or subtracting students' primary language and culture in the process of assimilating them to the dominant culture. (1989, p. 113)

Although these words are not specific to ECSE, they can be easily paraphrased: Practitioners who see their role as adding to families' and children's behavioral and linguistic repertoires are likely to empower them more than practitioners who see their role as replacing or subtracting from these repertoires in the service of promoting desired developmental goals.

Shifting the focus of conversation is the second strategy for establishing reciprocity in support of 3rd Space. A great example of this strategy comes from a conversation that the first author had with, a graduate student and practitioner:

In the middle of our discussion about 3rd Space, Janet, the graduate student, unexpectedly asked, "Is that something like the idea of a common denominator?" stopping me in my tracks. Only when we went back over our conversation did we realize that as she sought to anchor her understanding, she had intuitively succeeded in establishing reciprocity. As long as I continued to talk about 3rd Space, the power between us was implicitly unequal: I remained the "expert," and she was the novice. When she shifted the focus to common denominators, a concept with which she was familiar, I had to stop and remember what little I know about that mathematical reality. At that point we both became learners on an equal footing. The topic—3rd Space—remained constant, but our conversation shifted its focus to common denominators. This is not an easy strategy but it is a highly effective one.

Exploring how contradictory behaviors or perspectives can be complementary is the third strategy that helps establish reciprocity in relation to 3rd Space. This means that both are true at the same time (e.g., involvement can be expressed as both engagement and no engagement).

The complementary nature of contradictory behaviors can be explored by asking how one behavior or perspective balances the other. As discussed earlier, chaos appears to contradict order, yet actually balances it (i.e., keeps it from freezing into rigidity) and, thus, produces creativity. When split apart, each—order and chaos—becomes distorted and stops short of its full potential.

How might Karen's behavior (i.e., not participating in Maya's intervention activities) balance Betsy's (i.e., working directly with Maya)? What might be the result of that balance? Betsy might say, "You know, maybe there's a way that your behavior complements mine. When you leave Maya and me, you are supporting her development of independent problem-solving skills. If you stayed, she might look to you to help her out, and I think that she is emotionally and cognitively ready to begin solving simple problems on her own."

A statement such as this could potentially shift Betsy's and Karen's interactions. Their interactions can move from not supporting each other's goals toward being collaborative. How might both Betsy's and Karen's goals be met without sacrificing either? Perhaps Betsy and Maya could accompany Karen when she leaves the room and consider it a "field trip," during which Maya could learn various concepts, movements, or words. Although each is still in her own room—Betsy wants Karen to stay and Karen continues to leave—a door has been opened between their two perspectives. A reciprocal "right-right" rather than a "right-wrong" perspective has been established.

RESPONSIVENESS

Responsiveness and Anchored Understanding of Diversity

In relation to AUD, the quality of responsiveness addresses one's ability to communicate others' perspectives with empathic understanding (i.e., to tell their story from their perspective). Such understanding does not necessarily connote agreement, however. For example, Margie and Connie do not need to agree with Mr. and Mrs. Flores' beliefs and practices. They may still prefer that Sara's parents, too, extend their repertoire of parental behaviors. Even so, Margie and Connie can be responsive when they can say, "If we were them (i.e., lived their culture), then we'd do the same," and no longer feel a need to ask the parents to give up their present behavior. It is at that point that they could begin to become authentically responsive to Sara and her family.

One of the first strategies to shape such responsiveness is remaining mindful of and open to mystery rather than merely trying to find an answer. Some questions that help at this stage include the following:

- Am I overly focused on my goals and my interpretations/judgments?

- What important information or alternative interpretations might I be missing as a result of this focus?

- To what degree am I willing to trust the process (and the families engaged in it with me) without needing to know exactly what will happen?

Remen (2000) noted that focusing too closely on where one is going makes it easy to miss what is before us along the journey. For example, a person may focus too intently on a child's obvious (to a practitioner) need to learn to feed him- or herself independently. In doing that, he or she may miss a parent's deeper need to feel that he or she can take care of his or her child competently. Or, as in a situation encountered by the first author, the practitioner may miss the rich trust and emotional connection between the parents and their child, a connection that has been facilitating their own work all along.

Remaining open to mystery requires asking the simple question that was previously introduced: "Is it true?" (Katie, 2002). In Sara's case, for example, one might ask, "Is it irrefutably in Sara's best interest to learn to self-feed now?" Practitioners may say that if she does not learn now, then Sara will be delayed in developing other skills—but is that true? How might practitioners interact differently with Sara and her family if they were not so certain that they knew best about what Sara needed to learn next? This is not to say that practitioners should dismiss their goals, only that they should hold them more loosely, leaving room for what might be "outside the box."

Mindful attention to mystery and uncertainty blends with the next two strategies—sustained listening and observing without seeking resolution too quickly. The goal at this point is not to reach a solution but to deepen understanding so that the identified solution can be best implemented. Sustained listening reminds practitioners never to seek clarification and confirmation of perceptions instead of making assumptions. Respectively, these two strategies address one's ability to 1) reflect back to others' nonjudgmental acceptance of their actions and 2) keep understanding fluid until feedback confirms that one indeed knows the meaning(s) of particular actions. Only then can it be said that one is truly responding.

Obviously, AUD is a process that cannot be developed in a brief interaction or perhaps even in several interactions, no matter how carefully these strategies are followed. It requires time for self-reflection and multiple dialogues—both difficult and skilled—with diverse people. The exchange of stories (my story, your story) through conversations over time assists the anchoring of understanding in a unique way (Sanchez, 1999). This does not, however, mean that nothing can be done until one's understanding is fully anchored. Immediate actions, such as calling in social services or conducting interactive activities with children, can and should occur even as this process is ongoing.

Responsiveness and 3rd Space

In relation to 3rd Space, responsiveness addresses the creation of 3rd Space options that both gain access to and leverage the strengths of the existing choices/perspectives. The strategies described up to this point set the stage for these options. Strategies for responsiveness focus more specifically on generating responses to particular situations that integrate diverse perspectives and provide access to their strengths.

The first suggested strategy is to accept that a third choice can be found, even if there seems to be no choice other than the two contradictory ones already identified. That is, trust the possibility of options that honor diversity by not forcing choice. This is not always easy. The authors have yet to encounter a situation or scenario in which a third (and often fourth and fifth) choice could not be found.

The second strategy is a key one: Explore responses that integrate contradictions. The question at this point is, "What response incorporates both your perspective and mine?" Two metaphors that may be used to communicate this goal are the metaphor of half empty, half full and the metaphor of a musical chord.

Two common perceptions exist when we look at a bottle of water that is only partially filled—half full and half empty. We can try to choose between them or we can focus on the bottle, which contains both perceptions, and realize that each perception is, in fact, defined by the other. The bottle is half empty precisely because it is only half full. A 3rd Space perspective shifts our perspective from the boundary where water and air meet to the container that holds them—the bottle. Like the elephant encountered by the men in the dark, the bottle is the greater whole that contains both apparently contradictory perspectives (i.e., empty and full). This is similar to how a musical chord integrates various notes into a greater whole while respecting and retaining the unique nature of each. Practitioners can apply this approach to working with families who do not speak English at home by shifting from a "use English at home" perspective to a collaborative one focused on language development that leverages existing language skills and uses them to support the development in the language in which they do not yet appear.

A special type of jigsaw puzzle provides a concrete metaphor for 3rd Space. Photomosaics™ are composed of numerous small puzzle pieces, each a complete picture in itself. When integrated and placed in just the right position, these pictures form a bigger and different picture without being changed themselves. This type of integration is the aim of 3rd Space. The idea is to take two people's stories or perceptions and integrate them so as to form a bigger, different story or picture that honors the similarities and differences of the individual pictures and is, in fact, created by their juxtaposition and integration.

Reframing techniques constitute a third strategy for exploring the integration of contradictory perspectives. DeBono (2008, 2009), Fletcher and Olwyer (1997), and Perkins (2001) provided exercises for using reframing. Although not always possible, reframing is nevertheless a powerful strategy. It entails changing the point of view from which one defines a problem. Perkins remarked, "If the way you've been coding or representing the situation to yourself is not going anywhere, perhaps the problem is unreasonable—so why not try something different?" (p. 132). Laziness, for example, can be reframed and perceived as efficiency. After all, the goal of both laziness and efficiency is the same—the conservation of energy. Such reframing would increase the probability of a positive response to the person conserving his or her energy.

The following scenario illustrates reframing by telling different stories about the same event. Imagine that you are in a bank one afternoon. You are tired and ready to get home. The person in front of you, who is carrying a small child, cashes her check and then continues to chat with the bank teller. At one point, the woman even hands over the child for the teller to hold. This goes on for several minutes, with the person giving no indication that she is ready to leave. What story might you tell yourself about this situation?

One possible story might sound something like this: "How inconsiderate can this person be? Doesn't she have any awareness of people around her? Does she think that she can just stand there and block the line?" There is, however, another possibility. Imagine that when you finally get to the teller, she turns to you and says, "I am so sorry. I am a single parent. My husband died suddenly last year, and I had to return to work. That was my baby sitter with my daughter. This is the only time that I get to see her after I leave home because she is often asleep by the time I return from work." How would your response to the earlier actions change? The additional information reframes your perception of the situation. What additional information might reframe your perception in a given situation? Can you think of other stories to explain the situation?

Using different lenses to perceive situations can be another aid to reframing. Perkins provided an example of this in his presentation of the following puzzle.

> There's a man with a mask at home. There's a man coming home. What's going on here? This is thin information, so perhaps you would like to hear some questions answered. Is the man with the mask a thief? No. Does the man coming home live there? No. Is the man with the mask going to hurt the man coming home? No. (2001, p. 28)

Processing this information with a lens that translates *home* into *domicile* makes solving this puzzle unlikely. If you are using a sports lens and thinking about baseball, however, then the answer is clear.

There are multiple lenses available in any situation. For example, using a cultural lens to understand a behavior such as not speaking up in class may lead to the perception that such behavior is appropriate, although more effective in some contexts than in others. Using a developmental lens without reference to culture might lead to a different answer (Brown & Barrera, 1999)—perhaps that there is a language delay, self-esteem is compromised and needs strengthening, or the student is not engaged.

Finally, brainstorming techniques can also be used to explore potential 3rd Space options. It is not always easy to arrive at responses that truly provide access to and integrate the strengths of diverse perspectives, however, even with this technique and those previously described. Translating the mindset of 3rd Space into concrete responses is like learning to see the pictures hidden in 3-D illusion picture books (e.g., N.E. Thing Enterprises, 1993) in which one stares at a picture until a "buried" image appears. It takes continued practice and often requires what Perkins termed "breakthrough thinking," a type of thinking that purposely challenges "key assumptions" and seeks to represent "problems in a new way, broadening or shifting the boundaries of the search [for possibilities]" (2001, pp. 9, 55). It does not happen without intentional practice and some patience.

CURRENT STRATEGIES

The development of Skilled Dialogue strategies started with a focus on how to best achieve and maintain the qualities of respect, reciprocity, and responsiveness as identified through the observation and analysis of two practitioners the authors judged to be exceptionally culturally responsive and competent. As initial strategies were developed and field tested over time, however, it became clear that there was a need for a clearer and more systematic operationalization of the Skilled Dialogue process. This realization led to the development of the six strategies presented in our 2009 text. The following discussion briefly overviews these strategies, noting connections with those just discussed.

The six strategies introduced in this section—Welcoming, Allowing, Sense-Making, Appreciating, Joining, and Harmonizing—reflect the evolution of the original strategies as practitioners asked for further clarification. Although the original strategies can still be easily connected to the current ones (see Tables 7.1 and 7.2), the latter are now both more precise and more comprehensive. Readers interested in more detail on this aspect of their application are referred to our 2009 text.

Three strategies are associated with the expression of each disposition (see Figure 4.1). Each strategy targets a different quality or outcome. The three associated with Choosing Relationship over Control include Welcoming, which targets the development and maintenance of respect; Sense-Making, which targets establishing reciprocity; and Joining, which is designed to develop responsiveness.

The three strategies associated with Setting the Stage for Miracles include Allowing, which extends Welcoming and, in similar fashion, targets the development and maintenance of respect; Appreciating, which extends Sense-Making and is designed to establish reciprocity; and Harmonizing, which extends Joining and targets the development of truly responsive options. Each of these strategies is discussed in the following sections.

Strategies Associated with Choosing Relationship over Control

Welcoming   Welcoming focuses on promoting and sustaining respect (i.e., honoring identity) through Choosing Relationship over Control. It emphasizes the importance of communicating not only the opportunity to interact with another, but also a specific welcoming of the other person as an individual worthy of respect. How we first approach people is often the key to the nature and outcome of our subsequent interactions with them.

We may not agree or even like others' decisions or the resulting behaviors and/or perspectives. We may clearly see those behaviors and/or perspectives as inappropriate or limiting. Nevertheless, communicating our respect for another person cannot be fully accomplished without welcoming that other person not only as someone we can teach, but also, and more critically, as someone from whom we can learn.

The presumption of equal ability to craft a behavioral repertoire adaptive to a given context is a key characteristic of Welcoming. This presumption extends to the acceptance of another's behavior and/or perspective as legitimate within a given context and a willingness to communicate unconditional respect. The connection of Welcoming to mindful listening, previously discussed, is a clear one as we cannot feel welcomed if we do not perceived we are being listened to.

Sense-Making   Sense-Making draws our attention to finding ways of, quite literally, making sense of another's behavior, beliefs, and/or values. It invites us to search for and find the meaning(s) that underlies and structures that behavior, belief, and/or value. Sense-Making affirms the fact that another's behaviors make sense in some way, although it may not be initially clear to us just how it does that. Again, the connection of this strategy with those previously discussed (e.g., clarifying our understanding of another's perspective) is clear.

Having a curious attitude is the first requisite characteristic of Sense-Making. Such an attitude helps us to interact with another as a learner who seeks information rather than as an expert who is there only to give information or promote change. Attentive listening to the stories, experiences, and thoughts that support the other person's particular behaviors and perspectives is a second requisite characteristic. It is through honoring another person's voice as he or she tells his or her story that respect deepens into reciprocity.

Joining   Joining invites us to identify the larger shared context within which our beliefs and those of another person are connected as an expression of a single reality. Joining acknowledges the recognition that all interactions are constructed and enacted within a joint context (i.e., are connected) and that, consequently, the behaviors that compose them are not isolated and independent but rather are linked in some way. We do not act in isolation, one from another.

Joining rests on the previous strategy of Sense-Making and helps achieve responsiveness by honoring that which connects diverse perspectives. It seeks to establish a common shared space within which people are connected even when holding radically different perspectives. Connection cannot be honored until we make sense of another's behavior. Until then, the person's behavior remains in the "not like me at all" and "I can't relate to it" category. It is relatively easy to resist Joining (i.e., connecting) with what we cannot relate to or with what we perceive to be of little value. Until then, there is only "them" and "us."

It is necessary to relate to others' behaviors as somehow interpersonal (i.e., connected and connective) in order to honor connection. Until then, it is, unfortunately, all too easy to situate the problem out there—in the other and having nothing to do with us (e.g., "It is their behavior or perspective that is problematic and needs to change"). Senge, Scharmer, Jaworski, and Flowers captured the pitfalls of this tendency to disconnect the problematic from our own particular self in the following words.

> If you feel you've got a problem to solve that is "out there" and you don't see or want to see any possible relationship between the "you" who is trying to solve the problem and what the problem actually is, you may wind up not being able to see the problem accurately [and] unwittingly contribute to maintaining the undesired situation rather than allowing it to evolve and perhaps dissolve. (2005, p. 51)

Joining thus presents the challenge of identifying how another's behavior or perspective links with our own. It focuses on identifying and acknowledging the joint field within which current interactions are taking place. Joining is about seeing beyond the walls of our personal space into the common room within which both people stand.

If, for example, a practitioner perceives a person's behavior as inattentive but that person perceives it as attentive, then what is the context within which both perceptions exist? What is the whole reflected in each of the perceptions? One way of answering these questions is to realize that both people are standing in a single room called attention. One person perceives the absence of attention and the other perceives its presence; however, both are focused on attention. Senge and colleagues called this "understanding the whole to be found in the parts" (2005, p. 46). They used the metaphor of individual leaves—each different from the others yet all within "the living field" (p. 46) of the whole plant or tree. Joining challenges us to shift our focus from the parts to the whole, from half empty or half full to the container that holds both perspectives as one.

Joining asks us to affirm that a given solution is not about changing them; rather, it is about changing our perception of them so that new possibilities can emerge. Its two requisite characteristics are 1) an acknowledgment that every interaction is mutually constructed and maintained and 2) a willingness to identify specific aspects of how our own behavior and beliefs contribute to and sustain that interaction.

Block stated, "When we honestly ask ourselves about *our* [emphasis added] role in the creation of a particular situation that frustrates [or confuses or challenges] us, and set aside asking about *their* [emphasis added] role, then the world changes around us" (2002, p. 21). It is then possible to be participants in a mutual context within which the possibilities for change become both clearer and easier to access. Identifying this mutual context through Joining is key to the strategies associated with expressing the disposition of Setting the Stage for Miracles.

Strategies Associated with Setting the Stage for Miracles

Three strategies are associated with the expression of Skilled Dialogue's second disposition of Setting the Stage for Miracles: Allowing, Appreciating, and Harmonizing. This disposition deepens and extends the disposition of Choosing Relationship over Control through its focus on literally setting the stage for transformational shifts in the conceptual and perceptual paradigms that inform and shape interactions between diverse individuals. Its three strategies, also address respect, reciprocity, and responsiveness, but they do so in a distinct fashion. Their aim is to reframe existing contexts and relationships rather than to only relate with them. Current understandings that were gained from Choosing Relationship over Control can be moved into new integrative and inclusive frames within which novel, even miraculous, outcomes can be coconstructed (Jaworski, 1996).

Allowing   Allowing promotes respect by honoring identity. Its purpose is to make space for what is diverse, not only so that it may be welcomed, but also that it may be allowed to be what it is—diverse. Allowing supports the establishment of respect by letting others be who they are without first requiring compromise or change. This does not mean a simple passivity in the face of behaviors and/or beliefs that are less than optimal in a given environment. Rather, it means allowing what is to be as it is before determining how it may or may not need to change.

Typically, Welcoming and Allowing strategies are used almost simultaneously, with one reinforcing the other. No matter how we approach someone, Welcoming cannot be fully articulated if we do not at least momentarily suspend the promotion of our own agenda over the other person's agenda. That is the goal of Allowing—the suspension of the need to privilege our agenda (i.e., give it priority), however subtly, over someone else's agenda.

Allowing challenges our understanding and use of power. If someone listens to an interaction, for example, could they tell whose agenda was most important? Would it be ours? Do we perceive and communicate that we somehow have more power or competence than those with whom we are interacting? These questions hint at what is perhaps the most challenging aspect of Allowing—"staying with the tension" (i.e., allowing more than one agenda on the table simultaneously without forcing a choice between them). It is this sort of suspension of the need to fix, resolve, or defend that begins to quite literally set the stage for miracles by creating conceptual and emotional space within which diverse identities can be honored without needing to be erased or merged.

Our research and fieldwork on Skilled Dialogue has highlighted three characteristics that are necessary to creating this type of interpersonal context. The first is the one just discussed—the willingness to suspend judgment and simply remain present without fixing or judging others. Perhaps they appear careless of their responsibilities, yet there is always at least a 1% possibility that our judgment of this fact is based on insufficient or incorrect information. Even 60 seconds given to that consideration can set the stage for miracles.

Related to this characteristic is the willingness to release our stories and interpretations about another's behaviors and beliefs. Wilson (2001) provided an excellent illustration of how easy it is to assume quick judgments and let first impressions tell us all we need to know. Wilson tells the story of a mother who was arrested and sentenced for driving without a license. At first glance, those trying to help her judged her as a typical thoughtless person who was unwilling to do the necessary work to obtain a license. As the people involved obtained more information, however, they learned that their initial judgments were far from complete. Wilson commented on how easy it can be, even for those of us who are intelligent and have caring hearts to make assumptions based on what seems apparent rather than on what is true. The strategy of Allowing focuses on loosening the preconceptions and presuppositions that so easily lead to those assumptions. Only then can we make room for unimagined and/or unexpected truths.

Appreciating   Appreciating builds on Allowing by focusing on the value and worth present in what is, as it is. Another's perspective, no matter how diverse or unfamiliar, is acknowledged as an evidence-based expression of his or her competence because it is based on life experiences and knowledge, just as our own perspective.

Appreciating, like Sense-Making, also seeks to establish reciprocity and honor voice, even when significantly diverse from our own. It does so by going beyond the understanding gained through Sense-Making and acknowledging the inherent value and potential contribution of what another brings to the table. Appreciating deepens interpersonal connection and space so that the worth of diverse identities can be brought to the stage that is being set.

The strategy of Appreciating expresses the belief that everyone has something of value to contribute to a given interaction, even if that something is only a wake-up call to the limitations of current behaviors. It includes not only recognizing the sense and value of a behavior and/or belief for the person exhibiting it, but also the value of that behavior and/or belief in relation to ourselves and the goal(s) we wish to attain.

In Skilled Dialogue, this recognition is referred to as finding the gold nuggets. What unique example or lens (i.e., gold nugget) does someone bring to a situation that can enrich our view not only of this particular interaction, but also of the larger world? For example, can someone's insistence on only his or her own perspective be a reminder of the value of our own perspective, which perhaps we tend to undervalue except when clothed in the guise of "expert advice?" Or, perhaps, might it bring with it an invitation to reflect on our own misuse of power? It is difficult to truly honor another's voice until we can acknowledge the value of another's behaviors and/or perspectives in relation to ourselves.

Appreciating can be further defined through its critical aspects. As previously discussed, the first is the willingness to explicitly communicate our perceptions of the value and worth of another person's behaviors and/or perspectives. Doing this involves first identifying those aspects of another's behavior that have the potential to enrich our sense of the other person. Statements may be as simple as, "I see" or as detailed as, "I understand how difficult coping with your child's situation can be."

A second aspect focuses on identifying what another's diverse behaviors and/or perspectives can teach us (i.e., identifying the value of another's behaviors and perspectives in relation to ourselves). This aspect requires acknowledging that every behavior or perspective encountered may, in fact, mirror something within us (Hatfield, Cacioppo, & Rapson, 1993; Jaffe, 2007), although perhaps in an exaggerated form. Time and again in working with practitioners learning to use Skilled Dialogue, we find that the behaviors they identify as the most challenging are those that call attention to some aspect of themselves that they do not wish to acknowledge or that they have struggled with in the past. Sometimes the behaviors may reflect a hidden strength that they have yet to acknowledge in themselves; at other times, they may reflect something they always admired but have not felt able to express; and at still other times, they may reflect a weakness that causes pain or shame. Whatever is reflected, we will remain unable to honor another's voice in ways that set the stage for miracles if all we can hear is the echoes of our own.

A third aspect of appreciation is acknowledging that, from at least one perspective, all negative behavior can be understood as a good behavior exaggerated. What seems to be "indecisiveness," for example, may actually reflect the love of learning as much as possible and a reluctance to miss out on anything.

Zander and Zander (2000) gave an example of a student who disengaged from class participation because he cared too much about the subject to fail.

One person's "obnoxious" questioning can be another's positive "inquisitiveness" (Payne, 2005). With the understanding that every negative behavior is in almost all cases a positive behavior exaggerated, we might learn from a parent who allows children to yell and argue the value of allowing children self-expression, though perhaps not the value of allowing the behavior to that extreme. Or, perhaps, we might learn the value of allowing ourselves to express disagreement or frustration, although perhaps in a more skillful manner.

Appreciating completes the honoring of voice first addressed through Sense-Making by going beyond just understanding the value of diverse perspectives or voices. It is at this point that we can finally be authentically responsive, the goal of the final strategy and of Skilled Dialogue as a whole.

Harmonizing   Harmonizing complements Joining because it builds responsiveness through honoring connection. Its goal, however, is not only to create contexts in which we recognize interconnections, but also to shift the focus of interactional contexts from the noncomplementary aspects of diverse perspectives (i.e., the contradictions) to their complementary, albeit paradoxical, aspects. This shift allows for the transformation of the exclusive either-or nature of contradictions into the inclusive multidimensional nature of paradoxes within which third (or even more) option(s) that are responsive to initial differences as well as to desired circumstances can be generated.

Harmonizing redefines interpersonal contexts as complementary rather than oppositional to leverage and integrate their strengths. Harmonizing is, in some ways at least, the least familiar and most challenging of Skilled Dialogue's six strategies. It requires going beyond what seems apparent on the surface and, "paradoxically looking inside, and sometimes [individuals] aren't ready to do that" (Senge et al., 2004, p. 113). It is related to what Pink called the aptitude of symphony: "Symphonic thinking is a signature ability of composers and conductors, whose jobs involve corralling a diverse group of notes, instruments, and performers and producing a unified and pleasing sound" (2006, p. 130).

Similar to integrating the color blue with the color yellow to make green or integrating individual musical notes into a chord, Harmonizing seeks to integrates disparate perspectives into a larger and more inclusive whole in which each can remain itself while simultaneously becoming part of a third as yet unrealized option. Using this strategy transforms interactional contexts by finding and leveraging the complementary aspects of existing behaviors and/ or perspectives. It resolves the tension between diverse perspectives that has been allowed to continue up to that point as the gifts and connections within contradictions have been explored.

It is here that the use of 3rd Space is called for most strongly (see Chapter 6). In summary, Skilled Dialogue strategies form a symphony of their own.

Choose Relationship over Control through

- Welcoming—extending unconditional respect as an expression of honoring another's identity as legitimate and evidence based

- Sense-Making—searching for how others' stories, behaviors, and understandings make as much sense within their context as mine do within my contexts

- Joining—giving explicit attention to how one person's perspective and another's are joined (i.e., two sides of the same whole)

Set the Stage for Miracles through

- Allowing—allowing differences to stand without trying to change them or to defend my side

- Appreciating—finding the value of others' behaviors/perspectives not only for them but also for myself

- Harmonizing—integrating the "poles" of the identified contradiction and leveraging their complementary aspects so as to generate previously unimagined options

The strategies are reiterative and nonsequential. For example, without the strategy of Welcoming, it is difficult to establish a context of reciprocity within which you, as well as those with whom you are interacting, can appreciate and make sense of each other's diverse perspectives. Yet, it is much more challenging to welcome that which we cannot understand and which does not make sense to us. Each strategy supports and stimulates the others.

Although just discussed in a vertical sequence in relation to each disposition (i.e., Welcoming followed by Sense-Making and Joining), these strategies may also be examined in a horizontal, by quality, sequence (i.e., Welcoming followed by Allowing, then Sense-Making followed by Appreciating). This sequence is one that has proven the most successful for initial learning and practice. Each type of organization has something distinct to offer. The horizontal organization (by intention) can be read as follows:

I promote and sustain respect through

- Welcoming—extending unconditional respect as an expression of honoring another's identity as legitimate and evidence based

- Allowing—allowing differences to stand without trying to change them or to defend my side

I promote and sustain reciprocity through

- Sense-Making—searching for how others' stories, behaviors, and understandings make as much sense within their context as mine do within my contexts

- Appreciating—identifying the value/strengths of others' beliefs/behaviors for them as well as for myself (e.g., asking, "What I can learn?")

I promote and sustain responsiveness through

- Joining—giving explicit attention to how one person's perspective and another's are joined (i.e., two sides of the same whole)

- Harmonizing—coconstructing unimagined options that leverage the strengths of both sides of the identified contradictions

SKILLED DIALOGUE STRATEGIES IN ACTION[2]

Although they can be used to enhance any interaction, Skilled Dialogue strategies are especially useful for interactions in which different beliefs or values generate miscommunication, dissonance, or tension, regardless of whether these beliefs or values stem from cultural, personal, experiential, or other sources. Returning to our vignette of Betsy, Karen, and Karen's child, Maya (see Chapter 3), the following discussion broadly illustrates how the strategies might work when all put together. The scenario follows a horizontal sequence as this tends to be the one that flows most naturally.

Welcoming

Before meeting with Karen, Betsy (i.e., the person using Skilled Dialogue) focuses on developing her awareness that her viewpoint or perspective is not necessarily the only right or desirable one. She examines any assumptions about Karen or Maya that she may be bringing into the interactional context (e.g., "I'm the expert," "I know just the level and type of engagement between Karen and Maya that will yield the best results," "Karen obviously needs help").

As Betsy meets with Karen, she makes every effort to communicate that she welcomes both her and the opportunity to explore her perspective as a legitimate one, given her cultural context and life experiences. Betsy expresses respect both verbally and nonverbally based on her recognition of Karen's unique identity and not solely on the level of agreement or similarity of perspectives.

Allowing

Betsy intentionally drops her stories (e.g., "Here we go again; she's still insisting that I'm the expert," "She just isn't interested enough to engage in the activities I've planned") as she listens to Karen. These stories may also include

---

[2]See Barrera and Kramer (2009) for additional scenarios showing the application of Skilled Dialogue strategies.

thoughts such as the following: "I'm really frustrated and angry." "This must mean that she really doesn't like what I am proposing." "I wish that she would join us just once before she left."

Betsy uses the strategy of Allowing and simply tells herself, "These are my thoughts and I have to remember that I don't really know Karen. It is neither necessary nor desirable to express agreement or disagreement at this point. What is important is to listen without trying to change Karen's mind, defend my own perspective, or move to conclusions and action before further interaction." Allowing does not, however, mean delaying necessary actions in situations that require immediate change, such as one in which child abuse is present. It simply means that an oppositional stance is not necessary.

Sense-Making

Betsy consciously reminds herself to be a learner and release her role as expert so that she can listen attentively and with curiosity to what Karen says without making judgments about what it means just yet. She moves from, "I know what that means" (e.g., this person believes that it is okay to remain unengaged) to "I wonder how that choice makes sense to her; I'll just ask more questions and listen more carefully so that I can understand it from her perspective."

Or, conversely, Betsy might think, "She sounds just like me when I'm tired and don't feel competent; I wonder if she is making that choice for the same reasons I would." Betsy realizes that to truly make sense of Karen's words and behaviors, no matter how similar or dissimilar to her own, she must drop her assumptions about what they mean and, instead, obtain direct information. Questions such as, "What do you think (and/or feel) when I talk about joining me as I work with Maya?" and "What do you think might happen if you didn't leave and instead stayed to work with me?" can be helpful. It is also okay to say things such as, "I think very differently, but I really want to hear how you think about it." Or, "It sounds like we think in similar ways."

Appreciating

As Betsy starts to understand Karen's perspective and sees the situation through her eyes (and this may take several visits), she begins to recognize how much Karen actually has to contribute to the situation. She realizes, for example, that Karen believes in her child's ability to learn and become competent much more than she does, grounded as she is in assessment and developmental data. Betsy learns from Karen that child rearing is shared in Karen's cultural context and it is not unusual to distribute learning activities (i.e., one person does some types of tasks and another takes the lead on other types of tasks).

Betsy also learns some things about herself. She learns that just as Karen insists on her own perspective and resists opening to new perspectives, Betsy has that same tendency—and is, in fact, doing just that in this situation when she forgets about Skilled Dialogue. As a result, Betsy is able to communicate her appreciation for what Karen has to offer (e.g., telling Karen how much she appreciates her persistence in her views because that has been really helpful in establishing collaboration and reciprocity) and for what she herself is learning (e.g., Betsy telling Karen how much she is learning about her own persistence through this exchange of ideas). In expressing her appreciation in this manner, Betsy honors Karen's voice and sets a tone of partnership rather than one of helper and helpee or teacher and learner. She starts to listen as a learner herself, not just talking about collaboration (e.g., "You need to collaborate with me") but actually modeling it (e.g., "I'll collaborate with you").

Joining

Having come to appreciate the other person's diverse understandings and behaviors, Betsy initiates the strategy of Joining. She looks for ways in which she and Karen's behaviors/perspectives are connected (i.e., share a common context), a process already started as she learned to appreciate Karen's perspective and behaviors. She starts by asking questions about her own behavior.

- How am I contributing to the current miscommunication?

- Am I modeling the same inattentive or resistant behaviors that I am asking Karen to change?

- Am I not really listening and not willing to change my mind, which is fueling the other person's need to advocate for unconfined expression?

Betsy also looks for times when she has been where Karen seems to be; that is, times when she has been inattentive or resistant (i.e., has shared that same perspective that so frustrates her now). In doing this, Betsy moves from a nonjoint perspective (i.e., "One of us has a problem, and it isn't me") to a joined perspective ("We're in this together; it is a joint problem, as much mine as yours"). This shift requires looking for similarities in the stated differences (e.g., "Oh, I see—we're both really frustrated with this situation," "Oh, we're both really wanting control").

Harmonizing

Once a joint perspective is achieved (i.e., once Karen and Betsy have joined forces, so to speak), Betsy turns her attention to searching for an inclusive perspective (i.e., solution) within which the strengths of the two existing mutually exclusive options currently in play can be harmonized. She starts by asking herself, "How can engagement (i.e., working with me and Maya) and nonengagement (i.e., not joining in our activities) be leveraged to create options that tap into the strengths of both so as to form something richer and more stable than either one along?"

Harmonizing is the final strategy in Setting the Stage for Miracles, and practitioners must remember that miracles are defined as outcomes not predictable from the existing conditions. The 3rd Space choices that are the goal of Harmonizing are therefore themselves not predictable, or as Einstein is reported to have said, "You can't solve a problem on the level on which it was created." Every outcome that is formed through Harmonizing, therefore, is unique to the specific interactions that take place as it is formed. Betsy's first step, then, is to know that she does not know the solution that will emerge as she and Karen join forces. She might start out by telling Karen something such as, "It seems that we're sort of stuck just now. I want to work with you, and you are more comfortable letting me as the expert work with Maya. It sounds like we can only choose one or the other, but I believe that there is a third, and maybe a fourth or a fifth, choice. Are you willing to work with me in finding that choice?"

In many cases, it is important not to answer that question right away but to allow time, adding something such as, "Let's think about it and we can talk about it at our next session." In the authors' experience over the years, 3rd Space options have occurred in many ways. In one case, the problem just dissolved. As the practitioner came to accept a mother's behavior, allowing herself to appreciate that behavior and join forces with the mother, the mother changed her behavior without further issue. In other cases, 3rd Space emerged through the application of creative technologies (e.g., the use of cell phone cameras for a mother who was upset that she was not there to see her child's milestone). In still others, behaviors were reframed. Betsy could, for example, redefine Karen's behavior as engagement (e.g., she could see that Karen was engaged with her in letting her take the lead and making space and time for that to happen). The key aspect of Harmonizing is that outcomes are not conditional (e.g., "I can't really help Maya unless you work with us," "You need to change for Maya to progress"). Change happens not as a forced precondition but as a natural unforced outcome of connection.

Harmonizing requires recognizing the strengths of the perspectives involved and then finding ways of leveraging those strengths in service of the desired changes. It is not an easy strategy to implement. It is, however, one that can transform both interactions and outcomes when successfully applied.

A LOOK AHEAD

This chapter finishes Section II and our direct look at the mechanics of Skilled Dialogue. The chapters in the next section focus more directly on how to craft respectful, reciprocal, and responsive assessment and instruction of young children with exceptionalities whose culture and/or language differs from that reflected in early childhood settings as well as from that of practitioners themselves. The chapters in this section will discuss best practices for ensuring that both assessment and instruction of children from diverse cultural linguistic backgrounds are crafted in ways that honor identity, voice, and connection.

Collaborative and Culturally Inclusive Assessment and Instruction of Young Children

Section III focuses on using Skilled Dialogue as a tool to assist in crafting specific responses to the assessment and instruction of young children whose backgrounds differ significantly from those of their practitioners due to cultural linguistic differences. It is important to reiterate that Skilled Dialogue is a process and not a mechanical technique. Attempting to trace a process (i.e., to capture its flow in words) is a hazardous endeavor. Processes are by definition fluid and dynamic operations that are responsive to the specifics of a given situation. For that reason, the materials in this section are not designed to be either linear or tightly prescriptive. Rather, they are intended more as general guidelines to help organize the assessment and instruction of young children. Similarly, the forms suggested are intended to serve as supports to the process. They are not meant to add one more layer of paperwork to an already extensive documentation process. Use them as necessary

Chapter 8 sets the overall structure for using Skilled Dialogue in relation to assessment and instruction. Chapters 9 and 10 then focus on these two activities, providing extensive suggestions for practitioners. Finally, Chapter 11 focuses on issues of culture and trauma. Although these issues are not explicitly a part of assessment and instruction, they are a critical aspect of our interactions with children. It becomes particularly important to examine these issues when these children's backgrounds are diverse from our own. Unfortunately, neither the scope nor the length of this book allow for a full discussion. Cited references, however, can be a helpful resource for further information.

Chapter 8

Skilled Dialogue and Culturally Linguistically Respectful, Reciprocal, and Responsive Assessment and Instruction

We must learn of the simplest [artist] a parable. There is no great art without reverence. The real [artist] has great technical knowledge of materials and tools [but also] something much more: he has the feel of the wood; the knowledge of its demands in his fingers; and so the work is smooth and satisfying and lovely because he worked with the reverence that comes of love. (Vann, 1960, p. 19)

The Skilled Dialogue framework and its strategies can be applied in two distinct contexts: contexts of general interactions between practitioners and families and contexts specific to assessment and instruction. The distinction between these contexts is somewhat arbitrary as assessment and instruction also involve general interactions between practitioners and between practitioners and families. It is nevertheless a useful one for our purposes as it allows us to better address specific aspects of assessment and instruction such as selection of materials or data gathering, which are not typically part of general interactions. It is the latter context that is primarily addressed in this last section; the former will be reviewed only briefly. Readers interested in more information on using Skilled Dialogue in relation to general interactions are referred to our 2009 text, in which this is discussed at length.

At its core, of course, all assessment and instruction is a dialogue. This chapter describes and illustrates the applications and implications of Skilled Dialogue for determining how to best address specific cultural linguistic variables associated with a particular child and family during assessment and/or instruction. Of course, other resources exist that discuss many of the issues involved and offer general recommendations. The material in this chapter is designed to augment these by providing procedural and strategic recommendations for honoring identity, voice, and connection. Its emphasis is on best practices for establishing respect, supporting reciprocity, and developing responsiveness in relation to a specific child. Because most families are more or less diverse from the various cultural categories to which they are assigned (e.g., Hispanic, American Indian), the authors address the identification of specific cultural linguistic variables presented by individual families/children and the link between these and specific assessment and/or instructional adaptations/modifications to typical assessment activities and procedures as well as to instructional strategies, activities, and curricular content.

The material in Chapters 8, 9, and 10 are written for practitioners who already possess the basic knowledge and skills associated with assessment and instruction of young children. It is our assumption that, in general, this knowledge and skill remain the same for all children with the exception of those aspects that need to be modified or added in order to honor diverse identities, voices, and the connections between these and typical practice in early childhood service settings. Four distinct steps shape assessment and instruction as informed by Skilled Dialogue (see Figure 8.1).

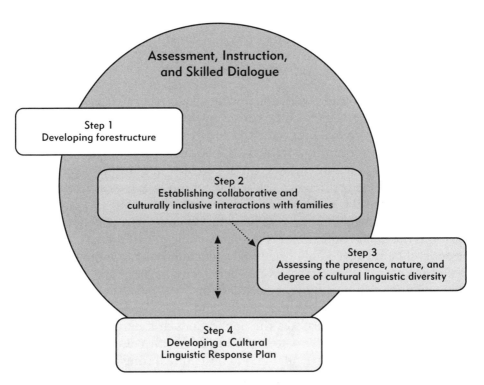

Figure 8.1.   Steps for integrating Skilled Dialogue into assessment and instruction.

1. *Developing forestructure:* This step focuses on acquiring the Skilled Dialogue dispositions and gaining knowledge about the affect of culture and language on assessment and instruction. It is a preparatory step that helps to set the Skilled Dialogue dispositions in place and is best completed prior to initiating any assessment or instruction.

2. *Establishing collaborative and culturally inclusive interactions with the child's family:* This step is designed to ensure the quality of the interactions between practitioners and families as well as to ensure reciprocity, which allows families' funds of knowledge and skills to be integrated into assessment and/or instruction so any assessment or interaction is optimally respectful, reciprocal, and responsive. This step is only briefly reviewed in this section. Readers are referred to our 2009 book for more detailed information.

3. *Assessing the presence, nature, and degree of cultural linguistic diversity present in any given situation:* This step offers suggestions and procedures for obtaining specific cultural data about individual children and their families in order that critical assessment and instructional variables and decisions can be optimally responsive (e.g., appropriate learning strategies, languages of assessment) to the children/families involved.

4. *Developing a Cultural Linguistic Response Plan:* This step focuses on taking the information gathered in Step 3 and using it to determine how to best craft assessment/instruction so as to optimize targeted outcomes.

This chapter's content provides an overall view of the steps, with a stronger focus on the first three. It concludes with an illustrative case study showing the use of specific data-gathering tools for Steps 3 and 4. Chapters 9 and 10 then focus more closely on developing a Cultural Linguistic Response Plan, the fourth and final step.

The four steps are not strictly linear; nor are they intended to be rigidly prescriptive. Rather, they serve as a useful framework for learning and practicing Skilled Dialogue. It is important to remember that their true goal is to support understanding of the skill that is developed with practice over time as the steps are applied, rather than to require mastery prior to its application. Skilled Dialogue, like language, cannot be truly learned prior to being applied and experienced (i.e., anchored). Langer's comment on the value of uncertainty in relation to teaching can be equally applied to learning these steps.

> Teaching skills and facts in a conditional way sets the stage for doubt and uncertainty and an awareness of how different situations may call for subtle differences in what we bring to them. We can learn a skill by accepting at face value what we are told about how to practice it or *we can come to an understanding over time of what the skill entails* [emphasis added]. (1997, pp. 16–17)

Readers are encouraged to implement the various steps from the start, however unskilled they may feel at first. First attempts may seem far from successful, yet each deepens practitioners' understanding and skills. This is especially true for Steps 2 and 3. Initial attempts to complete the forms for these phases may not yield the amount of data given in the examples. Any additional data, however, no matter how slight, enhance practitioners' understanding of and response to specific families and their children. Discussions of how to identify other data also stimulate greater reciprocity between practitioners and families. The following section discusses each step in greater detail.

STEP 1: DEVELOPING FORESTRUCTURE

Developing a meaning base from which to examine cultural diversity and its challenges is a critical first phase to learning and using Skilled Dialogue, especially its dispositions. All too frequently, practitioners find that they are like pilots trying to fix a plane while in flight. They focus on developing cultural competency while in the midst of specific situations, encumbered by constraints of time and immediate needs and without sufficient information. Nakkula and Ravitch (1998) used the term *forestructure* to describe the meaning base from which people draw their understanding of subsequent events. They pointed out, "We are projected forward into new activities with prior expectations based on internalized interpretations of our archive of life experiences" (p. 25).

Skilled Dialogue is a proactive process in which success is determined by the quality of the forestructure that practitioners build prior to interactions with specific families and children who are diverse from themselves. A significant aspect of forestructure is the two Skilled Dialogue dispositions—Choosing Relationship over Control and Setting the Stage for Miracles. Developing these dispositions can and should occur outside of, as well as within, actual professional interactions with diverse families. Four practices support the development of these dispositions.

1. Reflecting on your own current skill levels

2. Becoming knowledgeable about foundational concepts and specific to culture and cultural diversity

3. Engaging in conversations with culturally diverse friends, colleagues, and others to anchor general information

4. Practicing the Skilled Dialogue strategies, especially those of Joining and Harmonizing, in everyday situations with friends, colleagues, and strangers

Reflecting on Your Own Current Skill Levels

There will always be situations and people whose diversity challenges even very competent practitioners. Paradoxically, Skilled Dialogue is best practiced with what is, in some worldviews, called a "beginner's mind"—a mind clear or at least aware and mindful of preconceptions and open to the unexpected. Vaill referred to some of the reasons why should be so: life is "full of surprises," "complex systems tend to produce novel problems," and events "do not present themselves in neat packages" (1996, pp. 10–12). Kahane also referenced the need for an open mind that does not hold on tightly "to our opinions and plans and identities and truths" (2009, p. 4). These statements are especially relevant to encounters across diverse cultural parameters.

Appendix C contains a Skilled Dialogue Self-Assessment and Reflection Guide that can be used to get a sense of one's own current skill levels. In addition, Barrera and Kramer (2009) contains a list of resources and critical aspects for each disposition that may be used to assess the degree to which these have been learned (see Table 8.1 and Table 8.2). Of course, Skilled Dialogue is a process that is never completely mastered. Skilled Dialogue is a process learned through practice rather than a learned once-and-for-all skill set. There is always room to continue to refine skills as novel cultural perspectives are encountered. The authors have been working with Skilled Dialogue for more than 10 years and are still deepening and expanding their knowledge and skills. Self-assessment should not be done simply to measure achievement (i.e., as a summative evaluation). Rather, it should be done on an ongoing basis to monitor strengths and limitations, as well as to guide the practice of necessary strategies (i.e., in a formative fashion).

Becoming Knowledgeable About Foundational Concepts and Specific Cultural Expressions

The dispositions emerge from a deep understanding and awareness of interpersonal dynamics and are grounded in the nature of culture and its varied dynamics across different communities. It is, therefore, important to learn as much as possible about the constructs of culture and cultural diversity from as many different perspectives as possible (e.g., anthropological, psychological, educational, political). Chapters 1, 2, and 3 provide basic information on these

Table 8.1.   Critical aspects of Choosing Relationship over Control

- Assumption of equal competency to craft a behavioral repertoire adaptive to the given contexts
- Acceptance of diverse behavior(s) as evidence based
- Willingness to communicate unconditional respect
- Sense of curiosity about other people's stories and interpretations of reality
- A learner's attitude and mindset
- Nonjudgmental information gathering
- Perspective taking
- Explicit recognition of the messages sent
- Recognition that contradictory behaviors can be complementary
- Willingness to change verbal and nonverbal messages

From Barrera, I., & Kramer, L. (2009). *Using Skilled Dialogue to transform challenging interactions: Honoring identity, voice, and connection* (p. 60). Baltimore, MD: Paul H. Brookes Publishing Co.; reprinted by permission.

Table 8.2. Critical aspects of Setting the Stage for Miracles

- Willingness to stay with the tension (i.e., acknowledge another's perspective without needing to explain or defend one's own)
- Willingness to release stories and fixed interpretations about others' behaviors and/or beliefs
- Perception of diverse perspectives as potentially complementary rather than divisive or polarized
- Willingness to identify gold nuggets in others' behaviors and/or beliefs
- Recognition that every negative behavior is a positive behavior exaggerated
- Willingness to learn from others' behaviors and/or beliefs
- Willingness to reframe perceptions
- Openness to brainstorming
- "Thinking in threes" (i.e., 3rd Space thinking)

From Barrera, I., & Kramer, L. (2009). *Using Skilled Dialogue to transform challenging interactions: Honoring identity, voice, and connection* (p. 78). Baltimore, MD: Paul H. Brookes Publishing Co.; reprinted by permission.

foundational concepts. It might be useful to revisit this information now that readers are more familiar with the Skilled Dialogue process.

The goal of acquiring such cultural information is not merely to develop an understanding of the complexity and rich variety of cultural paradigms and their affect on behaviors and interpersonal dynamics (i.e., to arrive at a fixed answers). It is to do so in relation to the concrete and particular lives of individual families and their children (i.e., to come to an appreciation of that impact and gain access to its strengths in relation to specific behaviors within particular interpersonal contexts).

Becoming familiar with a range of diverse worldviews, values, behavioral scripts, social practices, and other cultural expressions is important for more than just learning certain characteristics of particular groups (although this knowledge can be helpful). More important, this practice can serve to facilitate adoption of the Skilled Dialogue dispositions by softening one's natural ethnocentrism. Choosing Relationship over Control and Setting the Stage for Miracles begin to make more sense as there is increased appreciation for culture's countless ways of structuring worldviews and behavior, all of which are as valid as or perhaps even superior to one's own. It is easier to release control in favor of relationship, for example, when it is recognized that there is not just one right way to address child rearing. Similarly, it is easier to work toward harmonizing alternate perspectives when their cultural strengths are acknowledged. All cultural information, whether or not it is specific to the families with whom practitioners work, can be placed into a reservoir of information from which 3rd Space options can subsequently be generated.

Engaging in Conversations with Culturally Diverse Friends, Colleagues, and Others to Anchor General Information

As discussed earlier, it is not enough to just know about others' cultural backgrounds. It is also critical to anchor that cultural knowledge as it influences and shapes individual behaviors amid personal preferences, differing life experiences, and other such variables. Discussing diverse perceptions, values, behaviors, and beliefs with friends, colleagues, and other willing listeners when not in "practitioner mode" is a great way to anchor cultural knowledge. For example, if practitioners have had conversations with people familiar with Hispanic culture in the Southwest prior to meeting with Hispanic families, then they will be better able to anchor their understanding of any diverse behaviors and values they encounter. Cultural understandings of words such as *family* and *education* will be more richly and accurately nuanced, for example. Distinguishing between behaviors that are normative to that culture and behaviors that are atypical will also become an easier task.

Of course, it is also productive for practitioners to discuss cultural dynamics with the families with whom they work. It is important, though, to differentiate between these discussions and those that occur outside of family–practitioner contexts. The distinct power dynamics of these two contexts need to be acknowledged and respected (see Chapter 2). In most cases, it is easier for a friend or colleague to tell a practitioner "I'm offended when I hear you say that" than it is for a member of a family receiving services from that practitioner.

Some families have reported significant discomfort, and even anger at times, when they perceived themselves as needing or being expected to be responsible not only for their child's care, but also for the practitioners' education about their culture. Although other families may find this type of interaction with practitioners to be a positive and rewarding experience, this should never be assumed. It is important to allow the choice to be voluntary rather than obligatory because practitioners have failed to be responsible in developing their own forestructures.

Practicing the Strategies of Joining and Harmonizing in Everyday Situations with Friends, Colleagues, and Strangers

Engaging in conversations about culture with diverse people in daily environments easily leads to the conscious practice of Skilled Dialogue strategies. The practice of these strategies, especially those of Joining and Harmonizing, which tend to be less familiar, is necessary to their skilled use in interactions with families. Practitioners who wait to practice these strategies until they meet diverse children and families increase their challenge (see Chapter 7 and Section III of 2009 text).

Behavioral and value differences are always present in interactions across cultural parameters. The strategies of Joining and Harmonizing are particularly useful in crafting respectful, reciprocal, and responsive interactions in any situation that contains differences. These strategies provide ways of celebrating and leveraging differences rather than getting stuck in confusion, frustration, or anger. Efforts to join across culture bumps as well as to harmonize diverse perspectives are at the heart of Skilled Dialogue (see Chapter 2).

Practitioners can work on identifying what specific differences may underlie dissonant interactions. Then, they can determine how best to join and harmonize those differences. For example, if a friend is often late for appointments and you value punctuality, then how might these two perspectives come to be understood as two differing sides of the same reality rather than as totally separate realities? How might one complement the other? How might one actually sustain the other? Similarly, how might being punctual and being late be harmonized (i.e., integrated so that there need not be a split into contradictory realities)?

What solutions might be generated that respect each person's boundaries and do not put the responsibility for change on only one person? Is it possible to break out of a dualistic my way (e.g., on time) or your way (e.g., not on time by your criteria) perspective? Chapter 6 provides a further discussion of exploring such 3rd Space options, and Chapter 7 discusses the strategy of Harmonizing in more detail. See our 2009 text for a full discussion of both options and strategies.

Joining and Harmonizing can also be practiced in relation to internal dissonance. For instance, a practitioner may think, "I know that I should be more accepting of this family when they skip appointments. Part of me wants to be accepting, but another part of me doesn't. It just isn't respectful of my time, yet I can also see that not accepting is not respectful of the family." How might Joining and Harmonizing apply in response to the internal contradictions reflected in such thinking? Remember that responses may not readily come to mind. Just stay with the question and continue to practice the strategies. Practitioners have reported finding both Joining and Harmonizing "Aha!" experiences that seemed almost independent of their effort (Barrera & Kramer, 2009).

STEP 2: ESTABLISHING COLLABORATIVE AND CULTURALLY INCLUSIVE INTERACTIONS WITH FAMILIES

The next step addresses the use of all six Skilled Dialogue strategies to communicate respect, establish reciprocity, and create responsive interactions. The important point of this step in this context is recognition that families need to be authentic partners in both assessment and instruction. Not only does this ensure that cultural linguistic diversity is honored, it also ensures that the strengths of such diversity can be both accessed and leveraged. Without using strategies that communicate practitioners' respect and acknowledgment of strengths, families are less likely to give optimum information or follow through on suggested practices.

Because this step is the main focus of our 2009 book, it will not be discussed in this book, other than to point out the need to work in true partnership with families if we are to serve our children optimally. Acknowledging, appreciating, and leveraging families' skills and resources, which this step addresses, is a critical part of establishing such partnerships.

STEP 3: ASSESSING THE PRESENCE, NATURE, AND DEGREE OF CULTURAL LINGUISTIC DIVERSITY

The presence, nature, and degree of cultural diversity cannot be accurately assessed until the nature and dynamics of culture across diverse communities is understood, at least to a moderate degree. Moving to this step too quickly risks stereotyping rather than true understanding. Once that is achieved, however, this third step, which focuses on gathering pertinent cultural linguistic data relative to specific children and families, can begin. Its primary purpose is to take cultural knowledge from the abstract to the concrete (e.g., Is there bilingualism? If so, how is it playing out in an individual family's unique context and experiences?). A corollary purpose is to alert practitioners to actual and potential culture bumps that might arise during assessment and intervention so that these can be eliminated or lessened through various modifications and adaptations. As stated earlier, there are four tools to assist practitioners in accomplishing this step (see Figure 8.2).

Step 3 often starts during initial contact and/or referral for services, which is one reason developing appropriate forestructure is so important. By the time practitioners meet the child/family with whom they are to work, time is of the essence. This step can also occur later when children come from other environments or programs. In either case, it needs to be completed prior to initiating direct assessment or intervention and instruction services, as its results are designed to inform such services. Three relatively sequential practices occur during Step 3.

1. Determine (rather than merely assume) the presence of cultural linguistic diversity.

2. Assess the nature and degree of cultural linguistic diversity.

3. Identify appropriate strategies for responding to this diversity during assessment and/or instruction.

Determine the Presence of Cultural Linguistic Diversity

Sometimes the presence of cultural diversity is immediately obvious (e.g., family speaks little or no English), whereas at other times it may not be as obvious. Whichever is the case, it is always necessary to examine the possibility that cultural linguistic diversity is present whenever practitioners make initial contact with a family.

As discussed in Chapter 2, the most reliable means of determining the presence of cultural linguistic diversity is to ask, "How likely am I to understand and attach the same meaning to behaviors as do the family and others from similar cultural backgrounds?" The lower the probability that practitioners will understand and attach similar meanings to behaviors, the more likely it is that culture bumps will occur and, consequently, the greater the need for

Skilled Dialogue. This question needs to be asked from the perspectives of individual practitioners as well as from the larger perspective of program services, procedures, and expectations.

It is not enough to establish that one or more practitioners are culturally knowledgeable and competent. It is also critical to examine program services, procedures, and expectations. The lower the probability that these services, procedures, and expectations reflect similar understandings or attach different meanings to behaviors (e.g., being on time) as does the family, the higher the probability of culture bumps and the greater the need for Skilled Dialogue.

There are some common indicators that there may be dissimilar understandings between families and the practitioners and programs that serve them. These include differences in ethnic background, usage of a language other than English in the home, extensive residence outside the United States, limited association with people for whom ENC is primary culture, and limited schooling in the United States. These indicators can be taken as "red flags" that signal the presence of cultural linguistic diversity. Baca and Cervantes (1998) presented the Acculturation Quick Screen (AQS): A Guide to Estimating Level of Acculturation, a tool that can be helpful in determining degree of diversity. The Family Acculturation Screen, a less formal instrument, is discussed later in this chapter.

It is not always necessary to use a formal instrument. Simple observations and practitioners' own experiences can be an equally reliable source of information because the purpose at this point is not to pinpoint exactly how families' and practitioners' understandings differ. It is, rather, only to get a sense of whether in fact that is the case.

For example, it is evident in Arturo's case, which is described at the end of this chapter, that there is at least some degree of diversity. Even so, the answer to the question, "Am I likely to understand and attach the same meaning to behaviors as would the family and/or others from cultural backgrounds similar to the family's?" might still vary, depending on the perspective from which the question is asked. From the perspective of the assessment process and curricula typical to ECSE services, the answer would, in all probability, be "no." This answer would be based on two facts. First, ECSE assessment and curricula typically reflect ENC values and beliefs (e.g., emphasis on parental decision making outside extended family, focus on early autonomy). Second, there is already some indication that Arturo's family reflects at least some aspects of Hispanic culture, a culture distinct from ENC.

From the perspective of individual practitioners, however, the answer could be "yes." Spanish-speaking Puerto Rican practitioners, for example, might answer, "Yes, to some degree," though, in some cases, they might instead answer, "No, I am unfamiliar with Hispanic culture outside of the Caribbean." A Hispanic staff member from the same community as Arturo's family, on the other hand, might answer, "Yes, without qualification."

Given the nature of the general population of ECSE practitioners, the probability is that answer would most often be closer to "no" than to "yes" in this and other similar cases, at least for the program in general as well as for some program staff. The next two practices become critical any time the answer is no for either individual practitioners or for the program in general.

Assess the Nature and Degree of Cultural Linguistic Diversity

Assessing nature and degree of cultural linguistic diversity is not a simple process of identifying a family's ethnicity and then looking up the characteristics associated with the identified ethnicity. Once practitioners determine that there is a strong probability of at least some degree of cultural linguistic diversity between the family and the program or individual practitioners, the need to assess the nature and degree of the identified diversity in more detail arises. It is not reliable to simply assume the nature and degree of cultural linguistic diversity based on external factors such as ethnicity.

Figure 8.2 shows the four tools developed by the authors to guide practitioners in assessing the nature and degree of cultural linguistic diversity in specific families vis-à-vis their own program. Each is addressed in the following discussion.

The Cultural Data Table is composed of a collection of specific questions, each focusing on a major curricular dimension: communicative-linguistic,

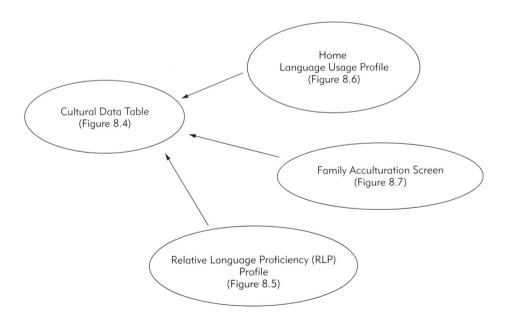

Figure 8.2.   Tools for assessing the nature and degree of cultural linguistic diversity.

personal-social, and cognitive-sensory (see Appendix A).[1] The questions within each dimension are further clustered into common factors such as degree of acculturation and child's relative language proficiency. Both the questions and the factors were generated from systematic observation and analysis of common situations in early childhood environments. A completed Cultural Data Table is provided in the illustrative case study at the end of the chapter.

Examining the detailed questions provided promotes respectful interactions and helps practitioners identify needed information and ameliorate or eliminate culture bumps specific to individual families/children. The range of cultural data that impinges on assessment and intervention/instruction is not exhausted by these factors or the questions associated with them. Nevertheless, these factors and questions do represent key aspects of such data. The ensuing discussions of each curricular dimension provide examples and strategies for using this tool.

Communicative-Linguistic   The Cultural Data Table breaks down the communicative-linguistic developmental/curricular area into five factors based on certain cultural dimensions. First, the language(s) of the child's caregiving environment(s) is practically self-explanatory. Language differences represent one of the more obvious aspects of diversity as well as one of its best recognized challenges. The Cultural Data Table presents two questions associated with this factor that prompt surpassing the simplistic question, "What language is spoken in the home?" encouraging and examining the complexity of bilingual and multilingual environments. Table 8.3 is a sample listing of various home language environments. Additional cultures and languages may be represented depending on the adults living with and/or caring for children at home (e.g., grandparents, nannies).

Second, the child's relative language proficiency focuses on the child's specific language skills. This factor prompts practitioners to go beyond the idea of language "dominance," which tends to carry the unrealistic assumption that once dominance is determined, only the dominant language needs to be addressed. Typically, no language is clearly dominant in bilingual environments. Typically, one language may predominate for discussions of certain things (e.g., home activities) and another for discussions of other things (e.g., world politics, conversations with in-laws). Children in bilingual and multilingual environments tend to alternate between languages depending on the content and context of situations and conversations (Harding & Riley, 1986; Tabors, 2008). Children may have similar proficiency in two or more languages. They also may possess critical, albeit small, pockets of knowledge (e.g., food or kinship terms) in the language that would not meet criteria as the dominant language (Miller, 1984). Using a Relative Language Proficiency (RLP) Profile is one way of documenting a child's relative language proficiency (see Appendix A).

---

[1]Blank forms are provided in Appendix A. Sample completed forms are provided within the chapter in relation to the illustrative case study.

Table 8.3.   Sample listing of non-ENC mixed home language environments

Type	Culture(s) represented in the home environment	Language(s) spoken by parents/caregivers	Languages spoken with the child
I	Diverse; not EuroAmerican Normative Culture (non-ENC)	Language other than English; no English	Language other than English; no English
II	Diverse; non-ENC; some ENC acculturation	Bilingual; English as well as other language	English only
III	Bicultural; non-ENC is dominant	Monolingual; parents speak English only; grandparents do not speak English	English only used by parents; grandparents mostly use a language other than English; child understands the other language but does not use it
IV	Multicultural; parents are from different non-ENCs; some ENC also represented	Limited English; each parent is fully fluent in his or her own language and understands some of the other's language	Multilingual; English is used as well as both of parents' languages
V	ENC dominant; some evidence of parents' non-ENC	Bilingual; both speak same language (other than English), mainly use English	Bilingual; both English and parents' other language are used

Source: Harding and Riley (1986).

Patterns of language usage in the child's primary caregiving environment (i.e., who uses which language for which purpose in the home) is the third factor in the communicative-linguistic area. Parents may, for example, use one language for discipline and another for teaching concepts. This factor extends those previously discussed by focusing on the contexts within which particular languages are used. This knowledge has important implications for both assessment and intervention/instruction because it helps to identify what content is known in which language. Using a Home Language Usage Profile can be helpful in obtaining and organizing this information (see Appendix A).

Differences related to the fourth factor—relative value placed on verbal and nonverbal communication—are often the source of significant culture bumps. ENC tends to value verbal skills and verbal communication compared with many other cultures (Bowers & Flinders, 1990; Philips, 1972). This value is reflected in assessment content (e.g., vocabulary carries more weight than social skills in many developmental assessment measures) as well as in intervention/instruction environments and expectations (e.g., "Tell me how you feel," "Ask for what you want").

The fifth factor addresses the relative status of languages other than English and the ability to speak more than one language. Subtle and perhaps not-so-subtle messages about this status can limit families' trust in practitioners and services. When parents perceive (incorrectly or correctly) that their home language is not valued as much as English, they may feel reluctant to report how much it is used at home. They may also feel that they themselves are less valued. They can also inhibit children's use of language for much the same reasons. The first author made this observation during interactions with children from predominantly Spanish-speaking homes in English-only early childhood environments. When first meeting these children and speaking to them in Spanish, the children's initial response was often to giggle or look away. This response is especially true in communities where Spanish is not commonly spoken in public settings. One older sibling actually articulated this impression by saying that Spanish was not supposed to be spoken in school, even though that was neither the intent nor the reality of the situation. Children may not be aware of language status in an abstract manner, but they are sensitive to implicit rules and expectations related to communication and language usage.

Personal-Social   Questions within the personal-social dimension address factors pertinent to anchoring one's understanding of diverse boundaries. The first factor highlights families' and children's degree of acculturation to ENC. To what degree are they experienced with and knowledgeable about ENC's values, beliefs, behaviors, and language? To what degree are they skilled in navigating within that culture (e.g., making appointments, meeting time expectations, requesting assistance from practitioners)? The Family Acculturation Screen (see Appendix A) was developed by the authors to assist practitioners to screen for families' degree of acculturation.

Similarly, the second factor examines the degree to which families are familiar with and knowledgeable about the early childhood education subculture: its expectations, beliefs, values, and language (e.g., terms such as *developmentally appropriate, assessment*). How skilled are they in negotiating within that culture (e.g., the referral process, expectations for turn taking in small groups)? When parents are not skilled in ECSE culture, they may not know how to question procedures, for example. Or, they may not understand why their child is determined to have inappropriate social skills.

The personal-social dimension also considers questions addressing several issues that underlie less obvious culture bumps. One is sense of self. Landrine (1995) and Markus and Kitayama (1991) referred to differences between ENC and other cultures in understanding self. Landrine advocated increased awareness of the "Western cultural definition of the self as well as the radically different way in which the self is understood by many ethnic-cultural minorities" (p. 402). Markus and Kitayama noted that in Japanese, "the word for self, *jibun*, refers to one's share of the shared life space" (p. 228), in contrast with ENC's notion of self as a separate and independent entity. Cross, Gore, and Morris (2003) and Gergen (2009) have also addressed this notion of self as separate and independent, showing the continued relevance of examining its implications.

A particularly evident expression of differences in sense of self is ENC's emphasis on independence as a measure of emotional development and its lack of focus on interdependence and communal decision making. This emphasis is implicitly reflected in valued developmental outcomes as well as in behavioral expectations for participation in early childhood environments. Asking questions such as, "How does this family or child understand autonomy?" and "To what degree are cooperation and group support or interaction valued?" helps anchor one's understanding of differences in this area. Gonzalez-Mena et al. (2000) and Trawick-Smith (2010) discussed some examples of varying values and beliefs in this area.

Examples of these variations include not making decisions before consulting with family elders or feeling uncomfortable traveling alone to medical appointments. Similar questions are associated with perceptions of identity and competence, a third personal-social factor. Developmentally appropriate curricula reflect certain perceptions of identity and competence that may not agree with those held by family members. Without a grounded understanding of diversity, practitioners may find themselves working at cross-purposes with families (e.g., advocating independent problem solving while parents discourage it at home).

Roles and rules associated with parenting and child rearing form another personal-social factor that must be examined because they can differ significantly across cultures. Common areas of difference have been discussed by multiple scholars, including Gonzalez-Mena (2000), Greenfield and Cocking (1994), and Trumbull et al. (2001). Gonzalez-Mena, a persistent voice in bringing this to the attention of early childhood practitioners, contrasted approaches to autonomy and discussed attachment patterns. She contrasted patterns that promote lifelong family dependence with those that stress producing individuals who are less family dependent and have more of a separate sense of self. In a similar discussion, she noted variations in patterns related to adult involvement in children's play. Some cultures believe that such involvement is essential; others see it as unnecessary and perhaps even inappropriate.

The remaining two personal-social factors are somewhat more general. Chapter 1 discusses how one of these, knowledge and experience about power and social positioning, affects interactions. This factor is critical because respect and reciprocity are defining characteristics of Skilled Dialogue. It can be difficult if not impossible to establish respectful and reciprocal interactions if power and social positioning dynamics are not carefully examined. In some cultures, for instance, it is considered rude to question someone who is perceived to have more skill or power. Taking the agreement of parents from these cultures at face value would be counterproductive to establishing reciprocity. Darder (1991) and Klein (1998) have both written seminal works on power and decision making.

The final factor in the personal-social area focuses on families' beliefs about and methods for gaining access to support. One type is instrumental support, which refers to external support such as additional services. Do family members believe that such support can only be obtained through informal kinship networks? Or, do they believe that it can be obtained through impersonal channels? And, do they have the requisite skills to do one or both? Emotional support refers to obtaining resources such as an empathic listener or time alone. This factor is particularly important given that a role of early intervention/ESCE services is to provide instrumental and emotional support. When such support comes in forms that are not understood or valued by families, however, it may not be perceived as support at all. Dunst et al. (1988) made reference to this in their seminal work on family support for families with children with exceptionalities.

Sensory-Cognitive   The sensory-cognitive dimension is the third dimension addressed in the Cultural Data Table. This area addresses beliefs, values, and behaviors related to reasoning and understanding and is broken down into four factors. The first factor is the funds of knowledge that a family possesses and values (see Chapter 1). Is knowing how to greet adult relatives properly in social settings a fund of knowledge that the family values and encourages for its children? Is using language to express oneself a valued fund of knowledge? Data on a family's fund of knowledge are critical for determining the degree of consonance between what is promoted in early intervention/ECSE environments and within individual families. Following Moll's (1990) seminal work on funds of knowledge, a range of sources have also discussed diversity of funds of knowledge across cultures (e.g., Greenfield & Cocking, 1994; Gonzalez, Moll, & Amanti, 2005; Lynch & Hanson, 2011; Maynard & Martini, 2005). No two families incorporate these funds into their daily lives in exactly the same way. It is therefore important to validate and anchor this information by getting specific information from individual families.

Two other factors in the personal-social area address preferred strategies for learning and for problem solving and decision making. Knowing preferred strategies in these areas can enhance practitioners' respect and responsiveness because learning, problem solving, and decision making are critical skills for both children and families receiving services. Are families conversant with strategies presented to them by practitioners? Can those strategies be easily integrated into home routines? Answers to these and similar questions determine whether families successfully carry out practitioners' recommendations regarding home activities.

Finally, it is important to obtain information on families' worldviews—how they believe the world works and what is right or wrong. A person's sense of right and wrong lies at the core of his or her response to others' behaviors as being either acceptable or offensive. For example, if someone's worldview is that human behavior is subservient to divine will, then that person experiences behavior that violates that law as insensitive or arrogant, perhaps even evil. Much of this information cannot be elicited directly, either because doing so might be perceived as rude or simply because families cannot readily articulate these aspects of culture.

The questions presented in the Cultural Data Table are not intended to be exhaustive, nor are they intended to be asked directly, one after the other, in an endless interview. They may be asked over time or even not asked directly at all. Asking a family, "What are your assumptions about how the world works?" will not always, if ever, elicit a useful answer. Such directness might even be perceived as offensive. Obtaining these answers may require observing family interactions over time and making cautious inferences. It is important not to expect that all answers be obtained in a single visit or interaction. An example of how these questions can be used in interactions with specific children and families is given in the case study at the end of this chapter.

As stated earlier, it is important to explore these questions not only with the families we serve, but also with friends, co-workers, and colleagues. Answering them will tend to have less emotional investment and lower risk levels for the latter than for families, who may feel intimidated or fear offending the practitioners on whom they rely for support and assistance. Discussing these questions with a greater number of people also makes it more likely that practitioners will make appropriate inferences and develop a more deeply AUD.

The RLP Profile (see Appendix A) is another tool designed to assess children's linguistic proficiency in both English and their language other than English. It is responsive to two needs identified by the first author in her work with young children. The first need is to separate receptive from expressive proficiency. These can diverge widely in children from bilingual environments, and most existing language proficiency tests do not yield separate scores for each. The second need is to distinguish between various levels of bilingualism on a spectrum rather than a continuum. With the RLP Profile, a child can be determined to be at one of seven levels of bilingualism, from monolingual in one language with minimal exposure to English to monolingual in English with minimal exposure to another language. These levels are shown at the bottom of the RLP form.

The RLP was field-tested with young Head Start children (see Metz, 1991). Using elicited language samples as its primary data source, the RLP Profile identifies three aspects of children's language proficiency. The first is the level of receptive and expressive proficiency in a child's language(s) other than English. The second is the level of receptive and expressive proficiency in English. Finally, these two are compared to determine the relative level of proficiency (i.e., the degree of bilingualism or multilingualism).

Completing a Home Language Profile (see Appendix A), a third tool, will be useful for documenting data related to this issue. The Home Language Profile was adapted by Barrera (1993) and field-tested in several Head Start programs in an urban area in the Northeast United States. However home language data is documented, it is important to recognize that the common question, "What language is spoken at home?" is woefully inadequate in a significant number of cases. In some homes, each parent may speak a different language with English as a third language. In others, two languages may be used simultaneously (see Table 8.3).

STEP 4: DEVELOPING A CULTURAL LINGUISTIC RESPONSE PLAN

This final step involves taking all of the previous information and using it to determine how best to assess and teach the particular child on whom it has been gathered. It is a step that will be discussed more extensively in Chapters 9 and 10. This chapter will look at the two tools that can assist with its implementation: the Cultural Consonance Profile (see Appendix A) and the Cultural Linguistic Response Plan (see Appendix A).

Completing the Cultural Consonance Profile is recommended once all available information is placed into a Cultural Data Table. Cultural Consonance Profiles rate the perceived degree of consonance between home culture and language and the culture and language reflected by practitioners and in early childhood settings. The higher the consonance rating, the less likely it is that significant adaptations to typical early childhood procedures and process will be necessary, though these can never be completely ruled out.

Ratings for the degree of consonance between home and early childhood environments are based on the knowledge and perceptions of the practitioners who completed the profile. Cultural consonance ratings are subjective, based on perceived similarities and differences between a child's home environment and the environment where the child will likely be placed. Many variables can affect these ratings (e.g., placement in a different environment, the addition of a Hispanic Spanish-speaking teacher, additional information from the family). The purpose of determining ratings is not to determine an exact degree of cultural consonance. Rather, it is to stimulate and structure team discussions about the needs and strengths of children and families. Lower ratings would indicate a stronger need to gain access to diverse family strengths and adapt existing procedures and materials so as to increase the probability of interactions with children and families that are respectful, reciprocal, and responsive.

Identifying appropriate strategies for responding to the assessed degree of cultural consonance or lack thereof is the next and final step. It is here that Skilled Dialogue dispositions, especially Setting the Stage for Miracles, become most critical as practitioners seek to honor the diverse values and behaviors that have been identified while simultaneously implementing ENC-based early intervention/ECSE procedures and goals.

The recommended approach is to develop Cultural Linguistic Response Plans. As shown in Appendix A, both assessment and instruction can be addressed on one sheet, or the two may be separated, based on what is most useful to practitioners. Figure 8.3 lists the types of items that can be addressed under each section. A completed assessment version is provided for the sample case discussed next.

Assessment/Instructional Cultural Linguistic Response Plan

Child/family: _____   Date: _____   Completed by: _____

Assessment Considerations

RE: Language and communication differences

Communicating with family
Communicating with child during assessment
Assessing relative language proficiency

Assessing overall language abilities/
communicative competence
Using language to assess other developmental/
performance areas

RE: Data-gathering procedures

Type of assessment format
(e.g., formal, informal)
Content to be assessed
Purpose (e.g., eligibility, instructional)

Number and roles of personnel to be involved
Pacing/use of time
Environment(s) in which data is gathered

RE: Interpretation of assessment information

Internal validity (norming)
External validity (alignment with sociocultural
expectations)
Translation/interpretation

Representativeness of funds of knowledge
Role of language in materials
Role of academic-cognitive skills

RE: Reporting assessment results

Need explicit information on adaptations/
modifications
Appropriate interpretation of standardized scores
(e.g., SEM)

Use of qualifiers and nonstandardized scores
Clear distinction between data on
English/ENC and other language(s)/culture(s)

Intervention and Instruction Considerations

RE: Language and communication differences

Language(s) for delivery of instruction (oral
and written)
Language proficiency for academic content/
context

Communicating with family
Communicating with child during instruction
(e.g., questions, directions)

RE: Teaching and learning strategies

Degree of familiarity/value of teaching/
learning strategies vis-à-vis child's home
culture(s)
"Bridging strategies (e.g., scaffolding)

Use of L1 and English language learner
strategies
Leveraging strategies that tap into existing
strengths as springboard for new learning

RE: Instructional content

Degree of cultural familiarity/value
vis-à-vis child's home culture(s)
Consonance to content familiar/valued by
child/family

Meaningfulness (i.e., social validity)
Vocabulary
Worldview(s) represented
Format/organization (e.g., linear, narrative)

RE: Teaching and learning materials

Degree contextualization and linguistic demand
Expected interactions (e.g., listen, answer
questions, solve problems)

Funds of knowledge: both those represented
and those assumed to be present for
understanding

Skilled Dialogue Reminders

	Choosing Relationship over Control/ Anchored Understanding of Diversity	Setting the Stage for Miracles/3rd Space
Respect	Welcoming range and validity of diverse perspective(s)	Allowing the tension of differing perspective(s)
Reciprocity	Making sense of diverse perspectives	Appreciating the strengths of diverse perspectives
Responsiveness	Joining across diverse perspectives	Harmonizing diverse perspectives so as to integrate and gain access to complementary strengths

Figure 8.3.   Combined Assessment/Instructional Cultural Linguistic Response Plan. (Key: SEM, standard error of measurement; ENC, EuroAmerican Normative Culture.)

A Cultural Linguistic Response Plan has three major parts. At the bottom is a reminder of the foundation on which each plan rests—the Skilled Dialogue framework and strategies. This framework and these strategies emphasize that all specific adaptations need to reflect the Skilled Dialogue process and not merely put together piecemeal. At the top are two sections, one addressing specific considerations related to assessment and the other to instruction/intervention. The content of this part groups recommended adaptations/modifications according to the major challenges posed by cultural linguistic diversity to assessment and instruction. These specific recommendations vary according to the cultural linguistic needs and strengths of individual children and their families (see Chapters 9 and 10). Cultural Linguistic Response Plans are not intended to replace individualized education programs (IEPs) or other existing protocols; rather, they are intended to guide the planning of assessment and instruction

ARTURO: AN ILLUSTRATIVE CASE STUDY FOR STEPS 3 AND 4

Five-year-old Arturo lives in an urban area in the Southwest. His mother, Tracy, used street drugs during her pregnancy and was incarcerated soon after Arturo was born. Arturo's 55-year-old grandmother, Vidalia, became his guardian at that time, and Arturo continues to live with her and his 8-year-old brother, Jaime, in a two-bedroom apartment. Tracy, now out of jail and on probation, "lives" with them also, although she spends little time at the apartment. Vidalia speaks both Spanish and English to the children. The family has regular contact with Arturo's great-grandmother, Delfina, and great-aunt, Hortensia, who use Spanish almost entirely in their interactions with the children. Tracy does not speak Spanish but understands it fairly well. Neither Arturo nor Tracy has any contact with Arturo's father, although there is irregular contact with Jaime's father.

At 2 years of age, Arturo was referred for early intervention services because of developmental delays in language and cognition. Preparations are underway for Arturo's transition into a school-based kindergarten, and he continues to exhibit significant language and cognitive delays. Assessments indicate developmental ages of 3 years for language and 2–3 years for cognition. An ECSE practitioner, a kindergarten teacher, a psychologist, a social worker, and an SLP are reviewing Arturo's file. These team members need to make decisions about placement and any additional assessments that may be necessary. They are somewhat concerned about both Tracy's and Vidalia's level of intervention involvement, which diminished once home-based services were discontinued.

Each section will first review the identified practice, then discuss it again in relation to this vignette. Completed tools (e.g., RLP Profile, Cultural Data Table) are shown as each is discussed.

Step 3: Determining the Presence and Nature of Cultural Linguistic Diversity

At least some degree of diversity is immediately evident in Arturo's case. Careful attention must therefore be given to the question, "Am I likely to understand and attach the same meaning to behaviors as the family and/or others from similar cultural backgrounds?" The answer to this question would probably be "no" from the perspective of the assessment process and curricula typical to ECSE services. Early childhood assessment and curricula typically reflect ENC values and beliefs (e.g., emphasis on parental decision making independent of the extended family, focus on early autonomy for the child). Arturo's family, however, probably reflects at least some aspects from one of the Hispanic cultures, which are distinct from ENC.

From the perspective of individual practitioners, however, the answer could be "yes." For example, some Spanish-speaking Puerto Rican practitioners might answer, "Yes, to some degree," whereas others might answer, "No, I am unfamiliar with Hispanic culture outside of the Caribbean." It is possible that a staff member from the same community as Arturo's family would answer, "Yes, without qualification."

Once practitioners determine that at least some degree of cultural linguistic diversity exists between Arturo's family and themselves or the program, they need to make sense of (i.e., strategy of Sense-Making) and appreciate (i.e., strategy of Appreciating) the types of differences evident in this particular child/family. These strategies require assessing the specific nature and degree of the identified diversity in more detail. At this stage they would begin to assess the nature and degree of the diversity.

Completing a Cultural Data Table is the first means of assessing the nature and degree of cultural diversity. Figure 8.4 illustrates a completed Cultural Data Table for Arturo. This table incorporates the information gathered through the other forms as well (e.g., RLP Profile, Home Language Usage Profile). The next three subsections address the data for Arturo in each of the developmental/curricular areas in the Cultural Data Table. The information that was initially available is shown in typed text. Additional information that was subsequently gathered through family interviews and observations is handwritten.

Communicative-Linguistic   Initial information indicated that Arturo's home environment is sometimes English dominant (e.g., interactions between Tracy and Vidalia) and sometimes Spanish dominant (e.g., interactions between Arturo and Delfina or Hortensia). Additional information gathered through subsequent family observations and interviews revealed that Jaime speaks English in most settings and situations. He was observed to speak Spanish occasionally and appears to retain a basic receptive vocabulary (e.g., responded to requests in Spanish). An RLP Profile (Figure 8.3) was completed

Cultural Data Table

Child's name: _Arturo_   Date completed: _1/16/11_   Completed by: _A. Nielsen and P. Howard_

Directions: Fill in responses to questions from the Guide to Identifying Cultural Data Related to Potential Culture Bumps.

Developmental/curricular area	Comments
Communicative-Linguistic Language(s) of child's primary caregiving environment(s)	Grandmother is bilingual (Spanish and English). Great-grandmother and great-aunt are Spanish-dominant. Mother understands Spanish but doesn't speak it. Jaime is 8 years old; he speaks English in most settings and situations and will occasionally use Spanish even though he retains a basic receptive vocabulary.
Child's relative language proficiency (degree of proficiency in English and other language[s] used)	Arturo understands both English and Spanish to some degree. Proficiency information (see Relative Language Proficiency [RLP] Profile) English: receptive (3) expressive (3) Spanish: receptive (5) expressive (3)
Patterns of language usage in child's primary caregiving environment(s)	Spanish tends to be used predominantly for daily living tasks, and English is used for academically related content (e.g., colors, numbers). The variety of Spanish is mostly standard with limited vocabulary and local idioms; the variety of English is standard with limited vocabulary. Discussion among adults in the home is mostly in Spanish. Conversations with children are bilingual. Mother and grandmother are the only ones who use English with the children, mostly for school-related topics (e.g., colors, numbers). Only Spanish is spoken when the great-grandmother or great-aunt are present, except on rare occasions (e.g., telephone calls).
Relative value placed on verbal and nonverbal communication	Interactions with extended family reflect a strong value on nonverbal communication. Mother and grandmother value verbal communication when in the home without extended family. Family values nonverbal communication; less value is placed on verbal skills.
Relative status associated with languages other than English and with bilingualism	Family places instrumental value on English (i.e., use to get things/information), the early intervention/early childhood special education (ECSE) program places instrumental value on Spanish (necessary until English is proficient). A strong value on bilingualism exists within the family. The larger community and early intervention (ECSE) environments place only instrumental value on Spanish (e.g., useful for certain purposes when English is not available) and reflect a stronger value on English.

Figure 8.4. Arturo's Cultural Data Table.

Personal-Social	
Degree of family's acculturation into EuroAmerican Normative Culture (ENC)	Initial information indicates the probability of a low-to-moderate degree of acculturation. Friends and community outside of the family are not mentioned. Jaime's level of acculturation is higher than Arturo's due to age and school experience. Great-grandmother and great-aunt have limited familiarity with ENC and tend to interact only within a circle of other Hispanic, Spanish-dominant friends. Grandmother has significant familiarity with ENC. She is a third-grade reading teacher and has many English monolingual friends. Mother, who has a GED, is less familiar with ENC.
Degree of family's acculturation into U.S. early intervention/early childhood special education (ECSE) culture	Previous contact with early intervention/ECSE programs and practitioners indicates at least a moderate degree of acculturation (i.e., expectations, beliefs, practices). Grandmother's and mother's diminished intervention involvement might indicate reduced acculturation into "family as key decision makers" aspect of that culture. Great-grandmother and great-aunt have little familiarity with early intervention/ECSE culture. Grandmother has moderate familiarity based on Arturo's 2 years in an early intervention program. Mother has less familiarity because of her reduced level of participation. Jaime has little to no familiarity, whereas Arturo has significant familiarity.
Sense of self (e.g., relative weight on independence, dependence, interdependence)	Grandmother's connection with extended family and care of her adult daughter and grandchildren indicate a strong value placed on family and interdependence across generations (i.e., sense of self defined within and by family context). Family observations and interview validate initial assumptions: A strong value is placed on interdependence and self-definition within a family context.
Perceptions and understanding of identity and competence	Identity seems to be family based, and competence seems to be highly correlated with caregiving and "taking care of one's own" rather than with more externally defined skills and achievements.
Roles and rules associated with parenting and child rearing	Prominent aspects of parenting and child rearing: cross-generational responsibility; child-rearing responsibilities not differentiated across family members
Knowledge and experience regarding power and social positioning	There may be some issues with authority due to daughter's experiences (e.g., family members may fear authority or feel powerless to interact effectively with them). Elders' authority is valued (e.g., grandmother's contact with her mother). Family members define themselves as middle-class Americans and do not label themselves as "minorities." Great-grandmother and great-aunt belong to an established family that has been active in both social and political arenas for several generations.

(continued)

Figure 8.4. (continued)

Values/beliefs/skills associated with instrumental and emotional support (e.g., gaining access to external resources, getting personal support)	Values seem to be rooted in family and interpersonal networks rather than in more external resources. Initial assumptions were validated by family observations.
Sensory-Cognitive Funds of knowledge: what type of knowledge is valued; concept structures and definitions (e.g., how family is defined)	Socioemotional knowledge appears to be valued over cognitive instrumental knowledge (e.g., individual skills such as reading a map). Observation confirms that socioemotional knowledge tends to be valued over cognitive instrumental knowledge. Cultural identities play a significant role. Grandmother values literature and reading. She has a wide range of knowledge. Family history and genealogy are frequent topics of discussion
Preferred strategies for acquiring new learning	Forestructure points to the possibility of valuing modeling over explicit verbal instructions and trial and error. Storytelling, modeling, and questioning are valued over exploration and trial-and-error learning. Teaching strategies tend to be implicit and indirect, both oral (e.g., storytelling) and nonverbal (e.g., modeling).
Preferred strategies for problem solving and decision making	Turning to family for assistance highlights the possibility of shared decision making. Great-grandmother is a key decision maker in the family. Problem solving tends to be inductive rather than deductive. The only male involved in family decisions is Jaime's father, who is occasionally consulted.
Worldview (i.e., assumptions about how the world works and about what is "right" and what is "wrong")	Forestructure predicts a strong possibility of culture bumps with ENC practitioners in this area (e.g., family's belief that it is appropriate for a grandmother to assume responsibility for a grandchild and seemingly let the mother off the hook). Mother's and grandmother's worldviews tend to be bicultural (e.g., they recognize both medical and spiritual reasons for Arturo's delays); great-grandmother's and great-aunt's views tend to be more traditional.

for Arturo using an elicited language sample and story retelling techniques. With Vidalia present, the SLP screened Arturo. The practitioner elicited language by showing him pictures of various activities (e.g., a baseball game, a picnic) and asked him to tell her all that he could about the pictures. Then, she told Arturo that she was going to read him a story and asked him to retell it after she was finished. Both procedures were done in Spanish and in English. The resulting RLP Profile (see Figure 8.5) showed that Arturo understands both Spanish and English. The story retelling activity, however, indicated significantly greater comprehension in Spanish than in English. His expressive skills in English were shown to be similar to his English comprehension skills. When retelling the story in English, Arturo evidenced consistent errors, especially in the use of tense and pronouns. Based on this information, Arturo is considered partially bilingual, with Spanish being his stronger language.

A Home Language Usage Profile (see Figure 8.6), completed during a home visit following the language assessment, indicated that discussions among adults in Arturo's home are mostly in Spanish, although conversations with the children are bilingual. Jaime and other neighborhood children around Arturo predominantly use English, sending a powerful message that English is the language of choice outside the home. This message may inadvertently inhibit Arturo's expressive skills in Spanish. Tracy and Vidalia are the only adults who use English with Arturo and Jaime in the home, mostly for school-related topics. Spanish is used almost exclusively in the presence of Delfina and Hortensia.

Interactions with the extended family reflect the high value placed on nonverbal communication, although Vidalia and Tracy value verbal communication in other situations (e.g., much discussion about daily experiences was observed). In addition, using both English and Spanish appropriately is valued, as evidenced by Vidalia's modeling and the family's insistence on continuing to use Spanish. Family members reported that speaking and understanding Spanish is important for family interactions and success in the larger community. English was considered important for successful participation in school and the English-speaking community. The implicit message seems to be that English is not as important as Spanish outside of that participation.

Personal-Social   Few questions in this area could be answered using the initially available data. Personal-social data usually are not explicitly gathered, although they may be known if the family has a long association with a particular program. As in Arturo's case, it is often necessary to gather additional information through observations and interviews and the completion of a Family Acculturation Screen (see Figure 8.7). The completion of this form occurred during two subsequent visits to the family.

Vidalia appears to have been the first family member to acquire significant familiarity with ENC. She was the first family member to speak English fluently and attend U.S. schools. She holds a master's degree and a teaching license, and she has worked as a third-grade reading teacher for more than 10

Relative Language Proficiency (RLP) Profile

Child's name: _Arturo_ _____ Date: _1/10/11_____ Date of birth: _11/15/05____

Chronological age: _5 years 2 months_____ Completed by: _J. Irish_____

Site: _Child's home_____ Instrument: _Elicited language sample and story retelling_

Proficiency in language other than English (specify language: _Spanish_____)

Receptive:	⑤	4	3	2	1
	Good; no significant errors	Mildly limited; some errors	Moderately limited; consistent/ significant errors	Severely limited; frequent and significant errors	Nonverbal and/or unintelligible
Expressive:	5	4	③	2	1

Comments:
Arturo seemed to understand Spanish at an age-appropriate level but had more limited expressive skills. His mean length of utterance (MLU) was below age expectations; he retained a simple noun-verb-object structure.

English proficiency

Receptive:	5	4	③	2	1
	Good; no significant errors	Mildly limited; some errors	Moderately limited; consistent/ significant errors	Severely limited; frequent and significant errors	Nonverbal and/or unintelligible
Expressive:	5	4	③	2	1

Comments:
Arturo's comprehension seemed limited (e.g. could not answer simple "who"/"what" questions). His expressive skills were similarly limited (MLU below age level; used mainly noun-verb structures).

Relative Language Proficiency (Write language other than English in blanks below.)

Spanish Monolingual	Receptive bilingual	Partial bilingual	Bilingual	Partial bilingual	Receptive bilingual	English monolingual
Has had minimal exposure to English	_Spanish_ dominant; understands some English	_Spanish_ dominant; limited English	_Spanish_ and English about the same	English dominant; limited _Spanish_	English dominant; understands some _Spanish_	Has had minimal exposure to _Spanish_

Comments:
Although Arturo's expressive skills are limited in both Spanish and English, his receptive skills clearly establish Spanish as the stronger, or "dominant" language.

Figure 8.5. Arturo's Relative Language Proficiency (RLP) Profile.

years. Tracy did not complete high school but obtained a general equivalency diploma (GED). Jaime's level of acculturation is strong; he has several close friends who are English monolingual and spends time in their homes.

Home Language Usage Profile

Child's name: _Arturo_　　　Date: _1/10/11_　　　Completed by: _J. Irish_

Person(s)	Only L$_x$ / Specify language other than English used in home: _Spanish_	Mostly L$_x$ (_Spanish_), some English	L$_x$ (_Spanish_) and English used equally	Some L$_x$ (_Spanish_), mostly English	Only English	Other language (specify) ___
				Languages used		
Mother				X		
Father					X Jaime's dad	
Siblings				X		
Maternal grandparents						
Paternal grandparents	_Not_	_in_	_contact_	_with_	_child_	
Caregiver (different from people listed above)	_None_	_used_	_outside_	_of_	_family_	
Neighborhood friends/peers				X		
Teacher(s)				X		
Social peers (e.g., at child care; at preschool)					X	

(Key: L$_x$ is the language other than English used in the home.)

Comments: _Based on observations and family interviews. Arturo appears to have little access to Spanish usage outside the home._

Figure 8.6. Arturo's Home Language Usage Profile. (*Source:* Williams & DeGaetano, 1985.)

The family's degree of acculturation in the early intervention/ECSE culture is more limited, based on their varying degrees of association with Arturo's early intervention program and practitioners. Family observations and interviews during a 2-week period validated the practitioners' initial assumptions regarding understanding of sense of self, perceptions of identity

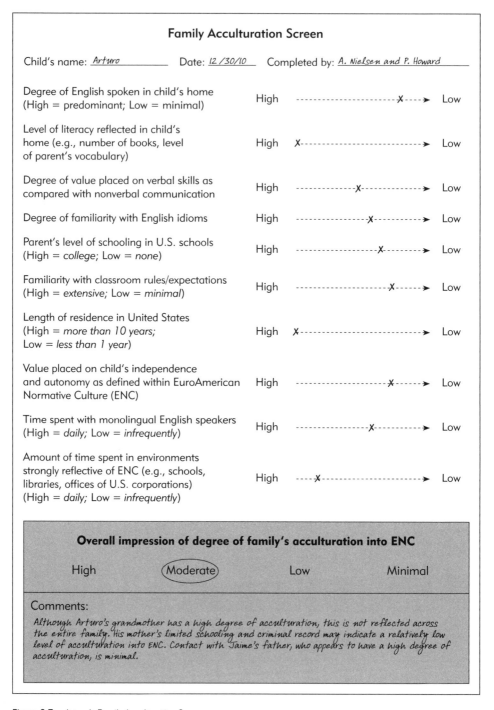

Figure 8.7. Arturo's Family Acculturation Screen.

and competence, and roles/rules associated with parenting and child rearing. These are more reflective of values and beliefs in Hispanic culture than in ENC (see Figure 8.4). Yet, the family members define themselves as middle-class Americans and do not label themselves "minorities." Delfina and Hortensia belong to an established family that has been politically and socially active in the Southwest for almost 100 years.

Sensory-Cognitive   Scant sensory-cognitive data existed in Arturo's case, so much additional information needed to be gathered. This is not uncommon, even though these data are especially relevant to practitioners' understanding of families' funds of knowledge (i.e., the skills and knowledge that they bring to early intervention/ECSE environments) and of the teaching/learning strategies valued and modeled in the home.

Arturo's sensory-cognitive data present an interesting bicultural portrait common to many Hispanic families in the Southwest. His family tends to value socioemotional knowledge over the cognitive knowledge and skills typically valued in ENC environments. For instance, they value social skills over years of formal schooling. Even though cognitive knowledge and skills valued in ENC environments are also considered important, they are perceived more as a means to an end than as an end in themselves. Storytelling, modeling, and questioning are the family's preferred strategies for acquiring new knowledge. Discovery and trial-and-error strategies were not observed except when adults helped Jaime with his schoolwork. Vidalia and Delfina used implicit, indirect teaching strategies. Yet, Vidalia was also observed to use the more direct, explicit strategies that she learned from early intervention practitioners who previously worked with Arturo.

Although 89 years old, Delfina remains the family's key decision maker. Her problem-solving strategies, as well as those used by other family members, tend to be inductive rather than deductive. Jaime's father is the only male involved in decision making; he is consulted from time to time when the family perceives a need for male representation (e.g., when needing to purchase a car, obtain insurance, or seek legal help).

The family's worldviews are generationally distinct. Tracy and Vidalia have worldviews that reflect both ENC and traditional Hispanic beliefs. For example, they recognize medical reasons for Arturo's developmental delays. Yet, they also recognize Delfina's belief that the delays resulted from Tracy's ignoring a dream about having her pregnancy blessed in the local church. They feel no need to choose between these two views. Delfina and Hortensia, conversely, hold to a traditional Hispanic worldview that might be judged as nonscientific ("untrue") within ENC. For them, a pregnancy without a spiritual dimension (i.e., a blessing) leaves both mother and child unprotected against negative influences and actions.

Cultural Consonance   Arturo's Cultural Consonance Profile (Figure 8.8) shows limited consonance between the program and Arturo and his family in the communicative-linguistic area. The moderate rating in this area was based on the fact that language and communication patterns in the home differed fairly significantly from those found in the kindergarten to which Arturo is being transferred. Spanish is often spoken at home; however, only one

Cultural Consonance Profile

Child's name: _Arturo_   Date: _1/08/11_   Completed by: _A. Nielsen_

	Highly similar to early childhood environment(s)/ practitioners' profiles					Highly dissimilar from early childhood environment(s)/ practitioners' profiles

I. Communicative-Linguistic Area   Comments

Language(s) used in child's home	5	4	(3)	2	1
Child's relative language proficiency	5	4	(3)	2	1
Patterns of language usage	5	4	3	(2)	1

Little use of direct question-and-answer routines

Relative value placed on verbal/ nonverbal communication	5	4	(3)	2	1
Relative status of language other than English and bilingualism	5	4	3	(2)	1

II. Personal-Social Area

Family's degree of acculturation	5	4	(3)	2	1
Sense of self/perception of identity/competence	5	4	3	(2)	1
Parenting/child-rearing roles and rules	5	4	3	(2)	1
Knowledge/experience regarding power and positioning	5	(4)	3	2	1
Values and beliefs regarding support	5	4	3	(2)	1

Familiarity with social and political power
Tend to rely on family and personal networks

III. Sensory-Cognitive Area

Funds of knowledge/concept definition/structures	5	4	(3)	2	1
Preferred learning strategies	5	4	3	(2)	1
Preferred problem-solving/ decision-making strategies	5	4	3	(2)	1
Worldview	5	4	(3)	2	1	*Bicultural*

Degree of consonance with early childhood environment(s)/practitioners' profiles

Communicative-linguistic area	High	(Moderate)	Low	Minimal
Personal-social area	High	Moderate	(Low)	Minimal
Sensory-cognitive area	High	(Moderate	Low)	Minimal

Comments: _Sensory-cognitive is moderate to low depending on the context and topic._

Figure 8.8.   Arturo's Cultural Consonance Profile.

practitioner speaks Spanish in the new early childhood environment. In addition, this environment reflects ENC values and beliefs regarding other aspects of language usage and patterns (e.g., an emphasis on verbal communication and direct questioning).

Consonance in the personal-social area was rated at the low-to-moderate level, based on available cultural data. The practitioners believed that the family's beliefs, practices, and values in this area reflect Southwest Hispanic culture more than ENC. This is especially true in the areas of sense of self, parenting roles, and values and beliefs related to obtaining support resources.

The sensory-cognitive area was also judged to have a low-to-moderate degree of consonance with early childhood environments and practitioners. Although Vidalia's and Tracy's funds of knowledge and worldviews included aspects of ENC, the funds of knowledge and worldview held by Delfina still wielded great influence in this area. In addition, both Vidalia and Tracy were observed to use teaching/learning strategies that reflect Hispanic culture more than ENC.

Arturo's Cultural Consonance Profile shows an overall pattern of low-to-moderate consonance within as well as across areas, which is fairly typical for many children from bilingual and bicultural families. These families retain many beliefs, values, and practices associated with their home cultures while acquiring ENC beliefs, values, and practices that are deemed necessary for successful participation in work and social environments. Some families keep each set of beliefs, values, and practices neatly distinct—just as some bilingual speakers keep their languages distinct. Other families "mix and match" beliefs, values, and practices—just as other bilingual speakers use two languages, rapidly switching them in response to personal and situational variables. In both cases, it is important to recognize which beliefs, values, and practices are operative at which times. Such recognition is critical for developing adaptations and opportunities that maximize the child's learning, family–practitioner collaboration, and adaptations and opportunities that are concrete expressions of respect, reciprocity, and responsiveness.

Step 4: Developing a Cultural Linguistic Response Plan for Arturo

Figure 8.9 is a sample Cultural Linguistic Response Plan for Arturo and his family that identifies four areas of consideration related to assessment. These are areas within which assessment dilemmas commonly arise. Five suggestions are given for Arturo's practitioners to consider in this area. These do not go into detail; greater detail is provided in Chapters 9 and 10.

Language and Communication   The first suggestion in this category responds to the fact that Arturo's language skills are not contained within a single language. The second suggestion recognizes that when items are pre-

Assessment Cultural Linguistic Response Plan

Child/family: _Arturo_

Date: _1/13/11_   Completed by: _P. O'Donaghue_

Specific Assessment Considerations

RE: *Language and communication differences*

1. Use both English and Spanish with slightly more Spanish, especially for directions, explanations, and non-school related content.
2. Test in less-proficient language first to minimize carry-over from one language to the other.
3. Probe all items missed in one language in the other language.
4. Match patterns of language usage in the home as much as possible.
5. Check for the influence of Spanish semantics and syntax on English.

RE: *Data-gathering procedures*

1. Involve family members in assessment; use familiar routines when possible.
2. Use less structured and more dynamic procedures in addition to standardized procedures.
3. Minimize the use of trial-and-error and direct-questioning procedures.
4. Increase the use of modeling and storytelling strategies that are familiar to the child.
5. Use peer-assisted and cooperative formats in addition to independent one-to-one formats.

RE: *Interpretation of assessment information*

1. Be aware of funds of knowledge reflected in pictures and objects; tap into familiar funds of knowledge unless explicitly assessing the ability to process unfamiliar material.
2. Include Spanish-language materials.
3. Use materials that are familiar to the child as well as less familiar materials that are common to early intervention/early childhood special education (e.g., a balance beam).

RE: *Reporting assessment results*

1. Identify which items were presented in which language; also note the language(s) used to respond to items.
2. Report adaptations to standard procedures.
3. Detail when results reflect linguistic or cultural variables and when they reflect developmental (delay or disability) variables.

Skilled Dialogue Reminders

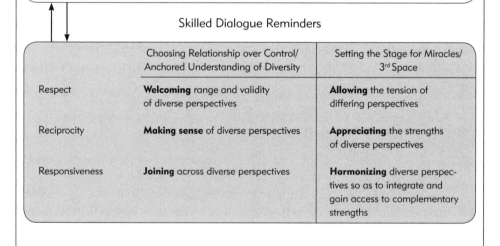

	Choosing Relationship over Control/ Anchored Understanding of Diversity	Setting the Stage for Miracles/ 3rd Space
Respect	**Welcoming** range and validity of diverse perspectives	**Allowing** the tension of differing perspectives
Reciprocity	**Making sense** of diverse perspectives	**Appreciating** the strengths of diverse perspectives
Responsiveness	**Joining** across diverse perspectives	**Harmonizing** diverse perspectives so as to integrate and gain access to complementary strengths

Figure 8.9.   Arturo's Assessment Cultural Linguistic Response Plan.

sented in a child's stronger language first, memory of those items can inflate scores for the weaker language.

The remaining three suggestions address recommended practices for bilingual assessments (see Chapter 9 for guidelines on interpreting and reporting assessment data). Considerations related to data-gathering procedures focus on two related aspects: 1) integrating family members and their perspectives into the assessment process and 2) integrating familiar strategies common in Arturo's home to control for the effects of unfamiliarity. The third set of considerations addresses the materials to be used in assessing Arturo's development and skills. Using Spanish-language materials that contain funds of knowledge familiar to Arturo will increase the probability of accurate and optimal assessment results. Finally, suggestions are given for reporting assessment results.

Data-Gathering Procedures   The first two considerations related to data-gathering procedures focus on integrating family perspectives and strategies into the assessment process. These two aspects of data-gathering procedures are not always easy but are, perhaps, the most critical if accurate data is to be obtained. The third set of considerations addresses materials to be used. Here, too, familiarity in both content and language is important as these are closely linked. Using Spanish language materials, for example, will increase the probability that these reflect the family's valued funds of knowledge. The accuracy of data collected will consequently also increase. The last two considerations provide more detail.

Interpretation of Assessment Results   It is not only data gathering that must be attended to. Accurate interpretation of results is also critical. Being able to identify which results reflect diverse cultural or linguistic variables and which may reflect developmental concerns is a key aspect of assessment. For this reason, being aware of the differences or similarities between Arturo's funds of knowledge and those referenced in assessment items is the first consideration. For example, did Arturo not respond to naming colors because this is not a developmentally stressed fund of knowledge or because he has failed to acquire this knowledge? Did he not understand the language used within a item or did he in fact not know that item? More will be said about these questions in Chapter 9.

Reporting Assessment Results   It is our belief that most assessment bias is not contained in the procedures or the materials used but rather in how assessment results are reported. When a score is reported without reference to the lack of an interpreter or when it is not noted that items were known when asked in Spanish, readers of the results will assume that a child's score validly reflects ability. It can, for example, be valid to give a Spanish monolingual child a test completely in English as long as results are interpreted to mean only as what that child can do in English and *not what that child can do, period.* Similarly, it can be valid to test that same child with English language story-books if the only purpose is to assess how well that child can handle English language storybooks—*neither comprehension nor general knowledge can or should be inferred.* These examples are not presented as suggestions but only as ex-amples of the role that assessment reports can have in promoting assessment bias. One suggestion (more are provided in Chapter 9), for example, is to add statements such as, "Though the child's normed score was 80, additional probing and use of different materials achieved successful performance. Had these results been able to be reported as standardized, the child's score would have been 95." Such statements promote a much more accurate understand-ing of children's developmental levels.

Although certainly not exhaustive, these considerations can go a long way toward honoring identity (i.e., communicating respect) through recog-nizing Arturo's boundaries and funds of knowledge; honoring voice (i.e., es-tablishing reciprocity) through promoting equal voice and privilege for the family's boundaries and funds of knowledge; and honoring connection (i.e., promoting responsiveness) through creating inclusive and creative assess-ment options.

Planning and Conducting Culturally Linguistically Inclusive Assessments

The challenge is not simply becoming aware of the framework within which a culturally different family operates, but becoming aware of the cultural assumptions from which professionals derive their judgments. (Harry, 1992, p. 334)

As discussed in Chapter 8, early intervention/ECSE practitioners must develop forestructures and practice Skilled Dialogue on an ongoing basis. Practitioners cannot wait until they begin working with a family to develop and utilize these practices. Perhaps nowhere are the potential problems or dilemmas of waiting more evident than in the arena of assessment.

Evaluating and assessing infants, toddlers, and preschoolers has presented significant challenges to the early childhood education field (Losardo & Notari-Syverson, 2001; McLean, 2001; Sandall, Hemmeter, Smith, & McLean, 2005). This is particularly true when families' cultural linguistic backgrounds differ from those of practitioners (Catlett, Winton, & Santos, 2000; Santos, Corso, & Fowler, 2005). During any assessment process, a child's abilities must be considered within the family's cultural context and home environment. In an ideal situation, practitioners determine the degree of cultural consonance and the corresponding need for Skilled Dialogue prior to conducting any formal child assessment activities; however, this is not always the case. It is important to determine the degree of cultural consonance between families and ECSE services, as well as the corresponding impact on specific procedures and interactions, even when other programs or individuals have already conducted assessments.

Sections I and II examine the potential challenges that practitioners may experience because of culture bumps. Some bumps revolve around communicative-linguistic issues related to language(s) spoken, nonverbal communication, and the perceived status of languages other than English and bilingualism. Common personal-social culture bumps stem from limited acculturation into and familiarity with ENC and the ECSE culture, as well as from differences in how individuals perceive their own identity and competence. Sensory-cognitive culture bumps arise because the types of knowledge deemed valuable and necessary vary substantially across cultures, and the value attached to certain learning and decision-making approaches can differ significantly between practitioners and families.

This chapter returns to culture bumps that frequently create assessment challenges experienced by early intervention/ECSE practitioners and families. This chapter presents research-based responses to help practitioners consider ways to respond to the challenges that they may encounter in serving children and families from diverse backgrounds. These suggested responses, however, do not comprise a complete list. Consistent with the concept and practice of 3rd Space, it is important to note that other appropriate responses exist.

COMMON ASSESSMENT CONCERNS AND CONSIDERATIONS

Common assessment challenges for practitioners working with children from culturally linguistically backgrounds may be placed into four broad categories: 1) determining language and communication differences, 2) gathering assessment information and materials, 3) interpreting assessment results, and 4) reporting and using assessment results. The following subsections present each challenge as well as suggested responses. At the end of the chapter, several vignettes show how Skilled Dialogue can support practitioners and families as they confront these common assessment challenges and work through responses.

Language and Communication Differences

The most common assessment challenges result from the fact that many culturally diverse families in the United States are also linguistically diverse. That is, they speak a language other than English with their children. We can begin to think about multiple ways cultural linguistic diversity may be reflected in a child's communicative-linguistic development by using the Cultural Data Table (see Appendix A). As discussed in Chapter 8, we need to reflect on several critical questions. What is the language(s) of the child's primary caregiver? Which caregivers speak which language(s) with the child? What is the child's degree of proficiency in English and other languages used in the home? What patterns of language are used in the home; in what situation or topics is a language used? What is the relative value placed on verbal and nonverbal communication? Is being bilingual a desirable goal in this family? These are a few questions that need to be answered prior to planning and administering assessments.

Based on such information, a practitioner may find that a family and their children are monolingual in a language other than English or speak one or more languages in addition to English. Such linguistically diverse home environments affect both the knowledge that children bring to assessment tasks and the language in which they hold and can express that knowledge. Consequently, two aspects of assessment are especially challenging.

1. The assessment of language proficiency, especially when families' languages cannot be incorporated into assessment (i.e., when personnel fluent in the families' languages cannot be found).

2. The assessment of general knowledge/skills when items and directions can only be presented in English and/or when existing knowledge and concepts are not equivalent across languages.

Practitioners can review the information obtained (see Chapter 8) and determine the extent to which linguistic and cultural differences need to be factored into assessment. For example, as practitioners assess the degree of linguistic diversity, it may be necessary to conduct home visits and interview family members to determine how and when a child uses a variety of different languages. As discussed in Chapter 8, practitioners should utilize the Home Language Usage Profile (see Appendix A). Practitioners should use the RLP Profile to support the child's receptive and expressive skills in each language (see Appendix A) The following strategies directly address such language issues.

Suggested Strategies   It is critical that information about the language background and experience of all children be gathered from families using respectful, reciprocal, and responsive dialogue (i.e., Skilled Dialogue). The following suggestions are provided in order to support practitioners engaged in the process of assessing young children from cultural linguistic backgrounds different from their own.

Assess for Language Proficiency First   A child's language proficiency needs to be assessed first to determine which language(s) to use in presenting assessment tasks. Assessment for language proficiency is distinct from a comprehensive language assessment. Its purpose is to determine the degree to which a child understands and uses a particular language rather than to obtain a detailed profile of language skills within a single language. Although assessment of a child's language proficiency supports comprehensive language assessment, it cannot and should not replace it.

It is crucial to know a child's level of proficiency in English, as well as other language(s) used in the home, even when the referring concern has nothing to do with language. Only with such knowledge can assessment tasks be properly planned and assessment results be properly interpreted. The Individuals with Disabilities Education Act Amendments (IDEA) of 1997 (PL 105-17) and the Individuals with Disabilities Education Improvement Act of 2004 (PL 108-446) require administering assessment in the child's native language. If the child is bilingual, then many agencies choose to assess in the child's dominant language (Moore & Beatty, 1995). The results of an RLP Profile or other similar tools can help determine whether there is a dominant language or whether the child is similarly proficient in two or more languages (see Chapter 8). Table 9.1 presents a matrix to assist early childhood practitioners in selecting the most appropriate type of assessment.

Seek Bilingual/Multilingual Practitioners and Other Individuals   Whenever possible, practitioners who assess children from diverse cultural linguistic backgrounds should be 1) proficient in both English and the other language(s) spoken by child and family, 2) familiar with the child's home culture(s), and 3) knowledgeable about first- and second-language acquisition and development in bilingual or multilingual environments. Many practitioners believe that individuals with these qualifications do not exist in their geographic area;

Table 9.1.   Language assessment decision matrix

Consideration	Type of assessment			
	Balanced bilingual assessment	Bilingual-dominant language assessment	Modified single language assessment	Single language assessment
Child's relative language proficiency	Similar proficiency in both languages	Partial bilingual	Receptive bilingual	Monolingual
Home language usage	Both languages used to similar degrees	Consistent use of one language with regular but limited use of the other	Some use of language other than English	Only one language used in the home
Child's language usage and preference	Consistent use of both languages	Evident preference for or dominant use of one language	Dominant use of one language with only occasional use of the other (e.g., with grandparents)	No receptive or expressive use of the second language
Emotional/cognitive considerations	Both languages important for interactions with significant caregivers	Elimination of the less proficient language would preclude access to a particular fund of knowledge	Understanding of particular concepts/vocabulary tied to the less proficient language	No use of the less proficient language by family members or other caregivers

however, it is important to avoid this assumption. Practitioners and programs need to establish connections with other early childhood programs in their community (e.g., child care centers, preschools, Head Start programs) as well as with a variety of experienced community personnel (e.g., military spouses who may not be working, practitioners with professional licenses from other countries). Families with cultural linguistic backgrounds that differ from ENC typically live in communities with other families from similar backgrounds. Connecting with community programs can help practitioners identify individuals who share the language and culture of the families who seek assistance from them. The search for bilingual or multicultural personnel should be ongoing and may need to include the development of preservice or in-service materials to extend the skills of those identified.

Prepare and Utilize Knowledgeable Individuals   It may not be possible to identify bilingual staff immediately, but it is almost always possible to locate non–family members who are proficient in the desired languages and cultures. (Note: The practitioner may need to provide professional development specific to assessment of infants and young children.) Word of mouth often elicits more responses in the community than written ads. Although family members can provide invaluable help, they must have a choice regarding the degree to which they act as translators and interpreters (see Chapter 2). In addition, it is important to use families' skills respectfully. Bilingual practitioners typically comment on how programs expect them to translate papers and conversations with little notice. One Spanish- and English-speaking practitioner from Puerto Rico who was working in the Southwest United States said that she was expected to translate despite her unfamiliarity with the local culture and dialect. See Appendix B and sources such as Hamayan and Damico (1991) and Langdon and Cheng (2002) for more information.

Meet Beforehand with the Person Who Is to Assist   Make sure that everyone involved knows the tasks and items being used and what is being assessed before beginning the assessment process. Ensure that interpreters[1] are knowledgeable about the language, culture, values, and traditions of both the family and the service provider. It is equally critical that the interpreter understands the terms and concepts likely to arise during assessment. If necessary, the interpreter should first observe the practitioner conducting another evaluation. Remember that interpreters should not be expected to assume the practitioners' roles and responsibilities. That is, they should not independently facilitate play situations or administer test items without specific guidance. Although translators and cultural guides may assist in understanding cultural linguistic issues

---

[1]The authors recognize that *interpreter* and *translator* have distinct meanings. For the purposes of this text, however, the terms are used interchangeably to refer to any person who assists practitioners in bridging linguistic differences.

that may arise during the assessment process, practitioners remain responsible for making clinical judgments. See Appendix B for further information.

Avoid Simultaneous Interpretations   Avoid saying something in one language and then immediately having it interpreted in the other. This type of interpretation makes it difficult to determine which language a child is responding to and, thus, confounds the assessment results. Sequential interpretation—completing a portion of the assessment in one language before switching to the other—is usually more appropriate. Although standardized procedures should always be followed, valid alterations to these procedures (e.g., using another language) can be made following their completion. For example, after administering items in a standardized manner and obtaining a valid ceiling, practitioners can revisit missed items and readminister them in another language or through the use of prompts. Responses to these latter items cannot be used in computing standard scores. Nevertheless, they provide valuable information on a child's knowledge and skills. Additional suggestions are provided in the section on reporting results.

Use the "One Person, One Language" Rule   When possible, one practitioner should speak one language with the child and another practitioner/ translator should speak the other language. The practitioners may speak English with each other, although they must do so cautiously because this may communicate that English is preferable or more valued than the other language. Young children quickly learn what it takes to communicate with individuals; however, they do not grasp the abstract concept of language until after the age of 7 or so. This was demonstrated during a screening of bilingual children in a Head Start program. During this program, several English monolingual children approached the table where the screening materials were laid out and said that they wanted to play too. After being told that only children who spoke Spanish were playing that day, one child replied, "We speak Spanish." The practitioner assented and began speaking to them in Spanish. The children responded readily—in gibberish, which is probably what the practitioner's words sounded like to them. It was clear that they could not yet grasp the distinction between languages.

Use an Observer/Recorder   When feasible, one person should observe and record while the other interacts with the child. Practitioners must acknowledge that their own observations can never be truly objective because people make evaluations based on personal and sociocultural "lenses" (Barrera, 1993). An observer who considers how the information is gathered can highlight the assessor's unconscious values and assumptions. Similarly, videotaping can also be useful for collecting accurate data that go beyond mere scores. In addition, if an assessment is videotaped, then a careful review of the translation and transcript can be conducted at a later date.

Assess Items in a Variety of Languages.   Practitioners should always present items missed in one language in the other language, although only after standardized procedures are completed (if these are being used). Many children from bilingual homes know some items in only one of their languages (e.g., they may know colors in English and kinship terms in their other home language). Children who are bilingual may lag behind monolingual children when assessed in only one language yet may possess a total vocabulary and language skills similar to those of monolingual children when assessed across both or multiple languages.

Note the Language(s) Used in Assessment   Always note the language(s) used by the evaluator and the child when recording responses to assessment tasks. Practitioners should especially note when multiple languages were used. This information is important for the correct interpretation of assessment results (see the Interpreting Assessment Results section for more detail).

Discriminate Between Items that Tap Academic Readiness and Those that Tap Language Proficiency   Readiness and academically oriented items such as color and number awareness 1) test a child's knowledge base rather than his or her language proficiency and 2) may not have the same developmental value in other cultures as they do in ENC. Rather than demonstrating ability, responses to these items may reflect the knowledge that a family values or the time when a family believes it is necessary to acquire these skills (which may vary greatly from ENC's expected age). Being able to label geometric shapes, for example, may not be highly valued before age 6, but naming second and third cousins may be expected by age 4.

These suggested responses to dilemmas related to language and language difference are not comprehensive. Nonetheless, it is important that practitioners consider each one. These responses provide a critical link to how assessment information is gathered and interpreted and, ultimately, to how it is used.

Gathering Assessment Information and Materials

Other common assessment challenges result from culture bumps related to the content, format, and inherent values of assessment items, which may be unfamiliar or negative to children from a culture other than that common to the population(s) on which the items were standardized. If items are unfamiliar, then children will be less likely to demonstrate the target skills during the assessment process. Clearly, responses to individual items will be severely affected for children whose cultural background does not include or value those items.

The Cultural Data Table (see Appendix A) can help identify possible cultural bumps arising from assessment content and format that may be unfamiliar to or not valued by the child/family. For example, we can identify the child's/family's degree of acculturation in ENC, as well as their degree of acculturation to the early childhood/ECSE culture, in the personal-social dimension. How skilled is the family at accomplishing their desired goals? Does the family value personal independence, dependence, or interdependence within the family unit? What behaviors demonstrate a child's competence? What are the roles and rules for parenting and child rearing? We can identify the knowledge and skills (funds of knowledge) valued and supported by the family in the sensory-cognitive dimension. The child's/family's preferred learning strategies—direct or indirect, oral or nonverbal, modeling or questioning—provide valuable information for developing or selecting an appropriate assessment tool. What are the child's/family's preferred strategies for problem solving or decision making—cooperative or independent of others, deductive or inductive? Answers to these questions can reveal diverse cultural understandings of the child/family in the personal-social and sensory-cognitive dimensions, which can affect a child's ability to demonstrate the target skill during an assessment activity.

It is critical to identify cultural bumps that may affect assessment as the inherent values of the assessment process may run counter to the values, beliefs, and customs of particular families. The families may passively or directly refuse intervention services. Families may demonstrate their concerns about the process by simply missing assessment appointments or not being home when the assessment team arrives. Other families undergo the initial assessment process but choose not to follow through on suggested intervention strategies based on the outcomes of the assessment. Clearly, how assessment information is gathered can have a significant affect on a family's decision to participate in early intervention/ECSE services and on the delivery of appropriate services and intervention strategies for children and families.

While formal assessments provide critical information in assessing young children, practitioners need to gather additional information from families essential to understanding the whole child—their development, experiences, and preferred ways of demonstrating new learning and skills. The acknowledgement and consideration of any differences that exist between the families and practitioners increases the degree of reliability of the assessment information being collected. Regular and periodic assessment and observations of children in multiple settings provide much more accurate depictions of children's skills and knowledge than a one-time administration of standardized measures. See the following strategies for gathering assessment information from young children and their families.

Suggested Strategies   Although standardized measures play a valid role in assessing young children, practitioners should gather additional information from families and other caregivers about children's backgrounds and development. Having an anchored understanding of the differences that exist between families and practitioners significantly influences the quality of assessment information collected.

Note Other Possibilities in Test Scoring   Practitioners should not limit themselves to the information collected during standardized procedures. The information yielded by these procedures may be accurately interpreted only when combined with information obtained through other assessment methods. Children may not demonstrate a skill when a test item is culturally or linguistically unfamiliar. If a practitioner uses standardized procedures and reports scores according to the test manual, then he or she should add comments on items that a child passed when adapted and translated. For example, the practitioner might note the score obtained if adapted items could have been scored as correct: "Obtained score was 'X'; had the translated items been credited, John would have obtained a score of 'Y'." Such statements alert the reader to the fact that obtained scores may underestimate children's knowledge and abilities.

Delineate Between Overall Language Functioning and Language Proficiency   Overall language functioning is not the same as proficiency in any single language. A child's overall language functioning is best reflected by scoring all items passed, regardless of which language was used for presenting or responding to individual items. Proficiency in a particular language, conversely, is reflected by items passed in only that language. Of note, a speech-language delay or disorder refers to deviations in learning and using language, not to limitations in a specific language. A child may even have limited proficiency in two languages yet not have a language delay or disorder when "mixed" use of two languages is the norm in his or her community. Practitioners must differentiate between language delays/disorders and simple differences in language proficiency when they gather assessment information (Klingner, Hoover, & Baca, 2008). Hamayan and Damico (1991) and Metz (1991) provided information and references related to these differences.

Utilize Information Gathered by Alternative Means   As previously stated, standardized results in themselves cannot sufficiently describe a child's abilities and skills. Parent reports and observations of same-age peers should be taken into account in determining a delay or disorder, even when statistically normative data are available. Even when scores indicate below-age performance, a language delay may not truly be present when a child's language is peer commensurate and normative within his or her social environment. Determining that a child's language corresponds with that of peers does not, however, preclude the presence of other developmental issues.

Regardless of the assessment method(s) used, practitioners should avoid placing children in artificial situations. To the maximum extent possible, children's typical home and preschool routines and activities should be used to obtain assessment information.

Distinguish Between Expressive and Receptive Language Delays It is critical that practitioners work with the child and family to distinguish between expressive and receptive language delays. Research shows that mild-to-moderate expressive delays without co-occurring receptive delays often are not a sign of language disorders in children from bilingual environments (Metz, 1991). Yet, children who demonstrate moderate to severe receptive language delays should be immediately referred for a comprehensive language assessment because receptive delays tend to be more closely linked to communication disorders.

Interpreting Assessment Results

After assessment information is gathered, the practitioner/assessment team is tasked with interpreting the results. In addition to psychometric interpretations, the team must also carefully consider the child's and family's cultural linguistic context(s) as well as their broader environmental context. For example, some children lose a primary language spoken during early childhood because they may not have had opportunities to maintain it after entering preschool or primary school. These children become English monolingual, or they may demonstrate limitations in both English and their early home language (Guardado, 2003; Mattes & Omark, 1984; Nieto, 2001). The first case results from decreased use and lack of opportunity to advance proficiency and vocabulary; the second case results from insufficient learning time or an overly abrupt language shift.

Language limitations due to limited exposure can be differentiated from true delays or disorders on the basis of 1) knowledge about the child's language learning history and 2) a practitioner's clinical experience with similar children. When it is not possible to definitively distinguish between language differences and language disorders, a follow-up evaluation should be recommended after interventions such as speech therapy or speech-language improvement classes, English for speakers of other languages (ESOL) lessons, or bilingual instruction. These services result in significant progress for children whose limited proficiency stems solely from the loss of their home language, as their language learning abilities are not compromised. Children with true communication delays or disorders will continue to exhibit significant difficulties despite these interventions. See Mattes (2007), Klingner and Artiles (2003), and Roseberry-McKibbin (2002) for additional information on the interpretation of children's language performance.

Suggested Strategies The family and entire assessment team should be involved to the maximum extent possible in interpreting the assessment results. This may require utilizing Skilled Dialogue to ensure that 1) all diverse perspectives are acknowledged (respect), 2) an equal voice for all participants is present (reciprocity), and 3) responses are created that integrate and provide access to the strengths of diverse perspectives (responsiveness). The following suggestions offer support for interpreting assessment results.

Consider the Primary or Heritage Language   A judgment of language delay or disorder must always take into account a child's proficiency in primary or heritage language. Behaviors that seem to indicate a language disability or delay may have cultural or linguistic interpretations (Billings, Pearson, Gill, & Shureen, 1997; Kritikos, 2003).

True communication delays and disorders cross languages and cultures. Their impact can be assessed across linguistic and cultural contexts. In addition, it should never be assumed that a bilingual child with a moderate command of English can fully demonstrate his or her skills and knowledge in English. The differences between the language skills necessary for basic oral communication and those necessary for more abstract and decontextualized communication are well described by Chamot and O'Malley (1994).

Use Test Results Across Multiple Languages   The results of testing in a second or less familiar language should be added to total language performance or used only as indicators of second-language learning level when interpreting assessment information. Judgments of delay or disorder should never be based on performance in a second or less familiar language. Children who are learning a second language may retain significant pockets of knowledge in their first language or may switch between two (or more) languages. Assessments that are conducted only in one language are unlikely to reflect the true skills and abilities of these children across most domains.

Differentiate the Reasons Behind Missed Items   The content, format, and inherent values of assessment items may be unfamiliar or negative to a child who is not from the population(s) on which these items were standardized. Behavior(s) that appears indicative of disability or delay may, in fact, stem from cultural or linguistic differences (e.g., inability to ask questions in the proper verbal form) (Billings et al., 1997; Collier, 2005). It is therefore critical to obtain information on primary language and home culture to differentiate between items missed as a result of limited linguistic skill and items missed for other reasons (e.g., lack of familiarity with item/context, limited English proficiency, misinterpretation of item). Multiple perspectives can be voiced when a team interprets assessment results. It is important to acknowledge that there is a range of diverse perspectives that reflects both home and early intervention/ECSE settings, that each team member has an equal voice in the discussion, and that the responses integrate and provide access to the strengths of each of the perspectives present.

*Increase Awareness of Typical Language Development in Bilingual/
Multilingual Environments*   All languages contain both common and distinct
features at all levels—phonologic, semantic, syntactic, morphologic, and prag-
matic. Features within a particular language may vary according to dialectal
usage. Practitioners should be aware that mixing two or more languages (i.e.,
code mixing, code switching) is strongly rule bound. Its presence may actually
indicate strong metalinguistic skills rather than weak language proficiency. In
addition, code switching or code mixing can reflect the following.

1. Local usage norms

2. Affective-motivational factors

3. Differences between what one wishes to express and one's knowledge
   or skill in a particular language or in the structure/vocabulary of the language itself

4. The structure or vocabulary of the language itself (e.g., rapport was taken
   from French to express a concept that no English word could adequately
   express) (Genessee, 2000; Reyes, 2004; Wei, 1998)

Therefore, these features of language development in bilingual/multilingual
environments must be carefully considered before a delay or disorder is determined. Bilingual or multicultural language development is more than mono-
lingualism in stereo.

Reporting and Using Assessment Results

The most important—and perhaps the most challenging—component of assessment revolves around reporting and using this information to improve the
quality of intervention/instruction. It is at this level that misconceptions and
biases can be most strongly communicated.

   Although many standardized measures may delineate methods for tab-
ulating assessment results, practitioners nevertheless struggle with how to
report these results to families and other practitioners in a clear and comprehensible manner that is responsive to the unique parameters of cultural
linguistic diversity. Reports that contain large amounts of ENC professional
jargon are unreadable for families as well as for professionals from other disciplines (Harry, 2002; Parette & Petch-Hogan, 2000; Trumbull et al., 2001). In
addition, reports written by practitioners may fail to mention in a meaningful
way the procedures used to adapt and respond to children's cultural linguistic
needs or backgrounds. It is not uncommon, for example, to read reports of
bilingual children's vocabulary levels without finding specific information on
whether translators were used or on whether levels are similar or different
between languages. The meaning of the assessment results remains unclear
unless this information is provided. Similarly, each section of the report for
children who speak multiple languages should consider how language dif-

ferences affected both the selected procedures and the results of the assessment, as well as the implications for needed services. Simply put, the goal of any report should be to describe the measures used, the modifications to the measures, and the rationale for how the examiner(s) derived the assessment interpretation.

Neisworth and Bagnato (2000) also advocated that practical suggestions for supporting a child's development be included in all reports. Effective early childhood practitioners continually assess individual and groups of children and revise the activities and interactions based on the results of that assessment. Unfortunately, many of the assessment tools and procedures used by practitioners do not make clear links between the results of the assessment and the implications for intervention. As practitioners increase their understanding that assessment must be inextricably linked to intervention, so too must they realize that the results and interpretation of assessment are inextricably linked to a cultural milieu. Brown and Barrera (1999) noted that from a developmental perspective, a child may show a developmental delay. From a cultural perspective, however, that same delay may indicate "diversity rather than disability" (p. 39).

A well-written report can serve as a powerful catalyst for change. This is true whether assessment results determine that a child has a developmental delay or exceptionality. As previously discussed, children whose culture and language differ from ENC—and, therefore, from populations on whom many of the standardized tests were norm referenced—are at risk for inappropriate referral and classification (Hamayan & Damico, 1991). Assessment results are a valuable and valid tool for early childhood educators only when appropriate time and effort have been taken to assemble a thorough, sensitive representation of a child.

Suggested Strategies   Most states specify a minimum requirement for reporting assessment information, especially if it relates to information used for an initial evaluation and eligibility determination. The following components should also be included in assessment reports when adaptations to standardized procedure require a greater degree of professional judgment (Billings et al., 1997; VanDerHeyden & Witt, 2008).

1. A rationale for departing from the procedures and instruments commonly used to assess same-age peers with similar developmental concerns

2. Specifications of the alternative strategies used for assessment

3. A justification for use of the alternative methods

4. A statement of results

5. An explanation of an identified disability or delay that specifically rules out cultural linguistic factors as the cause of atypical cognitive and behavioral performance or an explanation of ineligibility, giving evidence of the

specific cultural linguistic factors that explain the cognitive or behavioral performance without identification of disability or delay

The following suggestions are provided to assist early intervention/ECSE practitioners in reporting assessment results.

Consider the Format of the Results Report   The most helpful reports are free of professional jargon and use strengths-based language that notes the child's skills (Santos et al., 2005). Every report should begin with clear identifying information, including the name, date of assessment, age and cultural background of the child, examiner(s) name, and language(s) in which the assessment was conducted. A short background should follow, which includes a brief overview of the family's cultural background along with a summary of the child's development across multiple domains and languages. Next, the results of the assessment should be clearly articulated. The results should note differences observed across settings, testing conditions, and language(s). The report also needs to contain a summary of the results. Finally, reports must include straightforward and comprehensible recommendations for environmental modifications, instructional practices, or intervention strategies that are responsive to the child's and family's cultural context(s).

Describe the Procedures Used to Respond to the Child's Cultural Linguistic Parameters   It is important that practitioners consider the cultural linguistic background of children in the assessment process. Cultural linguistic diversity influences the assessment process of all children and families because of the relational and contextual nature of diversity. If procedural changes are made or if specific items are adapted in response to culture and/or language, then these changes should be clearly described. If a child is in a multilingual environment, then the report should describe how the assessment process responded to this factor. For example, such a report would detail any translation procedures that were used. Similarly, if an interpreter/translator was used, then that person's background and training should be noted in the report. Statements such as, "Mary has a limited receptive vocabulary" must identify the language(s) in which limitations exist. It is important to know, for instance, whether Mary's entire receptive vocabulary, limited as it is, is Hmong. Or, does she understand five words in Hmong and five words in English? Are they the same five words? Is her total vocabulary across Hmong and English five words or 10 words? Such details immeasurably enhance the validity and usefulness of a report.

Indicate the Language(s) Used During the Assessment Process   It is critical to indicate the language(s) in which items were presented when practitioners report performance levels. As previously discussed, language functioning is not the same as language proficiency in a particular language. A child's language functioning can best be reflected by looking at all items passed, regardless of the language used by the child or practitioner. Practitioners should note possible discrepancies in the score obtained through standardized procedure and the performance level that was assessed using the two (or more) languages. An assessor might, for example, write,

> Angie scored "X" when items were presented in a standardized fashion. We could not credit the following items because of standardization violations. The score would have been "Y" had we been able to credit these items elicited using Tagalog (Angie's language other than English).

Ensure that the Report Includes the Child's Relative Language Proficiency Identifying a child's relative language proficiency (i.e., proficiency levels in all language[s] used) is an important first step in the assessment process. It is not sufficient to simply state whether a language other than English is spoken in the home. The assessment report should identify relative language proficiency levels and describe which procedures were used to determine these levels. Chapter 8 introduced the RLP Profile, a tool to help early intervention/ECSE practitioners assess language proficiency (see Appendix A).

Note the Degree to which a Child's Background Matches the Assessment Instruments' Norming Samples When practitioners use standardized instruments they should report normed scores without qualification only when the child's experiential and linguistic background matches that of the norming sample (which is almost never). In all other cases, the report should qualify the assessment results (e.g., "Assuming validity, Tariq's standard score would be 'X'; had the translated items been included in the total correct score, Tariq's standard score would be 'Y'"). It is also helpful to report an instrument's standard error of measurement, as cultural linguistic differences heighten the probability that error will be present.

Clearly Identify Why Reported Performance Is or Is Not Interpreted as a Delay or Disorder It is critical that reports explain why the child's performance during the assessment process was or was not identified as a disability or delay (e.g., it is a disorder because the child is unintelligible in both languages at age 4 years, it is a delay because the child's performance is markedly different from same-age peers with the same primary language). Specific information should be included about the cultural linguistic factors that may contribute to seemingly atypical performance. In addition, an explanation of ineligibility should be provided when appropriate, giving evidence of specific cultural linguistic factors that explain why performance does not indicate exceptionality or delay (e.g., errors occurred in second language only, children from this population typically demonstrate a 3- to 6-month receptive delay).

Exceptionality or delays and cultural linguistic diversity are not mutually exclusive. Both may be present at the same time. When this is the case, each should be addressed in relation to the other.

Provide Recommendations that Address Children's Needs in All of Their Languages   If reports are going to support children and families, then tangible recommendations that link assessment to intervention must be provided. The recommended instructional practices and intervention strategies should address children's needs across both cultural linguistic contexts.

ASSESSMENT IN PRACTICE: FOUR VIGNETTES

In the following section, four vignettes highlight several common assessment dilemmas and culture bumps that practitioners are likely to encounter as they work with children and families from different cultural linguistic backgrounds.

   These vignettes are intended to illustrate how Skilled Dialogue tools and strategies may be used. Their "unfinishedness" is purposely designed to raise questions and prompt further exploration. Potential responses are examined for each vignette. The vignettes vary in detail, reflecting the reality that contextual and background information vary for each child and family served. The most detail is given in the first vignette to provide an opportunity to consider a family from a variety of perspectives using several of the available tools presented in Chapter 7. The steps that practitioners should take relate directly to the amount and type of information available and the point in the assessment process. Each vignette closes with additional questions that practitioners may wish to consider.

Xee[2]

Xee Ly, a 4-year, 2-month-old child, was born to her parents in a suburban community outside of Philadelphia. Mr. and Mrs. Ly came to the United States in the late 1970s after the reunification of Vietnam. The Ly family currently lives in a three-bedroom apartment, and Mr. Ly works at a factory that is a 1½-hour drive from home. Xee has five older siblings and one younger sibling. Hmong is the family's cultural linguistic heritage, and the family speaks Hmong as its primary language. Mr. Ly, however, is also fairly fluent in English.

   At birth, Xee was diagnosed as having Hirschsprung disease (congenital megacolon). She had a colostomy after birth. At the age of 1 month, she was hospitalized due to seizures. The seizures have been controlled with anticonvulsant medication. The church that sponsored the Ly family's immigration made a

---

[2]*Source:* Pennsylvania Department of Education (1994).

referral to the local ECSE agency after Mr. Ly expressed concern to a fellow church member about Xee using only a few words in both Hmong and English. None of the professionals on the initial assessment team were familiar with Hmong culture or language.

A certain member of the congregation who was a veteran of the Vietnam conflict and had become friends with many Hmong families assisted the team in understanding Hmong culture. He then suggested that a woman from the local Hmong community might be willing to serve as a cultural mediator and translator. She attended the same church and was affiliated with a Southeast Asia Service Center program. The team met with the mediator to learn more about Hmong culture and plan the assessment process.

An interview with Xee's parents was suggested as the first step. The goal was to determine the resources, priorities, and needs of the Ly family, as well as to complete an RLP Profile for Xee. The team decided that Mr. and Mrs. Ly should be present for the interview, as Hmong families emphasize the role of fathers in decision making. The interview would be conducted in Hmong by the mediator, and a member of the ECSE agency would be present. The mediator called the family to schedule the appointment.

The interview revealed that Xee's parents were concerned about Xee's failure to express herself verbally. Xee had limited receptive or expressive language in both Hmong and English. Her speech was often hard for family members to understand. Mr. Ly said that he wanted Xee and her younger brother to learn English because he thought it was important for them to do well in American schools. He expressed interest in having his wife learn ways to help with interventions at home so that Xee could enter a preschool program. Xee, however, was often fearful outside the home. She was most comfortable around other Hmong children with whom she played at church functions.

It was recommended that an SLP assist in determining Xee's language needs, and Xee's parents agreed to have such an evaluation. Assessment team members were to include Xee's mother and father, the mediator, the case manager, the SLP, an occupational therapist, and a Head Start teacher. Xee's skills in both Hmong and English would be assessed. During the interview, the mediator and the parents suggested several additional people who may be able to assist in the assessment and intervention processes.

This vignette describes many challenges that practitioners may encounter as they assess children from diverse cultural linguistic backgrounds that also exhibit developmental delays. Cultural linguistic diversity was clearly present in Xee's case (Step 2 in Figure 8.1). Xee's case manager asked herself, "How likely am I to understand and attach the same meaning to behaviors as would Xee's family and/or others from similar cultural backgrounds?" and determined that she probably would understand behaviors differently and attach different meanings to them. Therefore, Skilled Dialogue was likely needed. Then, she assessed the nature and degree of the cultural linguistic diversity between the practitioners and Xee's family (Step 2 in Figure 8.1). She and the early childhood team completed a Cultural Data Table, an RLP Profile, and a Cultural Consonance Profile to identify potential culture bumps and to consider approaches and responses for limiting the affect of these bumps. An initial Cultural Data Table for Xee (Figure 9.1) revealed a significant number of probable bumps in all three developmental/curricular areas. To confirm these potential bumps, the team determined the need to observe Xee and her family in a variety of settings as well as to observe and consider rules and values for behavior and communication in Xee's home and neighborhood.

The team also recognized that further language assessment was needed to determine more precisely Xee's level of proficiency in Hmong and English. Following a play-based assessment, which included both an extensive observation of Xee playing with other adults and children and a parent interview, the team completed Xee's RLP Profile (Figure 9.2). The RLP Profile confirmed that Xee's was equally limited in both of the languages available to her.

As they examined this information, Xee's team recognized the need to complete a Cultural Consonance Profile (Figure 9.3). Xee's Cultural Consonance Profile made it even clearer that extra attention was needed to limit the number of culture bumps (especially in the personal-social and sensory-cognitive areas) that might arise in gathering assessment information. To acknowledge the parents' competence in child rearing, for example, the practitioners needed to recognize their knowledge and skills with Xee. Similarly, activities and dialogue needed to be planned to build the family's sense of competence in navigating ECSE culture. Throughout this process, the family would be given extra time to consider all of the available choices.

Finally, the team created an Assessment Cultural Linguistic Response Plan for Xee (Figure 9.4). They considered whether translation of assessment materials into Hmong was appropriate and, if so, how they would do this. They had to choose their assessment strategies based on the family's funds of knowledge, child-rearing beliefs and values, and preferred strategies for learning and problem solving. It was decided that each team member would work with volunteers from the Hmong community and Head Start staff to lessen or eliminate potential culture bumps identified by the Cultural Data Table. The goal of this process was to determine Xee's skills and needs, as well as appropriate intervention strategies regarding family priorities.

Xee's story illustrates the principles of Skilled Dialogue in relation to a specific child and family. Forestructure is built prior to meeting with a family by means such as reading about first- and second-language acquisition. Initial information is collected and potential culture bumps are reviewed through tools such as the Cultural Data Table. Further information is gathered using other tools discussed in Chapter 8 as well as other strategies deemed appropriate (e.g., family interviews). Based on this understanding, an Assessment Cultural Linguistic Response Plan for assessment and intervention is developed (see Chapter 8).

Cultural Data Table

Child's name: _Xee_   Date completed: _12/11/10_   Completed by: _J. Sosa and M. Talbott_

Directions: Fill in responses to questions from the Guide to Identifying Cultural Data Related to Potential Culture Bumps.

Developmental/curricular area	Comments
Communicative-Linguistic	
Language(s) of child's primary caregiving environment(s)	Xee is 4 years old. Her family speaks Hmong as the primary language. In addition, her father speaks fairly fluent English.
Child's relative language proficiency (degree of proficiency in English and other language[s] used)	Xee uses only a few words in both Hmong and English. Proficiency information (see Relative Language Proficiency [RLP] Profile) English: receptive (2) expressive (2) Hmong: receptive (2) expressive (2)
Patterns of language usage in child's primary caregiving environment(s)	Discussion among adults in the home is entirely in Hmong. Conversations between the children and their mother are in Hmong; their father speaks both English and Hmong to them. In addition, the children use both English and Hmong at church.
Relative value placed on verbal and nonverbal communication	Interactions within the community demonstrate a strong value on nonverbal communication. Within the home, however, both parents encourage extensive verbal communication in English and in Hmong.
Relative status associated with languages other than English and with bilingualism	The interview with the family showed that Mr. Lg places a high value on having his children learn English but hopes that they will maintain Hmong as well. The early childhood program reflects a stronger value on English.
Personal-Social	
Degree of family's acculturation into EuroAmerican Normative Culture (ENC)	Mr. Lg has a fair amount of familiarity with ENC, however, Mrs. Lg generally interacts with other Hmong families from her clan who live in the same community. All of her friends speak Hmong. The children who are school age have a greater familiarity with ENC.

continued

Figure 9.1.   Xee's Cultural Data Table.

Figure 9.1. *(continued)*

Degree of family's acculturation into U.S. early intervention/early childhood special education (ECSE) culture	No one in the family has any significant degree of acculturation into the U.S. early intervention/ECSE culture. To this point, Mr. Ly has been the primary contact with ENC, interacting with other social service agencies in times of unemployment.
Sense of self (e.g., relative weight on independence, dependence, interdependence	The family apparently places a strong value on interdependence. However, as Xee is approaching school age, Mr. Ly expressed his desire for Xee to begin assuming greater responsibility for her own behaviors and increasing her personal-social and self-help skills.
Perceptions and understanding of identity and competence	Initial assumptions from family observations depicted Xee as an extension of her parents. Although Mr. Ly expressed concern about how Xee's delay reflects on the family, he is anxious for her to function successfully in American schools.
Roles and rules associated with parenting and child rearing	During the family interview, Mr. and Mrs. Ly discussed that their primary ties and responsibilities were to their children. Their role is to make sure that the children "listen and obey."
Knowledge and experience regarding power and social positioning	The family views itself as lower middle class. Mr. Ly explained that because of prejudice, many Hmong families in the community, including members of the extended family, are struggling to find and maintain employment.
Values/beliefs/skills associated with instrumental and emotional support (e.g., gaining access to external resources, getting personal support)	Mr. Ly indicated that up to this point, the family has relied on personal support from the Hmong community. However, he believes that there is a great value in gaining access to other community services, such as Head Start, to help Xee and her siblings succeed in school.
Sensory-Cognitive	
Funds of knowledge: what type of knowledge is valued; concept structures and definitions (e.g., how family is defined)	The knowledge and support of the immediate and extended family is most valued. The family's ancestry and ancestors are often discussed. In the family interview, Mr. Ly repeatedly expressed his concern that Xee and her siblings understand their roles within the family structure as well as in the larger society.
Preferred strategies for acquiring new learning	Most of the learning strategies tend to be nonverbal. Teaching strategies generally revolve around methods such as modeling.
Preferred strategies for problem solving and decision making	Mr. Ly is the primary decision maker in the family, especially for issues that affect the family outside the home. It appears that Mrs. Ly has more influence on the decisions that affect what happens within the home.
Worldview (i.e., assumptions about how the world works and about what is "right" and what is "wrong")	Mr. Ly seems to have a bicultural view. Although Mrs. Ly's views were not explicitly stated, they appear to be more traditional. Although Mr. Ly wants Xee and her siblings to follow the Hmong social and family order and responsibilities, he also wants them to learn English and to succeed academically at school and within ENC.

Relative Language Proficiency (RLP) Profile

Child's name: __Xee_____ Date: _12 /13/10___ Date of birth: _12 /10/05_

Chronological age: _5 years_____ Completed by: _W. Bircher_____

Site: _Child's home_____ Instrument: _Informal_____

Proficiency in language other than English (specify language: _Hmong_____)

Receptive: 5   4   3   ②   1

Good; no significant errors	Mildly limited; some errors	Moderately limited; consistent/ significant errors	Severely limited; frequent and significant errors	Nonverbal and/or unintelligible

Expressive: 5   4   3   ②   1

Comments:

English proficiency

Receptive: 5   4   3   ②   1

Good; no significant errors	Mildly limited; some errors	Moderately limited; consistent/ significant errors	Severely limited; frequent and significant errors	Nonverbal and/or unintelligible

Expressive: 5   4   3   ②   1

Comments:
Xee's use of English is also limited to fewer than 10 words.

Relative Language Proficiency (Write language other than English in blanks below.)

Hmong Monolingual	Receptive bilingual	Partial bilingual	Bilingual	Partial bilingual	Receptive bilingual	English monolingual
Has had minimal exposure to English	_Hmong_ dominant; understands some English	_Hmong_ dominant; limited English	_Hmong_ and English about the same	English dominant; limited _Hmong_	English dominant; understands some _Hmong_	Has had minimal exposure to _Hmong_

Comments:
Xee's environments—home and child care—are bilingual in Hmong and English. She communicates, and is communicated with, equally in each of these languages.

Figure 9.2. Xee's Relative Language Proficiency (RLP) Profile.

Cultural Consonance Profile

Child's name: _Xee_   Date: _12/16/10_   Completed by: _J. Sosa and M. Talbott_

	Highly similar to early childhood environment(s)/ practitioners' profiles			Highly dissimilar from early childhood environment(s)/ practitioners' profiles		

I. Communicative-Linguistic Area   Comments

Language(s) used in child's home	5	4	3	②)	1	_____
Child's relative language proficiency	5	4	3	②)	1	_____
Patterns of language usage	5	4	3	2	①)	_Few words_____
Relative value placed on verbal/ nonverbal communication	5	4	③)	2	1	_____
Relative status of language other than English and bilingualism	5	4	3	②)	1	_Family values highly as compared with ENC_

II. Personal-Social Area

Family's degree of acculturation	5	4	3	②)	1	_____
Sense of self/perception of identity/competence	5	4	3	②)	1	_____
Parenting/child-rearing roles and rules	5	4	3	②)	1	_____
Knowledge/experience regarding power and positioning	5	4	③)	2	1	_____
Values and beliefs regarding support	5	4	3	②)	1	_____

III. Sensory-Cognitive Area

Funds of knowledge/concept definition/structures	5	4	3	②)	1	_____
Preferred learning strategies	5	4	3	②)	1	_____
Preferred problem-solving/ decision-making strategies	5	4	③)	2	1	_____
Worldview	5	4	3	②)	1	_____

Degree of consonance with early childhood environment(s)/practitioners' profiles

Communicative-linguistic area	High	Moderate	(Low)	Minimal
Personal-social area	High	Moderate	(Low)	Minimal
Sensory-cognitive area	High	Moderate	(Low)	Minimal

Comments: _Sensory-cognitive is moderate to low depending on the context and topic._

Figure 9.3.   Xee's Cultural Consonance Profile.

Assessment Cultural Linguistic Response Plan

Child/family: _Xee Ly_

Date: _June 14, 2010_   Completed by: _R. Corso and I. Barrera_

Specific Assessment Considerations

RE: *Language and communication differences*

Assess Xee's language proficiency in both English and Hmong.

Utilize and train, as necessary, a cultural mediator to support interpretation needs of family and early childhood special education team.

Assess all items missed in English by Xee in Hmong.

For the items missed during assessment, discriminate between the items that test academic readiness versus language proficiency.

RE: *Data-gathering procedures*

Consider a play-based approach to assessment that utilizes toys and materials familiar to Xee.

Discriminate between Xee's overall language functioning and her language proficiency in both English and Hmong.

Consider parent reports and observations of other Hmong children who are similar in age and development to Xee before determining a delay or disability.

Determine if Xee has both receptive and expressive language delays.

RE: *Interpretation of assessment information*

Consider results of testing in both English and Hmong to get a total language performance.

Determine the reasons behind any items that Xee might miss during the assessment.

Work with the cultural linguistic mediator to increase awareness of any code switching that may occur.

RE: *Reporting assessment results*

Gain awareness about the funds of knowledge for Xee's family.

Clearly indicate when English is used for assessment purposes and when Hmong is used during the process.

Report assessment results in both Hmong and English to ensure Xee's family understands the results of the assessment.

Skilled Dialogue Reminders

	Choosing Relationship over Control/ Anchored Understanding of Diversity	Setting the Stage for Miracles/ 3rd Space
Respect	**Welcoming** range and validity of diverse perspectives	**Allowing** the tension of differing perspectives
Reciprocity	**Making sense** of diverse perspectives	**Appreciating** the strengths of diverse perspectives
Responsiveness	**Joining** across diverse perspectives	**Harmonizing** diverse perspectives so as to integrate and gain access to complementary strengths

Figure 9.4.   Xee's Assessment Cultural Linguistic Response Plan.

The following questions and exercise are provided to help practitioners further explore the application of Skilled Dialogue in relation to Xee and her family.

QUESTIONS FOR REFLECTION

1. Review Xee's Cultural Data Table and Cultural Consonance Profile. To what degree would cultural linguistic diversity be present if you were working with this child and family? What potential culture bumps would be critical to address?

2. Consider the assessment procedures that you typically use. What changes or adaptations would you have to make as a member of Xee's assessment team?

3. What additional information, if any, would you need to make these changes or adaptations?

Amad

Amad is a 4-year-old African American with mild-to-moderate autism. He was recently evaluated for a center-based special education preschool program in his urban community. Amad's mother and grandmother expressed their concern that members of the interdisciplinary team discussed "school learning" (cognitive growth) but not Amad's happiness. Amad's mother and grandmother want him to "have friends and like people and be okay when he goes outside when he is bigger." The family wants to hear how the program will nurture Amad's socio-emotional development so that he can fit in with the community and take care of himself. Amad's grandmother wants Amad to learn to deal with the difficulties in their community and be happy.

Only limited information was initially available to the ECSE practitioners about the cultural background, beliefs, and values of Amad's family. This is not unusual, of course; practitioners will likely feel that they have very little information on many families as they begin working with them. The mother and grandmother's reaction to comments of certain interdisciplinary team members, however, makes it clear that culture bumps were already present. The team decided to complete the Guide to Identifying Cultural Data Related to Potential Culture Bumps (see Appendix A). They realized that this was necessary to make respect, reciprocity, and responsiveness the foundation of their dialogue with Amad's family.

QUESTIONS FOR REFLECTION

1. Review the questions on culture bumps (see Appendix A). Which ones might be playing the most significant role in the interaction between

Amad's family and the practitioners? Which developmental/curricular areas (communicative-linguistic, personal-social, sensory-cognitive) seem key to the current issues?

2. How might you integrate the family's emphasis on Amad's happiness as a resource to strengthen his "school learning" (i.e., find 3ʳᵈ Space)?

3. What additional information, if any, would you need to work effectively with Amad and his family?

Abrish[3]

Abrish is a 2-year, 4-month-old boy who lives with his parents and two younger sisters in a rural area of central Pennsylvania. Abrish's family recently immigrated to the United States from Hungary. He attends a community child care program three mornings per week. Although Abrish is active, he is quiet in public. He has made few communicative attempts at the child care center during the past year. His mother and staff at the child care center noticed that Abrish has difficulty initiating communication or responding to directions and is quite fearful in new situations. Abrish rarely plays with other children at the child care center. He spends much of his time following the child care staff around and clinging to a toy cloth owl. Abrish's mother called the local early intervention agency because she was concerned about Abrish's development. She thought that Abrish might need special help to encourage interaction and the acquisition of skills for successful participation in preschool.

Although no forms (e.g., Cultural Data Table) accompany this discussion, readers are encouraged to practice completing these forms to consider how they would approach the assessment process with Abrish and his family and to consider how this approach resembles or differs from typical procedures. The early intervention agency responded to Abrish's mother by scheduling a developmental screening. An SLP and an early intervention specialist completed the screening, which took place in Abrish's home. Methods of screening included a parent interview, administration of a developmental checklist, an informal language sample in both English and Hungarian, and a brief observation of Abrish playing with his toys. In addition, Abrish's mother provided background information about home language usage and Abrish's birth history, medical history, and language development in both languages.

The screening results indicated that Abrish had age-appropriate cognitive, problem-solving, and adaptive skills. It also identified possible developmental delays in receptive language development (in both English and Hungarian) and social skill development. Abrish's parents and the early intervention team agreed that further evaluation was warranted to develop a more thorough

---

[3]*Source:* Pennsylvania Department of Education (1994).

understanding of Abrish's functioning and developmental needs. Before additional evaluation procedures were conducted, however, the team decided to complete a Cultural Data Table, an RLP Profile, and an Assessment Cultural Linguistic Response Plan for Abrish and his family.

As part of the Assessment Cultural Linguistic Response Plan, the practitioners assembled a team that included Abrish's parents, an early intervention specialist, an SLP, Abrish's child care provider, and a cultural linguistic mediator to translate language and potential culture bumps. An informal structured interview was used at the meeting to elicit the parents' perceived resources and needs related to Abrish's development. An assessment battery was then selected, and various team members agreed to complete specific assessment tasks. The SLP would administer several instruments and take a communication sample in English and Hungarian. The SLP was not proficient in Hungarian, so the mediator, who was bilingual in English and Hungarian, assisted with the Hungarian communication sample. In addition, the early intervention specialist planned to administer several additional developmental instruments, including observations of Abrish's interactions with his peers at the child care center, a rating of Abrish's participation and communication at the child care center and at home, and his level of general engagement in structured activities. The child care provider was asked to provide brief anecdotal records of Abrish's social interactions and behaviors related to his receptive language skills in English. Abrish's parents agreed to record an at-home language sample and to record how often Abrish initiated communication in certain situations, noting when communication attempts occurred and which language Abrish used for which purposes.

Initially, the early intervention specialist tried to conduct certain assessments without Abrish's mother present. When Abrish accompanied the specialist (who only spoke English) to a small room in the child care center, he became tearful, clung to his toy owl, and kept his head down. The specialist and the SLP found it difficult to conduct the assessment due to Abrish's fearfulness. The cultural linguistic mediator made the critical observation that Abrish's fearfulness likely resulted from his lack of acculturation into ENC and was compounded by separation from his mother, who was his secure base in unfamiliar situations. Eventually, the specialist noticed that Abrish became more cooperative when his mother was allowed to remain with him and when playful assessment processes were used in place of the initial highly structured tasks. For example, Abrish refused to complete a two-piece form board when he was directly asked to do so; he eagerly completed the task while playing with his toy owl, however, when his mother was present. Task compliance was achieved by Abrish's mother handing him the pieces, which they pretended were cookies to be put on a cookie sheet so that Owl could have a snack.

The early intervention specialist told the SLP about the effectiveness of this play-based approach. The SLP then readministered some of her earlier tasks by having Abrish put his owl in a toy car and point to certain pictures in a book. The SLP collected information in both English and Hungarian with the help of the interpreter. Abrish enjoyed this game and cooperated for 30 minutes. Both practitioners indicated in their reports that the scores were tentative because of the adaptive, nonstandardized administration techniques used. They focused on describing the abilities that Abrish showed in completing the tasks across both languages.

In these additional assessments, Abrish's play behavior and performance on nonverbal reasoning tasks indicated age-appropriate cognitive skills. Likewise, although Abrish was hesitant to interact with other children and unfamiliar adults, the team believed that his social skills were age appropriate in both ENC and home cultural contexts. Abrish's auditory comprehension in English and Hungarian and basic concept skills also appeared to be age appropriate, but his language and general communication skills in Hungarian and English were moderately delayed. He demonstrated an expressive vocabulary of approximately 25 words (15 in Hungarian and 10 in English), which were intelligible for his age. Abrish had difficulty answering various "wh-" questions in English.

Both practitioners felt more confident in the information that they gathered from direct observation than in the initial information that was collected in a more structured manner. The team reconvened when all of the assessment procedures were completed to discuss Abrish's developmental functioning, his family's strengths, and his needs.

QUESTIONS FOR REFLECTION

1. Abrish's vignette brings up issues of respect, reciprocity, and responsiveness. Can you identify them?

2. Review the steps of Skilled Dialogue (Figure 8.1). Which aspects of Skilled Dialogue, if any, do you believe Abrish's early intervention team overlooked?

3. Review the questions related to potential culture bumps (see Appendix A). What part, if any, do cultural linguistic factors play in this situation?

4. How would you complete an Assessment Cultural Linguistic Response Plan for Abrish and his family?

Peter

Peter is 4 years old. His father is a farm worker by day and cleans office buildings at night. Both of his parents were born in rural Mexico. They have lived in the United States for 4 years, immigrating just prior to Peter's birth. Peter's father has learned some English at work. He speaks Spanish to his wife and uses both English and Spanish with Peter. Peter's mother has very limited English. For the past 3 years, she has provided child care in their one-bedroom apartment for young children from other Spanish-speaking families in their neighborhood. With the additional responsibility of caring for her 4-month-old daughter, Maria, Peter's mother is very busy and has great difficulty keeping appointments.

A doctor at the county medical clinic referred Peter for assessment. Peter has a history of chronic ear infections (few were treated), is thin, appears depressed, and demonstrates very limited speech. He speaks to his parents and others only when he needs something. Peter's mother told the clinic doctor that her son is very shy. She is reluctant to have Peter evaluated, as she is adamant there is nothing "wrong" with her child, and has canceled six appointments. She was told that a Spanish-speaking staff member will assist her and Peter during the assessment activities. Peter and his mother have just arrived at the early intervention agency for the assessment.

The practitioners in this case have to make sure that they are respectful of the decision by Peter's family to delay the assessment. Despite the previously canceled appointments, it is critical that the ECSE team members consider all of the approaches available to support the assessment in both Spanish and English and ensure that they are responsive to the needs of Peter's family.

QUESTIONS FOR REFLECTION

1. Complete a Cultural Data Table for Peter and his family. What specific information is needed prior to conducting the assessment?

2. Review the assessment dilemmas discussed in this chapter. What dilemmas might be encountered during Peter's assessment? Of the suggestions reviewed in this chapter, which ones would be the most helpful at this point?

3. Which strategies would you use to determine the degree to which Peter's communicative behavior reflects cultural linguistic diversity? Which strategies would you use to determine the degree to which Peter's behavior reflects a disability or delay? If you believe that diversity and a disability or delay play roles, explain why.

CONCLUSION

This chapter has reviewed challenges that practitioners and families commonly experience as they engage in assessment activities across culturally linguistically diverse parameters. It has described dilemmas related to language and language differences, as well as suggestions for how assessment information is gathered and interpreted. It has also addressed how assessment results are reported. These are intended to augment sound assessment practices used for all children.

Vignettes and strategies have been provided to help practitioners consider various ways that they can respond to the issues that they will likely encounter as they serve children and families who are diverse. Given the enormous challenges of assessing young children, especially when their cultural linguistic background is different from that of practitioners, the importance of honoring identity, voice, and connection cannot be overstated. Practitioners must work to anchor their understanding of the families that they serve and, as needed, create 3rd Space options that gain access to and leverage family strengths and resources.

Chapter 10

Planning and Conducting Culturally Linguistically Inclusive Instruction

Promoting cultural diversity rather than ignoring it is an important classroom policy. On an individual level, the goal is to develop an extensive cultural repertoire. An individual who acquires understanding and develops competency in different linguistic and cultural systems is said to have an extensive cultural repertoire. [The development of such repertoires] is important to validate [a] child's experience, acknowledge linguistic and cultural differences, [and] integrate the community as a resource in development. (Perez & Torres-Guzman, 2002, p. 18)

As stated in the discussion on Step 1 of Skilled Dialogue, practitioners cannot wait until they are asked to work with diverse children and families to begin using AUD and 3rd Space. It is relatively easy to have interactions in which behavioral and value differences exist because they are always present—even within the same cultural group. When differences arise that generate bumps (e.g., confusion, frustration, anger), practitioners should seek to anchor understanding of these differences and explore nondichotomized response options (i.e., 3rd Space).

Step 2 of Skilled Dialogue focuses on determining the presence of cultural linguistic diversity and assessing its nature by gathering pertinent cultural linguistic data. These data are essential to inform assessment and intervention and to anchor understanding of actual and potential culture bumps. Step 2 ideally begins during initial referral; however, it often occurs later (e.g., when families come to programs after initial assessments have already been completed). Even so, it is critical that Step 2 begin prior to initiating intervention and instruction, as its results are intended to inform such services.

Step 2 of the Skilled Dialogue process includes 1) determining the presence of cultural diversity, 2) assessing the nature and degree of cultural linguistic diversity, and 3) developing cultural linguistic response plans (i.e., identifying strategies for minimizing potential culture bumps and maximizing a family's cultural resources). This chapter focuses on the second and third steps in relation to the development and delivery of appropriate intervention and instruction. Practitioners should consider using a Cultural Data Table and the Cultural Consonance Profile to explore the nature and degree of cultural linguistic diversity in specific situations (see Chapter 8). Once those considerations have been used to design an Assessment Cultural Linguistic Response Plan, an Instructional Cultural Linguistic Response Plan should be developed (blank forms are located in Appendix A). If Step 3 of Skilled Dialogue is necessary, then the process for critical incident analysis is the same whether it occurs in the assessment stage or the intervention and instruction stage.

It is important to recognize that many challenges are rooted in culture bumps. Examples include families apparently not following through on interventions, not being home for scheduled visits, or being vested in goals other than those outlined on an individualized family service plan (IFSP) or IEP. If practitioners question why a family does not follow an intervention plan without determining whether culture bumps are present, then they can miss critical opportunities to anchor their understanding of the child and family and become truly responsive to their needs. Similarly, 3rd Space options that honor those needs cannot be created unless practitioners gain awareness of their own perspectives in relation to families' perspectives. Culture bumps occur not only as intervention and instruction are planned, but also subsequently as practitioners interact with children and families to implement planned activities and services. The Cultural Data Table (Figure 8.4) is designed to be used whenever interactions between practitioners and children or families appear to be in conflict.

This chapter provides suggested responses for common intervention and instructional challenges that arise from culture bumps. Evidenced-based responses are suggested to help practitioners develop strategies for embracing children's and families' culturally based strengths. (Appendix A includes an Instructional Cultural Linguistic Response Plan specifically designed to support practitioners' consideration of potential intervention and instructional issues for the children and families.) Practitioners should not consider the suggested strategies a complete list. Indeed, the more skilled one becomes in the practices of anchoring understanding of families and creating 3rd Space, the longer one's list of possible responses becomes. The chapter also returns to the vignettes presented in Chapter 9 to illustrate how Skilled Dialogue supports practitioners and families as they move from assessment to intervention and instruction services. As in Chapter 9, these vignettes are intended only as a beginning illustration of how Skilled Dialogue can enhance interactions between practitioners and children and their families.

COMMON INSTRUCTIONAL CONCERNS AND CONSIDERATIONS

Challenges engendered by culture bumps typically arise in three areas: 1) language and communication differences, 2) teaching and learning strategies, and 3) instructional content and materials. The framework of the Instructional Cultural Linguistic Response Plan is specifically designed to focus practitioners on these three areas (see Appendix A for the blank form). The following subsections present each challenge as well as suggested strategies.

Language and Communication Differences

The most overt instruction and intervention challenges result from the fact that many culturally diverse families speak languages other than English with their children, either exclusively or in addition to English. These children may be monolingual in a language other than English or may speak languages in addition to English. Their linguistically diverse home environments necessarily affect the knowledge they bring to learning tasks and the language in which they hold and express that knowledge. Consequently, two aspects of teaching these children are challenging. The first is developing language itself. The second is using language (one or more) to teach particular skills and knowledge. These issues require understanding and addressing not only the dynamics of dual language acquisition, but also the role of language in acquiring and expressing knowledge/skills across developmental and academic areas.

Many of the language and communication challenges that are related to assessment (see Chapter 9) also arise when practitioners consider intervention or instructional practices for diverse children and families in early childhood environments. In addition, personal-social issues—including children's familiarity with the values reflected in intervention settings and procedures and their understanding of identity or competence—may lead to culture bumps. Other diverse cultural parameters, including types of knowledge valued and preferred learning strategies, can lead to misunderstandings or interactions that are less than responsive. These considerations are discussed in more detail in the following sections.

In many instances, the language(s) and/or communication style used in a child's home and community differs from the language(s) and/or communication style used by practitioners. These differences challenge practitioners to develop intervention and instructional strategies that recognize the multilingual environments that children must negotiate as they learn new skills. Planning effective instruction relies on collecting relevant information about the child's environment and language development during the assessment process.

Practitioners must use children's documented relative language proficiency in making decisions about the language of instruction, pace of an intervention, and ways to approach a child's performance errors. Children with limited or no English proficiency may be unable to respond to verbal instructions or interactions in English monolingual environments.

Similarly, early childhood and home environments may differ significantly in rules for nonverbal communication and expectations regarding appropriate behavior. For instance, some children are taught that when an adult speaks to them, maintaining eye contact for extended periods of time is a challenge to adult authority or a sign of inappropriate intimacy (Lynch & Hanson, 2011).

Conversely, practitioners may view failure to maintain eye contact as a sign of disrespect or even a developmental deficit. In fact, maintaining eye contact is an item on many developmental scales (Frankenburg et al., 1990; Newborg, Stock, Wnek, Guidubaldi, & Svinicki, 1984). Practitioners may even say, "Look at me when I'm talking to you," or position themselves directly in front of children so that direct eye contact is the only option. These situations may cause much anxiety and confusion for children as well as for practitioners.

In addition, the language and communication style reflected in early childhood environments, (e.g., addressing adults by their title and first name) may differ from that used in the child's home (e.g., addressing adults only by kinship terms such as aunt or uncle). These differences can make it difficult for the child to understand communicative intent appropriately. They can equally affect families' willingness to support and implement activities and interactions developed by practitioners. Differences in language and communication style also have the potential to make families feel unwelcome or shamed. Sending the message, even unintentionally, that a child's language is less desirable than English can severely affect the child's learning and the interactions with the family.

Language is the primary medium for making connections with others. For instance, when 5-year-old Pierre visited an early intervention program, he was asked which child he felt more comfortable playing with: Sammy, a nonverbal child with autistic behaviors, or Tony, a verbal child whose hands were at his shoulders because of thalidomide exposure. Everyone expected Pierre to say he was most comfortable playing with Sammy, who was attractive and charming. Yet, Pierre immediately answered that he felt more comfortable with Tony because he could play and talk with Tony. This incident highlights the critical role of communication in relationships, even early ones. The ability to communicate nonverbally and verbally plays a significant role in the ability to establish relationships—whether for playing, obtaining support, or gaining information. Personal-social bumps are sure to arise when a child's most proficient language is not understood or accepted in early childhood environments.

In addition to influencing the quality and quantity of relationships, language and communication bumps can negatively affect a child's sense of self.

For example, a practitioner who cannot pronounce a child's name may go as far as changing the child's name without recognizing the value that cultures place on names. The child's identity may be significantly altered for the practitioner's convenience.

As children leave familiar adults and comfortable environments and begin to interact with practitioners and other children, they likely experience both positive and negative feelings. In an English-only environment, children with limited English proficiency will be severely limited in their ability to express and communicate these emotions. Regardless of whether a child has an exceptionality or developmental delay, practitioners must determine the degree to which developmental concerns relate to language and communication differences rather than to actual developmental delays and exceptionalities (Landurand & Cloud, 1991; Metz, 1991). In all cases, practitioners need to consider which bilingual instructional strategy is most appropriate (see the following suggested strategies for various dual-language formats). Finally, it is important to recognize that exposure to or use of language(s) other than English never causes or contributes to a communication disorder (Arnberg, 1987; Harding & Riley, 1986).

Let's examine intervention and instructional considerations with respect to a child's language and communication differences. Review the child's Cultural Data Table. Information from the Language and Communication Differences section of the Assessment Cultural Linguistic Response Plan serves as a guide in thinking about key considerations in language differences in developing the Instructional Cultural Linguistic Response Plan. First, practitioners must consider language and communication differences when communicating with the family, becoming responsive to specific cultural communication patterns and social conventions (Phillips & Crowell, 1994). Mindful consideration must be given to communicating with parents who are not fluent in English. Practitioners need to identify any disparity between the language(s) used in early childhood environments and the language(s) used in a child's home when communicating with the family, encouraging the strengths of both languages and communication styles.

How the practitioner communicates with the child during instruction is a second consideration in developing effective instruction. The practitioner's use of language and nonverbal communication style when asking questions, giving directions, and providing feedback may be significantly different than that found in the home. The use of a modified single language approach, primarily the use of English as the language of instruction, but support by the child's first language demonstrates both respect and responsiveness increasing the effectiveness of instruction. Initially, a child learning English will benefit from "low demand" social and learning experiences, allowing the child to observe peer and adult interactions, process nonverbal communication styles, and adjust to the communication patterns in the new early childhood environment.

A third consideration is the language(s) used for delivery of instruction—oral and written. Practitioners who instruct all children in English or who rely on Spanish instruction primarily as a means of bridging the transition to all-English instruction may be viewed as promoting the primacy of the dominant culture and language. An alternative approach, demonstrating respect and responsiveness, would involve encouraging all children to acquire two languages.

A fourth consideration is the language proficiency a child needs to successfully learn the academic content of instruction. The practitioner should consider the child's relative language proficiency and well as the contextual support required for the child to be successful. Think about the attributes of the child to make a task more familiar or easier in some respect (e.g., prior experience, motivation, cultural relevance, interests). Also, consider your language and communication style during instruction. Does it assist or impede comprehension? Children with limited English proficiency benefit from language that is spoken clearly and contains a considerable amount of syntactic and semantic redundancy (Cummins, 1991). The following suggestions address the communicative and linguistic challenges that can arise as practitioners plan interventions and help practitioner's foster respectful, reciprocal, and responsive interactions

Suggested Strategies Collecting information about a child's language environment and language skills should be a standard part of the assessment process when exploring potential communication and language dilemmas that practitioners may encounter in their work. This information is critical for planning appropriate intervention and instructional strategies. If assessment information about a child and family's language background is insufficient or inappropriate, then practitioners must gather the necessary information prior to extensive intervention or instructional planning. Using the Instructional Cultural Linguistic Response Plan (Language and Communication Differences section) can assist practitioners in organizing this information when planning instruction.

Ensure Optimum Communication An obvious communicative-linguistic bump is the disparity between the language(s) used in early childhood environments and the language(s) used in a child's home. Practitioners should work with the family to select the communication format and language usage pattern that most closely match a child's relative language proficiency and home usage patterns. Depending on the family's goals, various approaches may be appropriate: 1) full bilingual, 2) dominant language bilingual, 3) modified single language, or 4) multicultural monolingual (see Figure 10.1).

For the purposes of this discussion, it is assumed that English is the dominant language of early intervention/early childhood programs, even though the authors recognize that this is not always the case. The alternative (i.e., a program in which a language other than English is dominant) is no less valid or valuable. In fact, this alternative may be more valid and valuable from

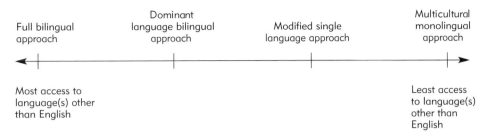

| Full bilingual approach | Dominant language bilingual approach | Modified single language approach | Multicultural monolingual approach |

Most access to language(s) other than English

Least access to language(s) other than English

Figure 10.1.   A continuum of language approaches. (From Barrera, I. [1993]. Effective and appropriate instruction for all children: The challenge of cultural/linguistic diversity and young children with special needs. *Topics in Early Childhood Special Education, 13*[4], 480. Copyright 1993 by PRO-ED, Inc. Adapted by permission.)

a research-based standpoint (Baca & Cervantes, 1998; Chamot & O'Malley, 1994; Cummins, 1989). Nevertheless, such programs are relatively rare and certainly are more challenging to implement, given available resources and the numerous languages other than English represented by children in many programs.

A *full bilingual approach* to instruction integrates children's home language(s) and English. For children who have limited or no English proficiency, this is often considered the best alternative when exposure to English is already taking place in the home. (Note that full bilingual approaches may use a language other than English only for a period of time; it is not necessary to use the languages equally during each day and activity.) Children are encouraged to maintain the development of their home language while they acquire skills in English. Ideally, programs hire practitioners who are bilingual in the languages of the child. Cultural linguistic mediators and skilled translators are needed when this is not possible (Barrera, 2000). It is important to note that being exposed to and learning more than one language from early childhood on is considered the norm in a majority of countries. No research indicates that exposure to multiple languages affects language development detrimentally; in fact, research indicates the contrary (Miller, 1984).

One language is used more frequently in the *dominant language bilingual approach*. Legitimate interpretations of the dominant language bilingual approach include both home language dominant with less English (e.g., a Spanish-dominant program) and English dominant with less of the child's home language. For consistency and ease of understanding within this discussion, the approach is interpreted as English dominant, meaning that it is the main language for instruction. ESOL and other such strategies must be used carefully to ensure comprehension and full access to existing skills. It is critical that the language other than English is not merely used informally but is also used in a planned manner to support learning and teaching. This approach is generally considered most appropriate for children who retain understanding of particular funds of knowledge in a language other than English yet have sufficient English proficiency to benefit from significant amounts of instruction in English. Similar to the full bilingual approach, the dominant bilingual approach requires practitioners or skilled cultural linguistic mediators who can understand and respond to children regardless of which language they use.

The *modified single language approach* relies primarily on English as the language of instruction. The language(s) other than English is used occasionally only to clarify or reinforce instruction. Practitioners using this approach with children who understand and speak a language other than English need to explicitly reassure children that they can still use languages other than English to communicate. This approach is most appropriate for children with strong proficiency in English yet with continued exposure to another language in the home (e.g., Hmong may be used at home but is not dominant).

Practitioners should be aware that children who are bilingual or multilingual often appear to have greater English proficiency than they actually do (Harding & Riley, 1986). Although these children may initially appear fluent in English, their ability to use it in an academic context may be much more limited.

A *multicultural monolingual approach* uses only one language (typically English) with diverse aspects of several cultures integrated into the curriculum. All early childhood programs should at least implement this approach, even when significant linguistic diversity is not present, as it sensitizes children to the existence and positive nature of cultural diversity. A multicultural monolingual approach is also appropriate for working with children and families who are culturally diverse when there is little or no linguistic diversity (i.e., both children and families are highly fluent in English). Under carefully structured conditions, it also may be used when such diversity is present. If access to children's language(s) other than English has yet to be identified, then practitioners may use an ESOL approach with limited or no use of language(s) other than English. Practitioners must pay close attention to the children's language development and concept comprehension when this is the case (see Chapter 9).

The multicultural monolingual approach is never ideal because children with limited proficiency in English must simultaneously deal with two different needs: 1) attending to the language itself (e.g., "What did she just say? What did it mean? Was she asking or telling me to do something?") and 2) attending to the content of instruction (e.g., "What is a square? What is a community helper?"). Children who are already proficient in English only need to attend to the latter. It is critical that implicit and explicit messages about diversity communicate strength, not deficit, whenever this approach is used. All children should be encouraged to explore multiple languages and ways of communicating and thinking (e.g., have CDs in a variety of languages, bring in children's family members who speak languages other than English). See Baca and Cervantes (1998), Barrera (1993), and Winzer and Mazurek (1994) for additional information on instructional approaches for children who are linguistically diverse.

Respond to Children's Communication Efforts with Words or Behaviors They Understand Children with limited proficiency in the language of instruction need to become familiar with an early childhood program's routines and environment before they are approached with questions or directives. Tabors (2008) noted that teachers initially may choose to include a child by using his or her name without directly asking questions that require responses (e.g., "How about we give Chun a chance," "Let's show Erich how to put this puzzle together"). Tabors referred to this strategy as a "low-demand" situation that gives the child time to adjust to the new cultural linguistic environment. Using this strategy does not mean that practitioners should not respond to the child's communicative efforts. On the contrary, practitioners should respond even if they do not fully understand the child's attempted message, as recommended with children who are nonverbal.

Use a Variety of ESOL and Other Language Improvement Strategies Practitioners need to consider a variety of communication strategies as they work with children and families whose primary language differs from their primary language. Many of these strategies are similar to those used with children who are nonverbal or have communication impairments. For example, practitioners can combine verbal (e.g., "Please get that truck") and nonverbal prompts (e.g., gesture, directed gaze). Other such strategies include the following:

- Repeat instructions to give a child more opportunities to understand.

- Ensure that communication focuses on the "here and now" so the child has a better chance of narrowing down what is being discussed.

- Expand communication attempts. For example, if a child says "cracker," then the practitioner may say, "These crackers taste good. Would you like another cracker?"

Cheng (1995), Echevarria and Graves (1998), and Tabors (2008) provided additional effective ESOL strategies. Ventriglia (1982) also provided a wealth of language development strategies designed especially for young English language learners (ELLs). These strategies can augment more familiar language development strategies.

Determine Relative Language Proficiency Practitioners should always assess relative language proficiency (i.e., proficiency in English and in language[s] other than English) prior to assessment or intervention. Sometimes the phrase "identifying language dominance" is used to characterize this step. The point, however, is to establish a working knowledge of the child's receptive and expressive skills in all languages used, rather than to single out one language as dominant. Determining relative language proficiency, as opposed to dominance, is particularly critical for young children. Children who are bilingual or multilingual often do not have a clearly dominant language but, rather, use two or more languages separately or in combination, depending on context and purpose. Relative language proficiency may be judged either formally through bilingual language screening/evaluation tools or informally through observations and parent interviews. In addition to probing the child's language usage, which may be minimal if severe disabilities are present, it is also important to probe language usage by others in the home (i.e., how much of which language is used by whom and in what contexts; see Chapter 8).

Distinguish Between Situations in which Language Is the Medium and Those in Which Language Is the Teaching Topic (e.g., Whether One Is Teaching the Concept of "up" or Teaching the English Word up)   Practitioners need to understand the purpose of language to determine when to use which language(s). New concepts and unfamiliar material are taught most effectively in the language that the child understands best. The less familiar language should be used primarily when the purpose is to teach known concepts and structures. For example, the concept "up" should be introduced and taught in the most familiar language. If English is the less familiar language, then the English word *up* could then be taught and associated with that concept. The less familiar language is best used, at least initially, only for teaching the language itself.

Learning both content and form (language) is simultaneously less efficient and more difficult for anyone, especially a child. Therefore, basic vocabulary for familiar items and actions should be known in the less familiar language prior to using it for instruction. Presentation of new concepts or skills, and demands for demonstrating learning of those concepts and skills, should be made in the more proficient language whenever possible. When this is not possible, which should rarely be the case, systematic ESOL strategies should be used to ensure optimal learning. As previously stated, languages in which one has limited proficiency are poor tools for learning anything other than the language itself.

Connect New Language and Content with Known Language and Familiar Contexts   Keeping the context familiar allows children to connect the unknown with the known. This connection maximizes the transfer of existing knowledge and skills to the new situation or language and enhances comprehension. Examples include using familiar discourse, behavior rules, and objects found in the child's home.

Create a Physically and Emotionally Safe Environment   Consider setting up learning environments as "safe havens" in which children can play. For instance, practitioners can select materials that are readily available for children (e.g., LEGOs, puzzles, blocks). Space should be available for children to interact independently with these materials if so desired. Coming into an unfamiliar environment with unfamiliar expectations and demands, in addition to lacking proficiency in that environment's language, can be a daunting experience for anyone. How much more daunting might it be for a 3- or 4-year-old whose problem-solving skills and experiential repertoire are only beginning to form? In many ways, Igoa's statements about immigrant children are equally applicable to all young children who are culturally linguistically diverse entering unfamiliar and "foreign" environments where demands to respond to an unknown language prevail:

> When immigrant children leave the country [i.e., environment] that was their home—a familiar language, culture, community, and social system—they experience a variety of emotional and cognitive adjustments to the reality of life in a new country. How dry and clinical that sentence sounds! It doesn't even begin to convey the paralyzing fear in a little boy from Afghanistan that he will never fully understand English, that he will always be on the outside looking in. It doesn't explain why an achievement-oriented girl from Vietnam will intentionally fail tests that might advance her in the educational system. (1995, p. xi)

Is this true only for children who are immigrants? Countless children born and raised in the United States have also lived that forced shift from the familiar to the unfamiliar. The first author entered first grade (in a school that was 100% Hispanic through the fourth grade) already speaking some English. Yet, the effects of cultural dissonance and needing to quickly master an unpredictable cultural linguistic environment remain with her to this day (see Afterword). Similar stories abound in culturally linguistically diverse communities of second- and third-generation U.S. citizens (e.g., Garcia, 2001). Chapter 11 examines some ways in which unsupported acculturation can be traumatizing. Delays and exceptionalities that delay or impede language and problem-solving abilities can further compound the trauma.

Expect a Silent Period Children should be given ample time and opportunities to orient themselves to the expectations of the early childhood providers and environments. Children entering an environment in which their home language is not dominant will speak little or not at all, depending on their personalities and other factors (Díaz-Rico & Weed, 1995). It is important to let them simply observe and/or interact nonverbally if they wish. Demands for verbal expression should be kept to a minimum until the child demonstrates spontaneous attempts at verbal interaction. Such attempts typically appear fairly quickly; if they are not evident in interactions with peers within 3–4 weeks, then other factors may be precluding them and practitioners should look more closely at the situation.

Avoid Direct Correction of Verbal Errors As children begin to express themselves in English, their utterances should be accepted without correction, although they may be asked to repeat something if it is not understood.

Approximations should be accepted to encourage continued expression. Children whose verbalizations are corrected may feel shame and decrease or stop attempts to communicate. In addition, many errors in a second language are developmental, responding more to time and practice than to correction (Díaz-Rico & Weed, 1995).

Provide Comprehensible Input   Practitioners should provide comprehensible input whenever a child's less familiar language is used. *Comprehensible input* refers to making the language directed to the child as easy to understand as possible by providing as many cues as possible (e.g., pictures, objects, gestures, familiar contexts and routines). The idea is to pair the spoken language with these cues to facilitate comprehension. This type of language exposure is very effective in helping children acquire communication skills in a second language (Cummins, 1984, 1989). Translating immediately after speaking is not effective for this purpose, although it is effective for learning concepts or content.

Realize that Expressive Skills May Exceed Comprehension   It is generally assumed that a child who says something in a language understands the content and has mastered the requisite language structures. For example, a child who says, "What is your name?" might be assumed to understand that question and to have mastered the forms for questions and pronouns. Children who are bilingual, however, frequently learn language in chunks and may be able to express more that they can understand. For example, they may have learned "What is your name?" as a single utterance without really understanding individual words or grammar. Therefore, they may sound more proficient than they actually are in their second language. It is important never to assume understanding based on expressive skills. Understanding should always be specifically assessed, especially across a variety of situations.

Recognize that Basic Interpersonal Communication Skills Are Distinct from Cognitive Academic Linguistic Proficiency   There are two distinct levels or facets of language skills (Chamot & O'Malley, 1994; Cummins, 1984). On the one hand, basic interpersonal communication skills (BICS) are present in face-to-face, informal, interpersonal interactions (e.g., talking with a friend about what one did yesterday). This type of communication is characterized by the availability of strategies and cues such as facial expressions, repetition or revision, shared referents, and suprasegmentals (vocal pitch, stress, loudness). On the other hand, cognitive academic linguistic proficiency (CALP) skills are necessary for competent functioning in academic environments. Preliteracy and literacy skills are major components of CALP, as is the understanding of formal oral discourse (Díaz-Rico & Weed, 1995). Many strategies and cues common to BICS are not common to CALP, for which reliance on extralinguistic cues is greatly reduced and the need to understand literate strategies (e.g., story grammars) is increased. A child may be very proficient at a BICS level and still have significant difficulty with academic work (e.g., following abstract discussions or directions, interpreting text).

Validate the Language Other than English Children quickly learn to associate a particular language with a particular person, environment, and/or activity. It is important, therefore, to pay attention to how often a language is being used in certain situations. It is especially critical to avoid communicating that English is a higher status language than the child's other language(s). This message may be inadvertently communicated when English is used in school and by professionals, whereas Spanish, for example, is used only when English cannot be used. This message devalues languages other than English and can inhibit a child's progress in those languages and in English. Languages other than English are validated when modeled by a variety of people—professional and nonprofessional—in a variety of environments. Exposing the child to literature and recordings in those languages is another effective strategy for validating them.

Cue Language Contexts Although language use should not communicate a difference in status, it should be predictable, at least in the early stages of learning (see Chapter 9). A child who is first learning English should be cued when English is to be used. For example, one person may speak English and another Spanish, or English may be used exclusively during a particular activity or time period every day. Puppets may also be used as visual reminders of which language is to be used at a particular time.

Teaching and Learning Strategies

Other challenges are related to using specific teaching strategies that may be unfamiliar to or not similarly valued by children and families who are culturally linguistically diverse. The following discussion clusters strategies into the three developmental/curricular areas used to discuss culture bumps.

Teaching is based on effective communication. Language is a primary medium for the transmission of information as well as for the self-talk that can be a critical aspect of learning. The language differences, dilemmas, and suggested responses are also highly relevant to this examination and should be considered in addition to the ones discussed in this section.

The language(s) in which a child can best learn a new skill is one of the initial factors that practitioners should consider when working with children who are bilingual or multilingual. Determining this may be especially challenging in ECSE environments in which children may come from a multitude of linguistic backgrounds. In these instances, practitioners need to consider how to incorporate all of the children's languages into the classroom.

Practitioners are challenged to recognize the limitations that they bring to the dialogue because it is impossible for them to be competent in the languages of all of the children and families with whom they work. Practitioners must realize that it is not just the children or families with limited proficiency in English who are "limited." Practitioners' low proficiency in the families' primary language is an equal limitation. This realization is critical to establishing reciprocity—a key characteristic of Skilled Dialogue. For example, it is important to communicate that translators/interpreters are necessary not because families have limited English proficiency but because practitioners have limited proficiency in the families' language(s).

The ALERTA curriculum (Williams & DeGaetano, 1985), which contains suggestions and protocols for practitioners' use, is a good guide to creating multicultural/multilingual early childhood environments. This curriculum contains forms and concrete suggestions for areas such as identifying and using community resources; preparing multicultural, bilingual language environments for young children; integrating strategies for language learning throughout the program; and observing children's interests, developmental levels, and language use.

Teaching is in many ways a relational endeavor. The importance of emotional intelligence in both teaching and learning is increasingly being recognized (Goleman, 1995; Greenspan, 1999). Practitioners need to examine how well their teaching strategies are responsive to children's personal-social funds of knowledge.

Practitioners tend to develop interventions and instructional practices based on the theoretical constructs accepted by their formal education and training. These constructs often do not account for different child-rearing practices, however (Bhagwanji, Santos, & Fowler, 2000). "Appropriate" social and instructional interventions are culturally defined (Fewell, 1996). For instance, Schneider, Parush, Katz, and Miller noted that families differ in the "the amount of auditory, visual, or tactile stimulation, whether play and movement are encouraged and in what way, and whether certain skills are actually taught or practiced" (1995, p. 20). Cintas (1995) stated that the cradleboards used by the Navajo and Hopi people illustrate a culturally based child-rearing practice designed to shape infant behavior for the parent's and the child's benefit. Practitioners must consider and incorporate such practices as they develop interventions and instructional practices for children and families. As Bhagwanji et al. noted, intervention activities aimed at increasing a young child's independence without also addressing interdependence and shared caring may conflict with the social and cultural preferences of many groups (see Chapters 5 and 7).

How practitioners present information highly influences the ability of children and families to understand the concepts or information provided. Similarly, how children and families communicate information may strongly influence the ability of practitioners to comprehend what is being communicated. Practitioners need to consider families' funds of knowledge and the types of knowledge valued within these funds. Are these primarily personal or communal? To what degree are funds of knowledge contained orally? To what degree are they contained in written form? Asking families that primarily value oral information to rely on written documents (e.g., IFSPs, IEPs) may lead to significant culture bumps.

Practitioners must also consider families' preferred strategies for acquiring new knowledge (e.g., modeling, questioning), as well as for problem solving and decision making. Practitioners must assess the degree to which learning strategies used at home are direct, indirect, explicit, or implicit. Observing how family members teach children what they consider important can give insight into which learning approaches are valued. How congruent are the preferred teaching and learning approaches used in a child's home to those in early childhood education programs?

For example, the nationally adopted response to intervention (RTI) program is a multitier approach to the early identification and support of students with learning and behavior needs. The RTI process begins with high-quality instruction and universal screening of all children in the general preschool and elementary education classrooms. This is a three-tiered model. Tier 1 provides research-based instruction in the general education classroom. Tier 2 provides children intensive assistance as part of the general education support system. Tier 3 is special education services. There are multiple assumptions about culture and learning embedded in the RTI model. Research-based practice providing the foundation is based on a cultureless knowledge base (Artiles, Trent, & Kuan, 1997). There is no acknowledgment of the preferred teaching and learning approaches a child brings to the classroom. The research that informs RTI does not consider the effect of race/ethnicity on special education placement or outcomes as many research studies did not specify the racial/ethnic composition of the sample or had too few minority children to measure effects by race/ethnicity (Donovan & Cross, 2002). Yet, we know a significant proportion of struggling learners and students in special education come from ethnic and linguistic minority communities. The RTI model requires all instruction be evidence based, but does not acknowledge that teaching and learning strategies work in relationship to the sociocultural contexts in which they are implemented (Artiles & Ortiz, 2002; Gee, 2001). RTI's view of students' low achievement is a result of poor teaching or a disability. Learning is understood as an individual process in which a student develops skills or knowledge through the use of instructional strategies. Culture is not acknowledged in RTI, yet practitioners are encouraged to be familiar with the beliefs, values, cultural practices, discourse styles, and other features of students' lives that may have an affect on classroom participation and success and be prepared to use this information in designing instruction (Donovan & Cross, 2002) Artiles (2007) suggested RTI and the current knowledge base be adapted while a new knowledge base is developed that is mindful of the learner's culture. Skilled Dialogue provides a way to respectfully acknowledge and leverage a student's first language and preferred learning strategies in the context of adopted curriculum.

Let's examine intervention and instructional considerations with respect to teaching and learning strategies. Review the child's Cultural Data Table. Information from the Assessment Cultural Linguistic Response Plan also serves as a guide in thinking about key considerations of teaching and learning strategies in developing the Instructional Cultural Linguistic Response Plan. First, practitioners must consider the degree of familiarity and how the family values the teaching/learning strategies used in school compared with those used in the home. For example, a family may rarely provide direct instruction to a child to complete a task, but rather use indirect instruction strategies and repeatedly model the task for the child. The practitioner designs instructional plans that provide multiple demonstrations, modeling the targeted skill and task completion for a particular child. A family's teaching and learning style may be "community based"—the child learns through interactions with siblings and other family members, rather than explicit instruction one-to-one with a parent. A practitioner would use peer and small-group learning strategies to leverage a child's learning experience if they seem to be the preferred strategies for acquiring new knowledge in the child's home.

Second, use the child's first language and strategies for ELLs. Teaching and learning strategies should promote the home languages of children as well as English. Children learning English need to interact as much as possible with English-speaking children in the classroom. Research shows that children learn a second language more easily if they participate in meaningful activities that require using the second language; thus, practitioners should encourage children to speak, read, and write the second language in meaningful ways (McLaughlin, 1995). ELLs are supported in a naturalistic learning environment when explicit strategies for language development are embedded within content lessons and daily classroom routines. The practitioner determines the background knowledge students need to know to understand the concept. Then, the practitioner seamlessly embeds the strategies into instruction by utilizing ELL strategies such as simplifying language, providing demonstrations and models, using graphic organizers, and displaying visual demonstrations and ongoing checks of understanding. A family may value oral language for gaining new knowledge and sharing information. Leveraging a child's learning from this culture, a practitioner would support this oral emphasis when presenting new information. Allow the use of a first language to support instruction in a second language when planning teaching and learning activities, and encourage students to share what they have learned.

Using "bridging strategies" is a third consideration when developing teaching and learning strategies. Bridging strategies require students to build on prior knowledge from past experiences. Practitioners help the students make connections or bridge the gap from prior learning, making new information relevant and linking it to some part for their lives. This strategy is critical for all young children, but is essential to second language learners. The goal for early childhood practitioners is to bridge a child's prior knowledge to new knowledge with culturally responsive teaching and learning strategies.

For example, scaffolding is a bridging strategy that provides support for learning and problem solving. The support can be giving children more time to speak, providing clues, offering reminders, giving encouragement, breaking a problem into steps, providing an example, or anything else that allows the student to grow in independence as a learner. Scaffolding strategies may be built into the lesson plan, taking into account where students currently are and where they need to be, or the practitioner may offer scaffolding during the course of instruction. Scaffolding is used in a classroom to ensure that students are able to take educational risks without having to feel scared of anything. Scaffolding is an instructional safety net that helps those students who are learning a second language as well as subject content.

Leveraging strategies that tap into a child's identified strengths to support new learning is a fourth teaching and learning consideration.

Juan is 5 years old, and information gathered from his Cultural Data Table reports Spanish is the primary language in the home, with his older siblings speaking Spanish and English. He is highly verbal in his first language, limited in English, socially confident, physically active, and enjoys drawing and coloring at home. His teacher carefully considers teaching and learning strategies that will best support his academic and social development as well as second language acquisition. Strategies selected support the continued use of both languages and the development of activities and lessons that reflect teaching and learning strategies used in the child's home. Building on his strengths, teaching strategies might include drawing pictures as a demonstration of knowledge, role-playing stories from texts, frequent opportunities for small-group work, using his first language among students who speak the same language, and guided reading and writing strategies. The practitioner identifies strategies that provide rich opportunities to listen, speak, and internalize the sounds, rhythms, and patterns of English over a period of time in order to leverage Juan's strong oral skills in Spanish. For example, Juan's family shares family experiences and history through storytelling. Teaching and learning strategies supporting ELLs can be leveraged to provide opportunities for Juan to share his experiences through storytelling. Such experiences provide Juan the linguistic information and the confidence he needs to develop his English language skills.

Suggested Strategies

RTI demonstrates the need for culturally linguistically responsive intervention and instruction procedures. This need is of particular concern in early childhood education. Only a limited amount of research exists, however, to help practitioners accomplish this. Fortunately, the practices of Skilled Dialogue can support practitioners in ensuring that they present culturally linguistically sensitive information in a respectful, reciprocal, and responsive manner. The following suggested responses can limit the impact of dilemmas that may arise from how information is presented to children and families who are diverse.

Establish a Relationship   Practitioners take time to build rapport with children and their families before beginning assessment or intervention. Although it is critical that a positive relationship be established to support the learning of all children, it is even more imperative that this occur when the cultural and/or linguistic background of practitioners differs from those of the children and families with whom they work. Many potential culture bumps are eliminated before they occur when families realize that they are respected, they have ample opportunities to voice their perspectives, and practitioners truly attempt to respond to their needs. Acknowledging that this process takes some time is an important first step. Practitioners should work to the maximum extent possible to build in opportunities for establishing this rapport prior to initiating academic instruction.

Set a Stable and Predictable Routine   Interacting with children via a consistent routine is one of the most helpful ways for practitioners to support children in managing a new or less-familiar language and communication environment. Routines make it easier for children to pick up subtle cues and use other children and adults as models of the expected behaviors. A stable routine gives children the opportunity to predict certain communications and instructions.

Use Teaching and Learning Strategies Familiar to and Valued by the Child and Family   Activities that are carefully selected to match the patterns of a child's and family's environment yield the greatest gains in overall development and early literacy (Kame'enui, Carnine, Dixon, Simmons, & Coyne, 2002; Williams & DeGaetano, 1985). Any attempt to address the learning strategies of a diverse group of children must offer a wide range of options. Gardner's (1993) multiple intelligences framework recognizes differences while reducing the risk of stereotyping children's abilities based on their cultural background. The materials developed and used by the Capitol School in Tuscaloosa, Alabama, provide an example of the application of this framework to early childhood (B. Roundtree, personal communication).

Match Communication Styles   Practitioners should match a family's pacing, level of directness, nonverbal behaviors, and other communication aspects to the maximum extent possible. Such matching requires that practitioners have developed a strong forestructure and an anchored understanding of specific differences based on the actual communication structures of the families with whom they work (see Chapter 7).

Be Responsive to a Family's Funds of Knowledge   Practitioners must closely examine the vocabulary and concepts used in intervention tasks and other communications for the degree of match with a family's funds of knowledge. If there is not a match, then there may be insufficient connections between the home and early childhood environments, making it difficult to transfer knowledge from one environment to the other. When unaddressed, this lack of continuity can put children at risk for academic problems as well as limit opportunities to develop the attitudes and skills necessary to succeed in a variety of environments.

Encourage the Continued Home Use of the Language Other than English   Some practitioners may believe that placing a child in an English-only environment is the best way to ensure fast acquisition of English (Quiñones-Eatman, 2001). Yet, research does not validate the belief that children who are second language learners should be exposed to as much English as possible (Baca & Cervantes, 1998). Research with both monolingual and bilingual children indicates that the richer the home language environment, the better the child's language development and school achievement. Cummins (1984) reported on a study of 108 Hispanic fifth- and sixth-grade students in which the relationship between maintaining Spanish as the home language and academic performance was examined. Results indicated that children from homes where Spanish usage was not maintained had "significantly poorer academic performance in comparison to students who had maintained Spanish as the main home language" (p. 112). Cummins reported on another study of 53 Chinese American 9- and 10-year-olds, which showed that increased exposure to Chinese outside the home correlated with better performance on a particular standardized test. Even more significant, the "amount of English used in the home was unrelated to [test] scores" (p. 112). Unfortunately, few studies such as these target younger children. Nevertheless, their implications cannot be ignored.

Parents should be encouraged to use the language with which they are most comfortable and in which they are most proficient in order to provide an optimum home language environment. The richer the language environment they can provide—regardless of which language(s) they use—the better their children will be able to develop and acquire new information. Home language patterns are also tied to self-identity and esteem, so the perceived demand to change them can have a significantly negative emotional impact.

Instructional Content and Materials

What practitioners teach in early childhood environments is often unfamiliar—and perhaps even inappropriate—for some children, based on their cultural and/or linguistic backgrounds. In these instances, culture bumps are likely regarding what practitioners and families expect and want in the learning environment. What practitioners value as individuals can strongly influence the content of instruction and the implementation of interventions. As practitioners learn to acknowledge and understand their own cultural lenses, they can begin to see beyond their particular frameworks. Thus, as practitioners incorporate Skilled Dialogue in their work, they can select content that is developmentally appropriate within ENC and respectful of diverse cultural values and beliefs.

Language, language level, and language style should be important parts of any content selection for instruction. Children and families need regular and frequent opportunities to communicate and share their ideas in order to maximize the appropriateness of selected content.

It is critical that practitioners avoid sending the message, either implicitly or explicitly, that one language holds a higher status than another. Rather, they need to ensure that all children learn the value of bilingualism and multilingualism. Similarly, practitioners should recognize the relative value that is placed on verbal versus nonverbal communication in the selected content for instruction. Finally, practitioners must understand that meaningful communication is essential to learning. It is difficult for young children to learn through an insufficiently developed communication medium. Stunting the development of one language to develop a second language in order to initiate instruction in that second language is an ineffective method both for developing communication skills and teaching concepts.

Practitioners must be aware that what they teach can either support or hinder the development of children's self-esteem and self-confidence. Instructional materials should offer many opportunities for learning activities that develop social responsibility and interpersonal skills in ways that honor and extend the values and beliefs of families. It is in these early years that practitioners and families lay the groundwork for young children's competence in Skilled Dialogue. At no point should families be made to feel that they must choose between what they know and value and what practitioners recommend. Equally important, children should never be taught that their language, knowledge, beliefs, and values are anything less than assets that can help them learn the unfamiliar.

The curricula or content of instruction should confirm that diversity in all of its facets is an asset to be tapped and not something that needs remediation. The content of instruction should reflect how children develop ways of observing, thinking, and experimenting within their environment and should support the funds of knowledge valued by their families. At an age-appropriate level, instructional content should engage children in determining an appropriate response to solving problems by using a variety of different decision-making strategies.

Teaching materials and curricula that adequately address diversity remain limited (Lynch & Hanson, 2011), despite increased awareness that practitioners must respond to the impact of culture and language on the educational process. Early childhood professionals face the challenge of finding quality early childhood materials to share with children, families, and their communities. To work effectively with children and families who are diverse, it is imperative to find or adapt materials with contents that respect, reflect, and include these families' values, beliefs, and customs (Santos, Fowler, Corso, & Bruns, 2000). Although authors and publishers of educational materials may increasingly acknowledge cultural linguistic diversity, practitioners still have the responsibility of selecting which materials to use. No one item is totally responsive to the full range of values and beliefs that exist across cultures. Therefore, the most challenging part of finding and effectively using materials is reflecting on their content and, subsequently, considering ways to adapt content to increase its cultural linguistic appropriateness for the individuals with whom the materials will be used.

The format of possible materials (e.g., print, video, audio) should be evaluated based on families' or children's preferred learning styles. In addition, the materials should be assessed to ensure the comprehension level is appropriate for the intended audience. Practitioners should specifically consider the degree to which technical terminology or early intervention/ECSE jargon is used in the material and whether it is adequately defined.

Many more efforts are underway to provide materials in languages other than English, but practitioners must carefully consider these materials. The vast majority are translations of materials originally developed in English (CLAS Early Childhood Research Institute, 2001). In an effort to provide materials in the family's preferred language, practitioners may be tempted to use any available resources in that language. As Santos, Lee, Valdivia, and Zhang wrote,

> In our quest to provide information that the family will access, comprehend, and implement, we may be inadvertently disseminating outdated, inaccurate, or even offensive information. Instead of setting the stage for an improved relationship between early intervention professionals and family members, we may further alienate the family by giving them inappropriate materials. (2001, p. 26)

According to Santos et al. (2001), effective translations

- Match the material's comprehension level with the intended audience's reading ability, education, social and economic status, and acculturation level

- Reflect regional and dialectical differences in the language spoken by the intended audience

- Recommend activities and examples that are familiar to the intended audience

- Use real stories and authentic voices and include visuals and photographs that are representative of the intended audience

- Make appropriate accommodations for the use of novel words and borrowed terms (e.g., IFSP)

- Do not distort, delete, or change the information

Materials must reflect families' characteristics, roles, backgrounds, and geographic location to be responsive to children and families served (Santos et al., 2000). Practitioners should consider children's or families' degree of enculturation in ENC and early intervention/ECSE culture as well as their skill in negotiating these cultures. Other issues that may affect which teaching and learning materials practitioners select pertain to the different roles that family members may play in child rearing, a family's experience regarding social and personal power, and the degree to which a family belongs to and identifies with a group with minority status.

Practitioners must assess the extent to which the materials reflect and acknowledge families' funds of knowledge. That is, do they address the diversity found in their community? Or, can they be adapted to acknowledge a specific group's concerns, beliefs, and practices? Materials that were once viewed as supporting best practice in the early intervention/ECSE field and other widely used materials may contain strategies that would offend some cultural linguistic groups (e.g., to question adults, to solve problems without adult assistance). Practitioners have to determine the degree the worldview described in the material matches the worldview of the child or family with whom the material will be used. They must consider whether the material's basic assumptions about how the world works and about what is considered right and wrong challenge or support the beliefs of a child or family. Appendix A contains a Funds of Knowledge Worksheet for Story Assessment. This form or one like it can be used to assess the types of knowledge reflected in stories and other print materials (e.g., materials that show and discuss only nuclear families).

Let's examine intervention and instructional considerations with respect to instructional content and materials. Review the child's Cultural Data Table. Information from the Assessment Cultural Linguistic Response Plan also serves as a guide in thinking about key considerations of instructional content and selection of teaching and learning materials in developing a child's Instructional Cultural Linguistic Response Plan. First, practitioners must consider the degree of cultural familiarity and value the child's home culture(s) has to the early childhood curriculum and routines. It is critical the practitioners have knowledge of immigrant parents' experiences with preschool in other countries that may influence their expectations about preschool in the United States.

For example, American parents are concerned about preschool children's social development rather than academic achievement (Pang & Richey, 2007). Child-centered curriculum and teaching materials value individualism, encouraging children to become independent and make free choices. Chinese immigrant parents usually have high expectations for young children's academic achievement, and they are expected to learn advanced academic subjects so that they are well prepared for kindergarten (Pang & Richey, 2007). Chinese parents spend more time teaching children to learn at home and believe a preschooler should spend time on learning academic subjects and instructed activities rather than free play (Huntsinger & Jose, 2009; Tobin, Wu, & Davidson, 1989). The typical child-centered, discovery learning, and free choice curriculum adopted by early childhood programs in the United States may be incongruent to the values, child-rearing practices, social validity, and worldview of families who are culturally diverse.

Second, consider the funds of knowledge represented in curriculum, as well as those that are assumed to be present for understanding. Decisions about curriculum are embedded in worldviews and value systems. Practitioners must engage in a dynamic and reflective decision-making process to craft an inclusive and relevant curriculum that honors the connections between homes, early childhood curriculum, and materials. This includes the critical recognition of the funds of knowledge (Moll, Amanti, Neff, & Gonzalez, 1992) each child brings to school that provides the context for new learning and a sense of belonging. Respecting and honoring the diverse funds of knowledge young children bring to school requires practitioners to reflect and evaluate instructional content and materials. Instructional content and materials must extend school knowledge beyond Caucasian, middle-class ENC to be engaging and meaningful. Effective practitioners should examine the instructional content's vocabulary, relevance to specific children in the classroom, projected worldview, assumed prior learning experiences, format and organization (linear, narrative), and the degree of contextualization and linguist demand, as well as the expected student–teacher interactions for listening, responding to questions, and demonstrating knowledge. It is critical for effective practitioners working with young children who are culturally linguistically diverse to consider the various characteristics, qualities, and assumptions embedded in instructional content and materials, ensuring the curriculum honors the diverse funds of knowledge children and their families bring to the classroom.

Suggested Strategies

Practitioners must consider which intervention and instructional content and materials best responds to children and families who are culturally linguistically diverse. Using Skilled Dialogue and examining these suggested responses can assist practitioners in selecting which information and skills they present to young children and families.

All materials inherently contain implicit and explicit judgments about which beliefs, practices, and funds of knowledge should be valued (e.g., by the people depicted or the events highlighted). Instructional materials influence what and how practitioners teach, and, subsequently, what children and families learn. Selecting culturally linguistically appropriate instructional materials implies that the content presented is congruent with local cultural and environmental knowledge. The material also should reflect current research. These two aspects may appear at odds in certain materials, but this does not necessarily mean the materials are not worthy of use. Instead, this situation may challenge practitioners to find 3rd Space to hold the seemingly contradictory information together. The following suggested responses can support practitioners as they face dilemmas in selecting content and teaching materials.

Teach the Value of Diversity   Practitioners should work to ensure that instruction content reflects the value of cultural linguistic diversity (e.g., through the stories and pictures used). Even in the youngest years—perhaps especially in these years—children are sensitive to what it feels like to be respected, to have reciprocal communication, and to have responsive caregivers. The actions that practitioners model and the content of instruction reveal their values to children and families.

Encourage the Continued Home Use of the Language Other than English   Children and families should be supported to continue using language(s) other than English at home. As previously noted, research with children who are monolingual and bilingual indicates that such continuity improves a child's language development and school achievement. Parents should be encouraged to use their preferred language with each other as well as with their children. In addition, home language patterns are tied to self-identity and self-esteem, so continuing them is important.

Allow for Exploration   The instruction content should encourage children to explore and draw conclusions in a risk-free environment. Doing so allows practitioners to build an environment in which children can safely try new things in a manner that is consistent with their cultural practices. Some toys and play materials that children use at home should also be a part of the environment to the maximum extent possible. As previously discussed, making children feel secure is a critical component for learning new skills. Early childhood environments should be structured so that children can choose which parts of their environment to explore (or not explore). It is important to note that exploration by infants and toddlers is not valued in some cultures. Therefore, practitioners need to create an environment where all children are not expected to conform to the same cultural practices and daily routine.

Provide Frequent and Varied Opportunities for Children to Communicate in English and Other Home Languages   Instructional content should allow children to share information about their feelings, knowledge, values, and beliefs in whichever language and communication style is most comfortable to the maximum extent possible. Communication should be thought of in a broad manner. Children who speak multiple languages may have a preferred language to communicate certain ideas or topics. In addition, children may prefer to communicate in nonverbal ways. Children who are learning a new language may begin expressing themselves with incomprehensible utterances. These should be accepted without correction, as correcting early communicative attempts may shame a child and decrease or stop further attempts to communicate.

Ensure that Assessment Information Is Ongoing During Teaching

Learning activities provide assessment information and help practitioners determine the extent to which children have processed information and can apply it to problem-solving strategies. As practitioners consider what to teach, how to assess the impact of what is taught should be simultaneously considered. This assessment process should help practitioners craft the next steps in the instructional process.

Many tools support practitioners as they continue to gather information about the children and families with whom they work. As an example, the Cultural Data Table can capture information about which teaching strategies seem to be consistent with a child's cultural linguistic background. Responses to the information noted on these tools should be considered dynamic. For instance, as children learn and develop, their expressive and receptive skills in English and other languages are likely to change. Therefore, these tools should be periodically reviewed and updated as part of an ongoing assessment process to help practitioners make decisions about what and how they teach.

Teach the Practices of Skilled Dialogue

The concepts of Skilled Dialogue could serve as a core for nearly any early childhood curriculum. It is never too early for children to learn about dialogue that is based on respect, reciprocity, and responsiveness. This is taught to infants and toddlers primarily through modeling. Practitioners can help preschoolers begin to understand the rich variety of cultural expressions (i.e., to anchor their understanding of differences). It can also be immensely helpful to teach children that there is always a third choice—the basic component of creating 3rd Space options. The ability to find third choices can be important developmentally (e.g., when one child wants to play and the other does not). It is also important culturally to emphasize that it is never necessary to lose one behavior (e.g., speaking Hmong) in order to gain another (e.g., speaking English).

Use Materials that Include Multiple Populations

An initial challenge for practitioners or programs often begins with simply finding up-to-date materials and information on specific topics. Several projects and professional organizations, however, have done much of the work to create substantial collections of materials (e.g., Catlett & Winton, 2000; CLAS Early Childhood Research Institute, 2001; Perry & Duru, 2001). These collections allow practitioners to make informed choices about which materials are most appropriate.

Carefully Consider the Selection of Materials Practitioners should ensure that materials and resources in the children's primary languages are accessible to the children and their families. Books, DVDs, posters, and other materials that are part of the early childhood environment should reflect the diverse languages of the children. When selecting materials, it is important that practitioners develop forestructures to become knowledgeable about the children, families, and community groups with whom they will share the material. Early intervention teams must realize that individuals and families are members of multiple cultures (Kalyanpur & Harry, 1999). Kalyanpur and Harry noted that "children are raised within a cultural framework that imposes rewards and sanctions for efficient learning of the group's norms and expectations" (p. 3); however, intragroup differences are often as large as intergroup differences. Therefore, there is not a simple "recipe" approach to selecting materials and practices with which practitioners can assume that a family from a particular culture should receive.

Practitioners must evaluate the overall strengths and limitations of the material's content. Practitioners should especially consider whether the material is responsive to the cultural linguistic background of the intended audience. Specifically, teams need to determine whether the values, beliefs, and practices highlighted in the material support or conflict with those of the children and families receiving the materials.

Practitioners also should determine whether the material's presentation and format are appropriate for the needs of the intended audience. For instance, families may prefer a DVD to printed material or material written in Spanish to English. If the material is translated, then teams should assess the accuracy and quality of the translation.

Adapt Materials to Make a Match After weighing the strengths and limitations of certain materials, practitioners will likely find something that approximates their needs. Instead of simply using a certain item as is, practitioners should reflect and consider how it can be made more suitable for the children and families receiving it. That is, how can practitioners create a match between materials and the values, beliefs, and practices of children and families? Although the content of some materials may be used as originally produced, others may need to be adapted to meet the intended objectives. It is important to keep in mind which kinds of adaptations can be made. Copyrighted materials may not be altered without permission from the copyright holder (typically the author or publisher); however, this generally does not prohibit teams from using parts of the original material or using it in conjunction with other materials. Teams have more freedom to adapt materials in the public domain (e.g., a government publication) as needed. It is always a good practice to cite the original source.

When considering adaptations to a material, several questions can help the community team determine what adaptations, if any, are necessary. Some questions that practitioners may ask themselves include

- Does the content match the child's learning needs?

- Is the content sensitive to diverse learning styles, values, and practices?

- Are there better ways to present the material to children or families (e.g., in print, in face-to-face interactions, electronically)?

- Can I address my concerns and identify appropriate ways of using the material through supplemental activities, discussion, or other materials?

- Can I use some but not all of the material and still produce desired outcomes?

- Can I use the material as a model to develop a new document, given my current resources?

Practitioners should rely on the benefits of the multiple voices in their agencies and communities to spark ideas and provide direction for adapting the materials that they have selected.

In adapting a material, practitioners should consider the values, assumptions, and beliefs represented as well as those of the participants and families with whom the material will be used. Adapting a material's presentation often enhances the material's clarity, comprehension level, format, and graphics, possibly making it more user friendly or efficient. Practitioners may continually refer to the question, "How can I adapt this material to best reflect the unique strengths and needs of children and families in this community?" as the process of selecting and using materials unfolds.

Allow Family Members to Interact with Materials   Too often, materials are simply given to families with no explanation about their content or purpose and with no follow up. Ideally, practitioners should consider a process that encourages the families to interact with the materials. Practitioners can specifically highlight portions of the material that may not be consistent with the family's beliefs and practices. This may facilitate dialogue between the family and practitioners around issues raised by the material's information.

Solicit Questions or Comments About Materials   Children and families should be asked what they liked about the material and what they think needs to be improved. With this input, practitioners can decide whether to continue using a material. In this reciprocal process, it is important to engage the voices of as many diverse stakeholders as possible. This allows the selection and adaptation of materials to be a shared responsibility, thus increasing the potential to use a material more appropriately with diverse populations.

INTERVENTION AND
INSTRUCTION IN PRACTICE: FOUR VIGNETTES

This section returns to the four vignettes introduced in Chapter 9 to discuss the culture bumps that practitioners are likely to encounter when implementing interventions and instructional practices. The components of Skilled Dialogue are explored to illustrate practices that might support the implementation of effective interventions. Again, each vignette is purposely "unfinished." Questions are provided at the end of each vignette to help practitioners consider potential next steps for working with the child and family.

Xee[1]

After Xee's assessment was completed, Mr. Ly requested that Xee be enrolled in a morning ECSE preschool and in an afternoon Head Start program. The team immediately realized that it was critical to review all relevant assessment information about Xee's environment and language development in order to plan effective instruction. The team decided to return to the completed Cultural Data Table and RLP Profile (see Figures 9.1 and 9.2 in Chapter 9). From this information, the team developed an Instructional Cultural Linguistic Response Plan to support intervention planning (see Figure 10.2).

The practitioners ascertained Xee's communicative-linguistic data from the initial assessment information. It was determined that Xee lives in a Hmong-English home environment, with Hmong as the dominant language. Yet, family observations and interviews revealed that Xee's older siblings often speak English when their mother is not present. Xee's RLP Profile showed that receptive and expressive language were very limited in Hmong and English. Her receptive and expressive skills in English were roughly the same. Nonetheless, the information gathered did reveal that Xee is partially bilingual.

The presence of a language other than English alerted the team that bilingual instructional strategies needed to be considered for Xee. Before they engaged in any detailed intervention planning, the Head Start teachers and the ECSE preschool teachers worked with the family to develop as ample an understanding as possible of the communication environment in Xee's home. The teaching staff were concerned about Xee's ability to handle verbal instructions and classroom interactions because none of them were fluent in Hmong. Having worked with other Hmong children and families in the community, some team members had developed their forestructures sufficiently to realize that nonverbal communication rules in Xee's home and in the classroom could be different.

Mr. Ly clearly expressed that he believed English was critical to Xee's participation in school and the larger community. The teachers determined through additional family interviews that the primary language used outside the home was English; however, the family considers speaking and understanding Hmong important for communication within the family and with other Hmong speakers.

---

[1]*Source:* Pennsylvania Department of Education (1994).

Instructional Cultural Linguistic Response Plan

Child/family: _Xee Ly_

Date: _July 12, 2010_   Completed by: _R. Corso and I. Barrera_

Specific Intervention and Instruction Considerations

RE: *Language and communication differences*

Determine how the language and communication styles used in a Xee's home can overlap with the language and communication style used in the early childhood special education (ECSE) and Head Start settings.

In both of the early childhood settings, consider using a modified single language approach, which will rely primarily on English as the language of instruction, but is supported with the use of Hmong.

Allow Xee to initially experience "low-demand" situations that allow time for her to adjust to the new early childhood settings.

Work with the ECSE and Head Start staff to support all of Xee's communication attempts, and avoid correcting any errors in Xee's communication efforts.

RE: *Teaching and learning strategies*

Use modeling and other indirect teaching strategies as much as possible as these seem to be the preferred strategies for acquiring new knowledge in Xee's home.

Support the oral-based emphasis of the Ly family in presenting new information.

Maintain a stable classroom routine that will help Xee predict and feel safe in the new early childhood settings.

Support the Ly family's continued use of both Hmong and English at home.

RE: *Instructional content*

Ensure that all children in the ECSE and Head Start settings experience a variety of languages in the early childhood environments.

Allow Xee frequent opportunities to share information about her feelings or experiences in either Hmong or English.

Provide regular and ongoing assessment of Xee's learning based on the different teaching styles and approaches.

RE: *Teaching and learning materials*

Utilize materials that reflect the characteristics and background of Xee's family.

Consider how current materials can be adapted to include the beliefs and practices of Xee's family.

Find materials in Hmong and English that allow the family to support the intervention strategies used in the ECSE and Head Start settings.

Skilled Dialogue Reminders

	Choosing Relationship over Control/ Anchored Understanding of Diversity	Setting the Stage for Miracles/ 3rd Space
Respect	**Welcoming** range and validity of diverse perspectives	**Allowing** the tension of differing perspectives
Reciprocity	**Making sense** of diverse perspectives	**Appreciating** the strengths of diverse perspectives
Responsiveness	**Joining** across diverse perspectives	**Harmonizing** diverse perspectives so as to integrate and gain access to complementary strengths

Figure 10.2. Xee's Instructional Cultural Linguistic Response Plan.

Xee's family did not have a long association with either the Head Start program or the ECSE preschool, so only a small amount of personal data was initially available. Therefore, Xee's team gathered additional information through some informal observations and interviews with family members. In addition, the team gathered information from the cultural mediator that was found through Xee's church.

Overall, the Ly family had a moderate level of acculturation to ENC. Mr. Ly was the first family member to acquire any degree of familiarity with ENC. Neither he nor his wife attended school outside of their country of origin, so their only connection with the U.S. public school system was through their children. Mrs. Ly had maintained her original way of life and beliefs to a large extent.

Family observations and interviews taken during a 4-week period revealed that some of the team's initial assumptions were more accurate than others regarding family members' understanding of sense of self, perceptions of identity and competence, and roles and rules associated with parenting and child rearing. The family members did consider themselves minorities relative to the larger culture of ENC. Because of the large Hmong population in their community, however, their sense of identity was not significantly affected by this feeling of minority status. The team initially believed that the family strongly valued interdependence. Yet, during the family interviews, Mr. Ly expressed a desire for Xee to begin assuming greater responsibility for her own behaviors, personal-social skills, and self-help skills. Xee's parents repeatedly discussed that their primary ties and responsibilities were to their children, and their role was to make sure that the children "listen and obey."

The team realized the need for cognitive data beyond what was collected during the initial assessment. This data was especially important to the preschool practitioners, who wanted to plan and implement instructional strategies that supported the family's funds of knowledge (i.e., the skills and knowledge that they bring to early intervention/ECSE environments) and the teaching and learning strategies modeled in Xee's home.

In their work with the early childhood education team, Xee's family tended to discuss as their priorities the cognitive knowledge and skills typically valued in ENC environments. Inside the family's household, however, the team noted that the social skills were highly valued. For instance, the children were expected to support their immediate and extended families above all else and to follow traditional Hmong beliefs about social and familial order. Modeling was the preferred strategy for acquiring new knowledge, as Mrs. Ly seemed to rely more on indirect teaching strategies. It was clear from interviews with family members that Mr. Ly was responsible for all decisions outside of the home, whereas Mrs. Ly was the primary decision maker for issues that affected child rearing within the home.

The family's worldviews differed across family members. Mrs. Ly and the two younger siblings had worldviews that reflected more traditional Hmong beliefs. Mr. Ly and the older siblings tended to have worldviews that reflected both ENC and Hmong beliefs. For example, although Mr. Ly wanted Xee and her siblings to follow the Hmong social and family order and responsibilities, he also wanted them to learn English and succeed academically at school and within ENC.

As the teachers planned their initial instruction strategy, they realized that the best course of action was to build rapport with Xee and to let Xee get comfortable in her new environments. Although the language of instruction would be primarily English, the team included some children's stories written in Hmong. The team decided to ensure that Xee was not initially put into situations in which her language delays would increase her anxiety. The teachers would combine verbal and nonverbal strategies to the maximum extent possible to help Xee negotiate the classroom. In addition, special attention would be given to ensure that they responded immediately to any of Xee's communication efforts.

QUESTIONS FOR REFLECTION

1. Review Xee's Cultural Data Table. Which learning strategies might be important to incorporate?

2. Given the family's level of acculturation, do you anticipate some culture bumps once intervention begins? What might they be?

3. What strategies could be used to ensure that Hmong is included in Xee's early childhood environments?

Amad

As noted in Chapter 9, Amad is a 4-year-old African American boy with the diagnosis of mild-to-moderate autism. Amad's mother, Regina, and grandmother, Doretha, expressed concern that members of the interdisciplinary team were more interested in Amad's "school learning" than his happiness. Regina and Doretha want to ensure that Amad has friends and is prepared to interact with people in his community. They want to hear how the ECSE program would nurture his socioemotional development.

Working with Amad during the ensuing year gave the ECSE team members numerous opportunities to enhance their understanding of the family's goals and cultural values. Regina and Doretha were very involved in implementing the team's intervention strategies. They also were instrumental in helping the team gather information about Amad's receptive and expressive language in English and his social functioning. Similar to many young children with autism, Amad had a much higher level of expressive language than receptive language. This led to many concerns about Amad's ability to follow verbal instructions. Amad had great difficulty communicating with his teachers and other children in the early childhood program. The team did not believe much understanding existed between Amad's family and the practitioners, despite the family–program staff interactions and increased awareness about Amad's learning styles.

This vignette illustrates how the principles and strategies of Skilled Dialogue come into play when planning interventions with specific children and families. As discussed in Chapter 9, members of Amad's ECSE team recognized that they were likely experiencing some culture bumps. These bumps had generated confusion and frustration between the team and Amad's family. Using the Cultural Data Table in Chapter 8 (Figure 8.4), they realized that the practitioners recognized the need to find 3rd Space so that the family's intervention goals could be integrated with and complement the team's academic goals.

The early childhood education staff engaged in the process of Skilled Dialogue to craft respectful, reciprocal, and responsive interactions with Regina and Doretha. To anchor their understanding of Amad's family, they built in time for more informal conversation and worked to establish interactions that allowed equal voice for all perspectives. The practitioners worked to communicate respect and understanding of the family's perspective. The team also revisited the questions about culture bumps and decided to review several questions with Regina and Doretha. The team members decided to explore the question, "How is autonomy defined by the family, and to what degree is it valued?" to improve their understanding of the family's "sense of self." In addition, the team believed that it was important to gather more information to answer, "How do the family members like to define themselves (e.g., by ethnic, professional, or other labels)?" Specifically, the team believed a key area of understanding that they needed to develop was related to, "What characteristics denote competence for Amad's family?" The ECSE team was beginning to think appropriately about the skills and definitions that led to competence in Amad's family and community.

QUESTIONS FOR REFLECTION

1. What do you think are some of the key challenges in this case?

2. What strategies could you use to develop AUD regarding Amad's family?

3. Which of this chapter's strategies and suggested responses would best integrate the family's concerns with the ECSE team's concerns during intervention planning?

Abrish[2]

Abrish's family recently immigrated from Hungary and lives in a small community in central Pennsylvania. Abrish attends a community child care center a few mornings each week but is reserved and makes few communicative attempts with anyone other than his parents. His mother and his caregiver have noticed that Abrish has difficulty initiating communication or responding to directions and is fearful in new situations. Abrish's mother called the local early interven-

---

[2]*Source:* Pennsylvania Department of Education (1994).

tion agency because she was concerned about Abrish's development. Abrish was 2 years old when he started receiving early intervention services.

Abrish's assessment results indicated age-appropriate cognitive skills, problem-solving skills, and adaptive skills. The results also showed developmental delays in expressive and receptive language development in both English and Hungarian, as well as in social skill development. As part of the assessment process, the team completed a Cultural Data Table, an RLP Profile, and an Assessment Cultural Linguistic Response Plan (see Appendix A for blank versions of these forms).

Prior to initiating any long-term instructional strategies, the early intervention developmental specialist and the SLP observed Abrish's interactions with peers at his child care program. Abrish was hesitant to interact with other children and unfamiliar adults, but his social skills were otherwise age appropriate. From the assessment, Abrish's language and general communication skills were found to be mildly delayed (see Chapter 9). A particularly important finding was that his auditory comprehension and basic concept skills appeared to be age appropriate.

Despite the efforts to gather complete assessment information, the early intervention team decided that more information was needed to determine Abrish's language use patterns. This would assist the team to decide on the best format for instruction. In addition, the team wanted to review the early childhood environment to recommend how to create a physically and emotionally safe environment for Abrish—one that would allow him to explore his environment at his own pace and in his own way.

Abrish's "silent period" lasted for several weeks, but the early intervention team worked with his child care staff to find ways for him to interact verbally and nonverbally. Similarly, the practitioners discussed ways to ensure a consistent classroom routine. This would support Abrish in managing the early childhood environment more easily so he could concentrate on the communication in his environment. Although Abrish's child care program was primarily monolingual (English), the team encouraged his family to continue using the language (generally Hungarian) with which they were most comfortable at home. The team understood the importance of a child's home language and language's relationship to a child's self-identity and self-esteem.

QUESTIONS FOR REFLECTION

1. Contrast Abrish's culture with ECSE culture. In which areas might major culture bumps occur?

2. Which of the strategies in this chapter might be responsive to the culture bumps you identified?

3. How could you help Abrish's mother develop Hungarian language skills at home so that existing funds of knowledge could be tapped and general language skills strengthened?

Peter

Peter's parents moved from Mexico to the United States shortly before Peter's birth. His father, Nelson, is a farm worker during the day and a janitor at night. Nelson has learned some English through his work but speaks Spanish to his wife, Yolanda, whose English is very limited. To make extra money, Yolanda provides child care for neighborhood children. Caring for Peter's 4-month-old sister, Maria, makes it difficult for Yolanda to keep appointments with practitioners.

Peter, now 4 years old, has a history of chronic ear infections but has received limited medical care. He demonstrates very limited speech—speaking to others only when he needs something. Yolanda has credited his limited speech to shyness and insisted that nothing is "wrong" with her child. Peter's case manager, Milagros, is fluent in Spanish and assisted during the assessment. Once the assessment was completed, Peter was diagnosed with a moderate hearing impairment.

Despite Milagros' presence at meetings, Yolanda had great difficulty sharing information about interventions for Peter's condition with Nelson. Although Milagros tried to explain the technical terms used by the audiologist at the clinic, Yolanda requested written information in Spanish that she could take home. The medical team discussed the possibility of tubes for Peter's ears or—even more confusing to Yolanda—cochlear implants. Yolanda felt frustrated by the team's focus on Peter's problems and deficits. She wondered if they saw Peter as she saw him.

Milagros was aware that some culture bumps were present and decided that Skilled Dialogue might help determine the degree to which they were caused by cultural linguistic differences between Peter's family and the clinic staff. During the assessment process, Milagros worked with the clinic team to complete a Cultural Data Table, an RLP Profile, and a Cultural Linguistic Response Plan. As the discussion moved to planning intervention, Milagros encouraged the team to develop an Instructional Cultural Linguistic Response Plan. Milagros searched for materials in Spanish that might help explain the medical procedures to Yolanda and Nelson. Unfortunately, all of the materials available at the clinic were only available in English.

Milagros searched the Internet for materials that explained these procedures in Spanish. She found several web sites with material that looked appropriate. Before she gave them to Peter's family, however, she reviewed the materials. In her review, Milagros noticed several points in which the implicit values of the material might conflict with the family's values.

QUESTIONS FOR REFLECTION

1. Where might Milagros have found resources to share with Peter's family? Identify specific web sites and other resources in your community.

2. Which issues might Milagros have considered before selecting materials to share with Yolanda and Nelson? (See the CLAS Institute web site at http://clas.uiuc.edu)

3. What special issues should Milagros consider when selecting materials that have been translated into Spanish from another language?

4. After selecting materials to share, what should Milagros consider when using this material with Peter's family?

CONCLUSION

Several vignettes have been used in this chapter to illustrate some of the most common dilemmas that stem from culture bumps related to intervention and instruction. Suggested responses to the dilemmas posed by these culture bumps have been offered to show how practitioners can develop strategies that embrace children's and families' culturally based strengths. In addition, the chapter provided an Instructional Cultural Linguistic Response Plan that is designated to support practitioners' consideration of potential intervention and instruction issues. Practitioners will greatly improve their ability to enhance intervention and instruction for the children and families they serve as they become more comfortable using these processes and more skilled in the practices of anchoring their understanding of families and creating 3rd Space.

Issues of
Culture and Trauma

This chapter strives to integrate two areas of literature whose relationship has received little attention within the early childhood field. The authors realize they risk being misinterpreted when connecting discussions of cultural diversity and trauma. Nevertheless, it is important to raise these issues if practitioners are to truly develop Skilled Dialogue and act in the best interests of the children and families with whom they work.

As discussed in this book, there are many challenges to understanding cultural diversity and developing Skilled Dialogue. The sociodemographic backgrounds of children in early childhood and ECSE settings are typically complex. Multiple experiences have already shaped these children's view of the world and themselves, including cultural diversity. Traumatic and stressful experiences also have profoundly altered the lives of many of these children. The prevalence and impact of trauma and stress are so significant that practitioners must consider these issues in any discussion designed to broaden understanding of the communication and interaction styles of children and their families. All efforts to develop respectful, reciprocal, and responsive interactions may be unsuccessful if trauma or prolonged stress is ignored or not sufficiently identified. Judgments and assumptions about individuals can be further complicated by the fact that trauma may be hidden or well disguised—sometimes even repressed beyond conscious awareness. Therefore, practitioners cannot assume that cultural diversity is the only issue that impedes establishing respect, reciprocity, and responsiveness when developing the necessary skills for cultural competency.

Much of the material in this chapter draws from years of work with culturally diverse individuals and families in a clinical mental health setting. Without changing the intent of the discussion, details of the vignettes have been altered for confidentiality. The observations and interpretations are based on professional experiences as well as many hours of training and applying research-based material. Unless cited specifically, these observations and interpretations are presented as a professional point of view and may or may not be supported by research in the field of trauma and extreme stress.

Trauma can be a life-altering experience that generates a unique world-view, along with a set of beliefs and values that may equal or exceed cultural diversity in causing discord in interactions. The discussion that follows is designed to contribute more insight into this complex interrelationship. It is meant to sensitize early childhood and ECSE practitioners, as well as other related professionals, to the overlapping issues of trauma and cultural diversity. It is in no way a definitive or comprehensive treatise of these interrelated topics. Most important, this information is not intended to prepare practitioners to identify or diagnose trauma as a mental health or psychiatric condition in this or any other context.

TRAUMA DEFINED

Deskin and Steckler explained *trauma* as

> An injury to the physical or psychological well-being of an individual or group. It means that the individual or group has been hurt or upset to the degree that the way they function, either mentally, emotionally or physically, or any combination of these, is severely affected. (1996, p. 6)

Much of what is known and researched about trauma pertains to adults. The impact of traumatic experiences or maltreatment on children is often minimized or ignored, despite the fact that, as a group, they are some of the most numerous, vulnerable, and voiceless victims. In fact, although the average person can frequently identify an animal that has been traumatized by its aggressive or fearful behavior, many times, traumatized children are not identified before they end up in prisons, psychiatric hospitals, or the grave.

In adults, traumatic experiences shatter basic assumptions about self, others, and/or the world. In children, early experiences such as cruelty, physical or sexual abuse, witnessing domestic or community violence, deprivation, and loss will inevitably define the adult by shaping and scarring the developing brain.

Trauma may refer to the event itself or to the event's sequelae (i.e., after-effects). It also may relate to a single occurrence of extreme stress or to multiple stressful events that can break down the functioning of an individual, a community, or a society.

Incidents such as being in a car accident or witnessing a crime may cause an acute stress reaction that is characterized by shock and temporary disruption in thought, feeling, and behavior. If there is no opportunity to process the trauma sufficiently when it occurs (e.g., to discuss with a trusted adult), then a delayed stress reaction may surface unexpectedly sometime after the trauma. Certain factors must be in place to process trauma adequately—the ability and the opportunity to express one's thoughts and feelings (catharsis), ample time to deal with these thoughts and feelings, and a validating environment. A very young child who experiences trauma lacks the verbal skills to express the associated thoughts and feelings, although art and play therapies may offer some preliminary opportunities. A woman who gives birth to her first child in a difficult delivery and then learns that her mother has died in a car accident the next day does not have time to deal with her mother's death. A young child who lives in an invalidating environment and begins to disclose details of abuse by a relative may be blamed for the abuse or not believed at all. A delayed stress response is almost inevitable when these types of situations occur. A child who experiences verbal or physical abuse by others who are intolerant of the child's cultural or ethnic identity also may encounter disbelief, or lack of support or empathy, especially outside the home. These relational injuries may further alienate and isolate a child who is vulnerable, disrupting normal emotional, behavioral, cognitive, social, and physical development. Though outwardly distinct, all of these situations can be traumatizing.

A single overwhelming, encapsulated experience as well as prolonged and repeated exposure to extreme stress or traumatic events can both result in a range of neuropsychiatric disorders (e.g., posttraumatic stress disorder [PTSD], dissociative disorder and attachment disorder) in the developing brains of children. These early experiences will become the template that defines the same adult many years later.

An individual with PTSD repeatedly recalls and reexperiences the trauma, perhaps throughout his or her life. "Normal" homeostasis (a baseline state of calm) may never be fully restored. Traits such as cognitive inflexibility, which makes it difficult to broaden or shift perspective, may be related to the freeze response in childhood, often leading to rigid and compulsive maladaptive behaviors such as aggression, addictions, and personality disorders in adults. The impact of a traumatic event is directly related to the individual's perception of the severity of the threat and risk of harm, sense of personal responsibility (i.e., blaming self for having been victimized), opportunities for escape, and feelings of helplessness, often caused by the disparity in power between the young victim and the perpetrator. Experience in adults alters the organized brain, but it organizes the developing brain in infants and children (Perry, 1994). In adults, new experiences have only a small component of new information and small portions of the brain are activated, superimposed on previous memories. In children, the total brain response triggered by trauma creates a harmful cocktail of core narrative, emotional, motor, and physiologic state memories, resulting in trauma-related neuropsychiatric signs and symptoms (Perry & Pollard, 1998).

The developmental stage of the child also dictates the severity of the response to traumatic or overwhelming stress. Very young children are totally dependent, nonverbal, and unable to escape or fight a dangerous situation, chronic maltreatment, or neglect. They are also particularly vulnerable to the effects of trauma because they lack the cognitive and emotional maturity to perceive and process these events accurately. The "magical thinking" and egocentricity of young children, as well as their tendency to idealize adults, form a collage of distorted perceptions and feelings that often persists into adulthood. Although young children may misperceive and misinterpret traumatic events, casting doubt on the validity of certain abuse allegations, some type of trauma probably has occurred in most cases. The exact details of the event, however, are subject to distortion and inaccuracy when reported by very young children who have been repeatedly traumatized.

TRAUMA AS A UNIVERSAL, CROSS-CULTURAL EXPERIENCE

Some form of trauma occurs at least once during the life span of most individuals and groups. Electronic, televised, and print media provide almost instantaneous news reports, which results in individuals worldwide witnessing traumatic events on a frequent, almost daily basis. This lessens people's ability to distance themselves from the images of war, terrorism, famine, and natural disasters. Sometimes individuals even witness horrors as they occur (e.g., attacks on and collapse of the World Trade Center towers on September 11, 2001).

Just as all people view the world through the lens of their cultural experiences, trauma also becomes a lens that may distort or impair the life experiences that follow the trauma. Many people agree that the September 11 attacks changed the world. The sense of safety and security of those living in North America probably has never been violated to such a degree in modern history. Not only did individuals experience the trauma of these events, various communities, cultural groups, and societies were affected to some degree as well. Arab Americans and others with a similar physical appearance became targets for discrimination, hatred, and even murder in retaliation for the acts of an extremist Islamic group. An American Muslim who lost a family member in the World Trade Center attacks might have had a much different experience with the trauma and its aftermath than a non-Muslim. This person may have felt cultural shame that significantly affected the grieving process. Although community support and validation existed for those who lost loved ones in this tragedy, this person may have experienced an invalidating environment. In addition, one can almost imagine a classroom of children struggling to make sense of this tragedy, talking about it with their teacher, ignorant of the private suffering—and perhaps even shame—of a student who is a Muslim and an American. Anchored understanding of different experiences with particular events is a critical component of ensuring emotional safety and lessening the sequelae of trauma for all children.

It has been said that "the song sung to the cradle is heard to the grave." In no case is this more true than for the child with stressful or traumatic early life experiences. By the time a child has reached 5 years of age, he or she may have experienced the extreme stress caused by one or more experiences common in modern society—poverty; homelessness; immigration; exposure to neighborhood crime; risk of death or injury; violent or premature death of a family member or friend; family violence; or physical, emotional, verbal, or sexual abuse. Also included are natural disasters, accidents, and vicarious exposure to trauma through family members who survived traumatic events (e.g., the Holocaust, the Vietnam War).

WHEN INVALIDATION OF CULTURE RESULTS IN TRAUMA

In addition to the trauma that anyone from any culture can experience, there is also the trauma that can result from the invalidation of one's worldview, beliefs, and values (i.e., culture). Many children's early life experiences may be traumatic when their cultural linguistic backgrounds differ from those of their peers and educators (e.g., not being able to ask to go to the bathroom in the practitioner's language, not being allowed to speak their home language). Such children may struggle to master developmental tasks in contexts that are not responsive to their cultural linguistic repertoire and, therefore, are confusing and nonsupportive. Differences in language, values, beliefs, and practices pose significant challenges for communication. Children are alienated from others in the environment, including peers and practitioners, when such diversity is not understood or respected.

Children from minority groups, immigrant families, and oppressed cultures (i.e., politically oppressed or persecuted) may experience the social environment as foreign, invalidating, and nonsupportive—sometimes even threatening. They may be shunned or bullied because they are different and do not have the power and status of their peers from ENC. Young children may feel disconnected, ashamed, and guilty for "causing" culture bumps when their interactions with others are not respectful, reciprocal, and responsive to existing differences. They may withdraw and try to blend into the crowd. They may become bullies to protect themselves from further victimization. Some children may retreat into their home culture, refusing to learn new customs and the accompanying language. Others may shun their home culture's language and traditions along with the skills and knowledge that those contain.

Children also may respond by becoming the communication facilitators between their families and the social environment, thrusting them into a role that is developmentally inappropriate (i.e., emotionally dissonant and cognitively premature). They become the adults to their parents, called on to act as translators and family spokespeople at an age when they should have limited responsibility and involvement in adult activities. Out of necessity, they become privy to information about family troubles, finances, and other matters in which younger children should not be involved. This involvement in adult matters can overwhelm and burden children with responsibility they often cannot handle. This role reversal further isolates them from their peers, who are just being children. Furthermore, they often have difficulty with authority figures, including parents and caregivers, who on many other occasions expect compliance with rules that are more age appropriate. These adaptations often are not recognized as inappropriate, much less traumatizing. Nevertheless, they place children who are culturally diverse, especially those with delays or disabilities, at added risk for failure in early childhood settings. Using an adult translator to engage in Skilled Dialogue with families can be invaluable for determining the degree to which such issues are present and exploring ways to reduce their impact.

PROBLEMS IN DIFFERENTIATING TRAUMA AND CULTURAL DIVERSITY

Trauma and cultural diversity often co-occur (e.g., a child of parents who speak a language other than English is sexually abused by a neighbor). Distinguishing their associated issues may become problematic. Many sequelae of individual and societal trauma are strikingly similar to the issues that emerge when cultural diversity is present and not honored, further compounding the complexity of the situations that practitioners must address. The following vignette illustrates how the elements of trauma and cultural diversity need to be understood if respectful, reciprocal, and responsive interactions are to develop.

> *Chantel, an African American woman, lost custody of her children because her chronic drug and alcohol abuse resulted in allegations of neglect. The children were in the care of Caucasian foster parents, and the Child Protective Services (CPS) case manager was also Caucasian. One day, Chantel learned that the foster mother had cut her daughter's hair, and she rushed to her daughter's school despite a court order forbidding contact with the children. The school called the police to have Chantel removed and reported the incident to CPS. The case manager documented the mother's violation of the court order and cited this as another example of Chantel's noncompliance and failure to follow the CPS plan to regain custody of her children.*
>
> *Chantel had been seeing a Caucasian counselor, to whom she reported a personal history of sexual abuse and rape in childhood and adolescence. Further investigation by the counselor revealed issues that may explain Chantel's behavior.*
>
> - *From the moment her children were placed in foster care, Chantel was upset that they had not been placed with an African American family.*
>
> - *Chantel had been chronically concerned about her daughter's hair not being properly braided and conditioned because of the foster mother's lack of understanding of African American hair grooming practices.*
>
> - *Cutting a child's hair in the African American culture, especially without the mother's permission, appeared to be a traumatic violation. Chantel acknowledged somewhat shamefully that in stark contrast to a Caucasian child's hair, her child's hair may take an extremely long time to grow back.*

- *This violation appeared to trigger memories of Chantel's past experiences with sexual violation, resulting in common symptoms of posttraumatic reactions—excessive irritability, rage, and desperate attempts to regain control.*

- *Chantel insisted that she was not going to accept this situation without a fight, saying, "I'm nobody's slave." This statement also recalled another time and carried particular meaning in her culture's history.*

This vignette illustrates how the overt manifestations of trauma can often be confusing and difficult to identify when cultural diversity is also present because there are many similar and overlapping sequelae. Traumatic elements of both personal and cultural history often interweave into a single, apparently seamless tapestry. Without understanding their various strands, responses become only reactions and intentions to be respectful are doomed to failure.

MANIFESTATIONS OF TRAUMA IN CHILDREN

Children who experience prolonged stress or trauma often develop predictable physical and emotional states and patterns of social interaction, as well as a certain cognitive style, which set them apart from their peers and put them at risk for future victimization (van der Kolk et al., 1996). Children who have experienced sexual abuse may internalize lowered perceptions of control and poor coping skills that may incapacitate them when faced with future stressful situations. In trying to effectively resist a coercive experience (as an adult), it seems imperative that the potential victim believes in his or her own ability to change a situation and can utilize adaptive coping strategies in doing so (Walsh, Blaustein, Knight, Spinazzola, & van der Kolk, 2007). In many ways, their baseline funds of knowledge are permanently altered, as in the case of a young adult male who, as a child, was sexually abused by a male relative for many years. He described himself as homosexual but often wondered if the events of his childhood had influenced his sexual orientation and, ultimately, his entire life experience. The losses for some of these children are profound, including the loss of what their lives might have been without the trauma.

Specific manifestations of trauma in children fall into five categories.

1. Social: Children may become withdrawn, avoidant, unable to tolerate being alone, aggressive, clingy, mistrustful, or too trusting. They may isolate themselves, act out, attempt to control and abuse peers, or demand excessive attention.

2. Physical: Children may experience chronic headaches, stomachaches, diarrhea and other somatic complaints, numbness and analgesia (the inability to feel physical pain), sleep disturbance and frequent nightmares, failure to thrive, poor appetite or overeating, or incontinence. They may daydream frequently, appearing dazed or in a trance. Or, they may engage

in self-injury and self-mutilation, repetitive reenactments through play, rituals, and compulsive behaviors.

3. Emotional: Children may be hypervigilant, hypersensitive, irritable, restless, hyperactive, depressed, angry, tearful, anxious, fearful, apathetic, or full of rage. They may also regress, develop new and sometimes irrational fears, act helpless, feel overwhelmed, feel excessive guilt and shame, or feel worthless.

4. Cognitive: Children may exhibit difficulty concentrating and focusing; experience memory lapses; appear confused, lost, or stuck in their thinking; deny or distort reality; live in a fantasy world; or have negative preoccupations.

5. Communication: Many children who have experienced trauma develop a code for telling their stories. They may begin to speak in metaphors with hidden meanings as they become more verbally sophisticated. They may attempt to hide their true feelings by saying that everything is fine, or they may become silent or even mute. Their language is often detached, as they lack words for the overwhelming feelings that they are experiencing. Lack of maturity also may impair children's ability to interpret and talk about traumatic experience. For example, when adults who were sexually abused as children are asked to report the age of their first sexual experience, few reply with the age at which they were sexually abused. Even adults have a hard time comprehending that their first sexual experience occurred at such a young age. Children also may speak negatively about themselves or others to shift the focus from what is really wrong.

In many ways, it seems that these patterns of thinking, feeling, behaving, and communicating form the basis for a disconnection and alienation from peers and other social contacts. This alienation and disconnection can be similar in many ways to the experiences of children from culturally diverse environments when the larger society does not understand or value these environments.

TRAUMA AS A CUMULATIVE EXPERIENCE

The best preparation for a bad experience is a good experience, not a bad experience. Those who function best under extreme stress have had minimal previous negative or stressful experiences and come from environments where they have been able to accumulate a reserve of resources, including self-esteem and effective coping skills. Individuals who have not had prior traumatic experiences are able to think and feel simultaneously and usually react appropriately to stressful situations.

Conversely, those who still carry the sequelae of high-stress, traumatic environments have limited reserves and marginal coping skills. They may even "fall apart" over time. Their thoughts and feelings have become disconnected, and subsequent traumatic experiences or even minor disruptions often immobilize them as they live in a persistent state of fear and hyperreactivity. For example, two individuals encounter a vicious dog during a walk. One of the individuals has been bitten by a dog; the other has not. It might be assumed that the first person would have an advantage in handling the situation because of previous experience. It is more probable, however, that this person would freeze or react foolishly by running or hitting the dog. The person who has never been bitten may be more likely to stop, assess the situation, and perhaps recall previous warnings about what to do in such situations. In other words, the person who was not previously traumatized might be frightened but able to think rationally. Cumulative trauma exposure, therefore, may predispose individuals to evoke ineffective coping responses (van der Kolk et al., 1996).

A high number of individuals and families from oppressed or minority groups have lower socioeconomic status and, as a result, have higher rates of exposure to stress-producing factors. Some of these factors include poor diet, hunger, poor education, exposure to crime, traffic hazards (e.g., playing in the street), unreliable or inadequate transportation, substandard and overcrowded housing, low-paying jobs, unemployment and underemployment, lack of health insurance, limited access to services, untreated or poorly treated health and dental problems, inadequate prenatal care, greater exposure to disease, premature death, higher death rates, and inadequate child care provisions.

These conditions of prolonged stress may adversely affect the physical and mental health of a child and his or her immediate and extended family, neighborhood, community, and cultural or ethnic group for many generations. As a result, a child who experiences a traumatic event, such as the death of a parent or exposure to a violent crime, may be predisposed to greater suffering because of the cumulative trauma, not just the most recent traumatic event. It is no surprise that children are being hospitalized in psychiatric institutions at younger and younger ages as their coping skills become exhausted. Imagine the horror and disbelief at hearing a 5-year-old girl, hospitalized in a children's psychiatric unit, recount her efforts to kill herself by sitting on a swing and twisting its chains around her neck to strangle herself, expressing a desire to die. Although it seems unlikely that a 5-year-old would be developmentally able to fully comprehend the nature and finality of death, this child seemed so bent on her own self-destruction that one can only imagine her previous experiences with death and suffering. "Warrior Child," a poem by Nanci Presley-Holley, eloquently sums up the cumulative effects of years of trauma:

I've never been a soldier
But I know what war is like
Having survived a childhood
Besieged by enemies
More dangerous and insidious
Than those

Armies face with guns
My foes were alcoholism and child abuse

And I was unarmed
I never got just the one-year tour of duty
In some battle torn country
I was there for the duration
From birth to age 18
Escaping like a prisoner of war
Only to be snapped back into the fold
When they'd find out where I lived
Or I broke down and told

Just like a soldier who has no life of his own
I was my family's possession
Theirs to send where they wished
Sometimes to grandma's, an aunt's, an uncle's
When the burden of raising three children
Pushed them to the limit
But it wasn't "rest and relaxation" for me
'Cause no matter where I went
The disease ran rampant
Through my family

"Army issue" was hand me downs
Or poorly made clothes by a woman
Trying to maintain her sanity
'Cause dad had drank what little money there was
Or spent it on some floozy in town

Bedroom inspections were always on Saturday
If everything was perfect
We could go outside for the day
But a comic book out of place or a messy bed
We'd pay dearly
What does a 5 year old really know
About dust and hospital corners?

Normal childhood activities, like play?
Not this child
I was always combat ready
Training myself to survive
I had to be on guard, alert
For the fist in the stomach, a slap upside the head
Because I'd spoken when I was supposed to be quiet
Or asked for something to eat
Or even colored over the lines
I never knew when the flak would hit

There was never any warning
I wished there'd been someone
To scream "incoming."

Nighttime was the worst
But unlike armed camps
There weren't any sentries
Laying in my bed
Hovering between exhaustion and sleep
Listening for the whisper of the intruder
Just in case he crept toward my room
Or waking to find he'd already infiltrated
And was laying on top of me
How could I do anything else
…Except play dead?

My childhood was a war zone
As frightening and devastating as Viet Nam
A battleground of fear
Where discord and conflict were the rule
Once in awhile
When I allow the feelings stored since childhood
To bubble to the surface
I have a hard time keeping them under control
I immediately want to fight or flee
Destroy something
Sometimes
     Even
        Me

(as cited in Middelton-Moz, 1989, pp. 71–73)

The hidden lives of many children come close to the nightmare portrayed in the "Warrior Child." These children become experts at surviving but have no opportunity for thriving. Their coping skills, which are learned in these environments, do not prepare them for a healthy life but, rather, to transmit a distorted view of the world to succeeding generations. Breaking the cycle of trauma becomes an even greater challenge when cultural diversity is present because an equal level of shame, pain, and worthlessness can result from a lack of acceptance of one's culture and identity.

DIFFERING CULTURAL PERSPECTIVES ON CHILD MALTREATMENT

The roles of children can differ dramatically across cultures. In some cultures, children are allowed to express themselves freely; in other cultures, children are given very little freedom of expression. Certain cultures advocate protecting children until they reach maturity while expecting them to behave like adults at a very young age. These norms may change over time and are influenced by factors such as the increasingly influential roles of women; population shifts with immigration; loss of economic status and power from war, unemployment, and natural disasters; or improved economic status. For instance, whether sanctioned by cultural norms or not, children begging in the streets may be the norm for a country in which economic status has declined because of civil war. Slave trafficking and child prostitution become commonplace when children are orphaned as a result of genocide of their caregivers or natural disasters such as tsunamis and earthquakes. It is in these ways that cultures themselves become traumatized and distorted.

Acceptable methods of disciplining children also vary widely among cultures and are subject to change. At one time in North America, the prevailing culture accepted the strap as an acceptable way to administer punishment in public schools. Excessive corporal punishment at home was also accepted by these same cultures (see United Nations, 2006). In the latter part of the 20th century, these practices were designated a form of child abuse subject to both criminal and civil penalties; however, some parents who were raised in these environments still believe that they have the right to discipline their children the same way. Many of these parents have so repressed the trauma of their own abuse that they are shocked when anyone suggests that they are mistreating their children. With therapy, these parents may begin to connect with their own feelings of pain and helplessness, allowing them to see the pain and helplessness in their own children (Miller, 1980; Stettbacher, 1991).

Now imagine what it must be like when a parent from a cultural group that continues to practice harsh discipline immigrates to a society or community where those practices have been outlawed. Such parents can quickly find themselves in serious legal trouble and these parents can also lose custody of their children, perhaps permanently, when CPS and the courts intervene. The dilemmas involved in cultural interpretations of correction/punishment versus abuse, and how those cultural interpretations correspond with state and federal law, pose a significant challenge for all practitioners in our multicultural societies. Fontes (2005) provided practical ideas for making child protection services equitable for families from diverse racial and ethnic backgrounds.

Some cultures practice noninterference when there is a problem within a family. They give primacy to the authority of parents or of only the father in the family. For example, if an American Indian child is being abused at home, then the extended family or clan may find a way to quietly move the child into the home of other family or clan members rather than shame the family in front of the entire community. If the child lives on a reservation and traditional ways have been preserved, then this resolution may be quite successful. If an outside teacher, counselor, or medical professional learns about the abuse, however, then state and federal laws mandate filing a report with the authorities. This policy of interference may result in the child being removed from the home as well as from the American Indian community. Culture bumps regarding intervention in the maltreatment of children occurs frequently, presenting a dilemma for teachers and service providers who must adhere to the law while serving families and children from many different cultures.

SECOND-GENERATION TRAUMA

It is important to note that many traumatic reactions are not the result of direct exposure to trauma. Trauma may be experienced vicariously through the lives of others, even those who are already deceased. These residual emotional reactions are often culture specific. People whose parents and grandparents lived through the Depression still may exhibit residual compulsive behaviors, such as not wasting food and turning out the lights when leaving a room (although there are certainly valid reasons for these behaviors in any time period). Very often, trauma that is experienced vicariously is related to an event that is part of the history of an entire culture. One example of this phenomenon involves descendants of people who experienced the Holocaust firsthand. These people may live under a cloud of unexplained sadness and doom, with a restricted range of feelings (i.e., blunted affect) and a sense of overwhelming shame whenever they make mistakes. At a Vienna outpatient clinic addressing trauma from the Nazi era, Dr. David Vyssoki said that some descendants live in an "oppressive climate of silence" (as cited in Jahn, 2002, p. A24). When the horrors are so unimaginable, sometimes there is no opportunity for catharsis by talking about what happened, and some survivors have no memories because they have completely repressed details of the Holocaust. Their children and grandchildren may never feel that they have permission to have fun and play and are often workaholics as adults. They may describe often feeling "survivor" guilt in their interactions with others, especially with members of their family, knowing that they escaped the hell that others experienced. When they connect these thoughts and behaviors to the past, it is as if their whole life begins to make sense for the first time. Their overreaction to things such as tattoos and the smell of barbeques, never before understood, finally begins to make sense in the context of second-generation trauma.

Another example involves American Indian and First Nation Canadian[1] children whose parents and grandparents were taken from their homes on reservations and sent to boarding schools across the country. These parents and grandparents were often prevented from going home to their families until age 18, and in many cases, their families never knew where they were sent. Sadly, many of these children also suffered emotional, physical, and sexual abuse by the caregivers and teachers who were tasked with indoctrinating them into the "White man's ways." According to Tsianina Lomawaima, head

---

[1]*First Nation Canadian* is a term adopted in the 1970s, referring to the native Indian people in Canada.

of the American Indian Studies program at the University of Arizona, the intent was to completely transform people, inside and out. "Language, religion, family structure, economics, the way you make a living, the way you express emotion, everything," says Lomawaima.

Lomawaima says the government's objective from the start was to "erase and replace" Indian culture, part of a larger strategy to conquer Indians. "They very specifically targeted Native nations that were the most recently hostile," Lomawaima says. "There was a very conscious effort to recruit the children of leaders, and this was also explicit, essentially to hold those children hostage. The idea was it would be much easier to keep those communities pacified with their children held in a school somewhere far away" (Bear, 2008).

Members of succeeding generations frequently experience prolonged depression, high rates of drug and alcohol addiction, and academic and behavior difficulties in school. The shame felt by the previous generations who experienced the trauma is passed on to the children and grandchildren as a secret that is never discussed. Beginning in 1990, newspaper articles and lawsuits describing the horrors of these boarding schools began to expose the hidden traumas of multiple generations of native people (see Mofina, 2001). Because this unspoken burden has remained hidden for decades, the average American or Canadian is most likely unaware of these events and their resulting scars. Practitioners working with American Indian or First Nation Canadian children in any school, whether on or off a reservation, should be aware of this legacy whenever home–school cooperation problems arise.

Frequently, a child who experiences trauma has a caregiver who was also traumatized as a child. This "double-jeopardy" situation requires the child to compete with the caregiver for limited resources to deal with the sequelae of trauma. The child almost always loses out. A caregiver whose own childhood was affected by trauma may be totally unavailable to the child, instead struggling with his or her own feelings of shame, anger, and low self-esteem. In addition, if the family lives in a high-stress environment where daily living is a struggle and danger lurks at every corner, then the child has little hope of finding a "good enough" stable, relational environment for recovery from current trauma and stress. Some practitioners also may struggle with their own traumas. If they do not address their own issues, then these practitioners may

- Fail to discern and respond to the child's distress

- Be insensitive to serious symptoms exhibited by the child, dismissing them as "normal"

- Avoid any discussions or experiences that might evoke memories of their own traumas, resulting in pressure to forget or "get over" the experience

- Rationalize that the child is too young to remember what happened or resilient enough to overcome the trauma without intervention

- Misinterpret aggression, especially in boys

- Fail to sense danger or intervene in dangerous situations

- Blame the child for what happened or excuse the adult

- Become so distraught that the child must tend to the adult's needs

- Focus on dangers or distractions outside instead of inside the home

- Force the child to suppress his or her feelings and "grow up"

- Create an environment of constant crisis and chaos that mimics the home environment

It is important to be aware of the potential for multigenerational trauma when dealing with the parents and families of children who have experienced trauma. Many children who are sexually abused have a parent who was also sexually abused as a child and may be unable to protect the child or recognize danger. This occurs because of the tendency to repress or deny traumatic information. For example, a woman who was sexually abused by her father may leave her children in her parents' care without making the connection that her children also could be abused. Assuming that this mother would know better than to leave her children in the care of a known perpetrator amounts to a cognitive error—that is, a way of thinking based on a faulty belief system that is designed to protect one's view of the world. Practitioners who have experienced sexual abuse are more likely to make cognitive errors. They may believe that perpetrators would never repeat their crimes, especially if caught or confronted, but there is no known cure for such behavior and perpetrators often abuse multiple children (Lanning, 1992). Practitioners who have dealt successfully with their own traumas are much less likely to make cognitive errors and can show great sensitivity toward these children because of their own experiences.

CULTURAL DIFFERENCES IN HELP-SEEKING BEHAVIORS

Once a practitioner has identified that trauma or extreme stress and cultural diversity are co-occurring issues, the next step is to begin formulating appropriate intervention strategies. Intervention must account for many variables, including subjective, wide-ranging reports of well-being and various help-seeking behaviors. There is no single cross-cultural approach to dealing with problems and seeking solutions. ENC coping strategies are not universally endorsed by all cultures. Both help-seeking behaviors and ways of disclosing problems are rooted in one's culture. The self-help movement has attracted mostly Caucasian, middle-class individuals who have become experts themselves on a variety of trauma-related issues (e.g., codependency, recovery). This new culture of help-seekers has spawned an explosion of print media and talk shows to support efforts to resolve childhood trauma. This "Oprah effect," however, may not have permeated the consciousness of many individuals and groups outside of the mainstream, culturally and linguistically. Conversely, individuals from minority cultures can be overrepresented in community mental health programs. These programs primarily serve individuals with low socioeconomic status or with chronic mental illness, as well as those whose treatment has been mandated by courts, probation, CPS, or the Department of Social Services. The overrepresentation of minority cultures in these programs is not a function of culturally based help-seeking behavior. In reality, minority status frequently correlates with low socioeconomic status and limited access to care. Sadly, individuals, as well as entire groups, may be labeled as having negative help-seeking behavior when these issues are misinterpreted or confused.

Suppression and/or denial of stress may be a function of an individual's mental illness as well as a coping strategy of a person who is oppressed. These two issues are frequently confused, and an individual may be labeled as resistant, manipulative, noncompliant, or controlling when the cultural aspects of self-disclosure are not considered. Members of various cultural groups may perceive self-disclosure as unsafe or as a sign of giving up control and independence; therefore, the tendency toward nondisclosure may limit help-seeking behaviors. Admission of a problem may be perceived as an acknowledgement of weakness in some cultures, which could lead to more vulnerability, oppression, or victimization (Neighbors & Jackson, 1996).

Fear of outside authorities may also affect help-seeking behavior. An African American mother with limited financial resources may be less likely to request help when she cannot take care of her children, knowing that she may risk losing custody of them. Conversely, a Caucasian middle-class mother facing similar circumstances may be more aggressive about seeking help, knowing that the risks of losing custody of her children are much smaller. Furthermore, there is an inherent (and experience-based) mistrust of agencies and helping professionals among many cultures. Those with limited resources and less sophistication in dealing with "the system" are frequently treated poorly or unfairly, whereas those with a greater degree of education, money, and access to legal aid have a distinct advantage. Justice is seldom blind for those who are disadvantaged and oppressed.

Laws against illegal immigrants in some states have triggered justified fears of deportation, and help-seeking from agencies or authorities has been curtailed significantly. As a result, any troublesome behavior or victimization involving a child is much less likely to be addressed and may even be hidden to avoid risk of deportation. Immigrant families, already experiencing high levels of stress, often cope by moving to other states away from the few supports that have helped to ease the trauma of illegal immigration.

Many variables appear to predict the extent to which stress is denied as well as preferred types of help-seeking behaviors. Social status (income, education, access to resources and third-party insurance), social roles (gender, age, personal competence), and group identification (social supports, extended family, religious affiliation, cultural affiliation) seem to play significant roles in determining which individuals are likely to disclose problems and seek help voluntarily. Preference for specific helpers is also determined as much by prior individual experiences as by the experiences and beliefs of one's entire culture. Members of some groups (e.g., ENC) tend to seek outside professional help. Other individuals have been socialized to request help from nonprofessionals such as extended family, friends, and church or community healers (Neighbors & Jackson, 1996).

When children and families are in crisis, it is important to understand the normative help-seeking behaviors for their culture before drawing conclusions about their level of dysfunction or planning interventions. It is also important to understand that culturally based help-seeking behaviors that functioned well when a culture was intact often become ineffective or inadequate when individuals are displaced or relocate beyond the boundaries of their original culture. As shown in the following vignette, this frequently occurs when families immigrate to a new country and find that their new environment does not support their traditional help-seeking behaviors.

Rosa, a Hispanic woman in her mid-30s, had been having thoughts of suicide, so she called the county crisis line. She was referred to a mental health crisis center for psychiatric assessment. Upon her arrival at the center, staff quickly determined that Rosa was a native of another country who spoke little English. A male mental health worker was also present to translate because the center's evaluator did not speak Spanish. Rosa had to sign numerous forms to complete the evaluation, none of which were written in Spanish. She appeared anxious and hesitant, stating through the translator that she wanted to leave because no one was home to care for her four children, ages 2–10 years. The evaluator determined that Rosa had been very depressed since her husband's illness and death a year earlier.

Rosa was very guarded in her responses throughout the interview, but several inconsistencies emerged. The evaluator noted that Rosa began responding to questions before the translator finished the translation. The evaluator questioned this, and Rosa eventually responded in fluent English. She admitted that she had been living in the United States since she was a teenager and was not a legal immigrant. Several family members resided in the United States while others, including her father, remained in Rosa's native country. She acknowledged a previous suicide attempt in adolescence while living in her native country, but she never sought help, nor did she disclose this to her family. Rosa finally admitted that her father, as well as several male relatives, had sexually abused her. She stated that her mother knew what had happened but they never talked about it. Rosa believed that the move to the United States may have been an attempt to remove her and her siblings from the abuse and agreed that this might explain why her father never joined the family in the United States. She was shocked when asked if the abuse had ever been reported to the authorities in her native country; she believed that the police would then abuse her, too. When asked whether she thought some of her emotional distress was connected to the abuse, Rosa agreed that it might be possible. She said that she currently felt overwhelmed by grief re-

garding her husband's death and did not understand why she could not just "get over it" as her mother and aunts advised.

Rosa admitted that she was having trouble going to work because of her depression and because her family members refused to watch her children while she was at work. When asked for more information about her job, Rosa admitted that she worked for an escort service, which was why her family did not support her job. Rosa found that she could make a lot of money at this job, however, even though she did not have papers to work legally in the country. In addition, the flexibility of her hours allowed her to spend more time with her children. Rosa then noted that her children were becoming defiant and unmanageable at school, adding to her stress. She also stated that her children could not receive any survivors' benefits from Social Security because her husband never worked legally in the United States. She had no health or disability insurance and would probably qualify for little financial assistance for mental health services or prescription medications. When Rosa was encouraged to apply for legal resident status in the United States, she said that she did not want to take chances on being deported or losing the house that she had purchased.

Several conclusions can be drawn from this example. Rosa's initial refusal to speak English and her refusal to consider becoming a legal resident indicated her distrust of "the system." She did not see herself as the traditional U.S. worker with a need for benefits and security for herself and her children. This worldview limited her access to services and resources in the United States.

Rosa's sociocultural background also did not support utilizing outside professional resources to solve problems, as demonstrated by her family's recommendation that she "just get over it." Rosa even appeared to believe that seeking help from professionals is dangerous, based on her beliefs about the police in her native country. Members of the U.S. psychiatric community would suggest that Rosa was moderately depressed and possibly needed medication to stabilize her moods. Based on her past history, she was at risk for another suicide attempt and possibly death.

Rosa did not view her job, working for an escort service, as a reenactment of her sexual abuse trauma, which was likely preventing her from addressing her grief. Not only was she minimizing her trauma to others but also to herself. She never had an opportunity for catharsis because she had not talked about the trauma and the environment was very invalidating. Many immigrants believe that they have left their traumas behind, but the "geographical cure" rarely lessens the sequelae.

Rosa's coping skills and help-seeking behaviors were severely compromised by her illegal immigrant status, the stigma of her chosen profession, and unresolved trauma issues. She was beginning to see problems with her children but probably did not realize just how unavailable she was to them because of her own grief and her broken-down family support system. Her cultural beliefs made it unlikely that she would seek outside help from professionals for herself and the children. In addition, it is possible that she would not recognize if her children were in dangerous situations and would not report suspected abuse to the authorities. The prognosis was not hopeful for Rosa's successful resolution of her mental health issues and her children's challenging behavior.

It is likely that Rosa's children would begin to experience emotional problems and receive little support from their mother or her extended family. In a classroom, practitioners would probably have only limited information about the extensive trauma issues that so clearly influenced the mother's coping skills and help-seeking behaviors. Engaging her in getting help for her children, if needed, would at least require a basic understanding of the interplay of cultural diversity and trauma issues.

CULTURE AS A PROTECTIVE FACTOR

Culture provides a structure for normalizing experiences, renders life predictable, and defines rules for emotional expression and grieving. Without this structure, the individual and the family may become more vulnerable to the effects of extreme stress and trauma. Unfortunately, some cultures and societies, especially those in the Third World, seem more prone to such experiences as a result of ongoing civil wars and limited resources to recover from natural disasters. An entire culture may be severely disrupted or even devastated to the point that recovery seems impossible when such catastrophic events occur. One must begin to consider the following questions when examining the aftermath of such events (deVries, 1996).

- When a culture is intact, does it protect against the effects of stress and trauma?

- What happens to individuals and families when the culture has been disrupted or destroyed?

- What happens to individuals and families who become separated from their culture?

- How are these issues relevant for early childhood and ECSE providers in the classroom?

Almost every classroom in North America has children whose families have experienced some disruption in their culture as a result of immigration or relocation (Igoa, 1995). Catastrophic events elsewhere in the world often result in an influx of immigrants to North America, who are seeking sanctuary for themselves and their families. Many others come looking for a better life and the "American Dream." American Indians were forced to relocate to reservations far from their established homelands and support structures. Individuals and families who immigrate or relocate outside their culture often must rely on themselves to survive. Without the bond to their culture, there may be no mechanism to stabilize and restore functioning, especially when the events precipitating the immigration or relocation were extremely traumatic, perhaps even catastrophic.

Many factors protect individuals and families with a strong cultural affiliation from disintegration in times of extreme stress: norms and beliefs, rituals, social roles, prescribed tasks during the life cycle, stories, legends, ceremonies, concepts of emotional illness, a religious context that involves a belief in a higher power or a spiritual realm, rules for grieving, the support and involvement of extended family, and a medical treatment system. Many children from first-generation immigrant families come to school with these protective factors disrupted or distorted, thereby reducing the children's ability to adjust to their adopted culture. As a result, children may exhibit emotional problems and challenging behavior, and the family may be unable to cope without resorting to maladaptive responses. This situation is illustrated in the following vignette.

Anna and Jacob were well-educated professionals who had considerable professional status in their homeland and adequate financial resources despite the overall poverty in their country. Regardless of their success, they believed that the future was bleak for their two children in their native country. Jacob remained there, working to provide for his family, but Anna and their children immigrated to the United States. Anna was pregnant and determined to give birth to the child in the United States even though she was not a legal resident. Jacob, reluctant to give up his job because he would have to learn English to work in his profession in the United States, was not present for the birth of their son. After 2 years, however, he eventually joined Anna. When the family's money ran out, Anna took a job that would allow her to obtain legal U.S. residency. Anna's employer promised to pay back wages as soon as she received her Social Security number but did not follow through. Thus, Anna was forced to work in a factory and clean houses to feed her family. During this time, Jacob refused to work, became increasingly depressed, and started drinking heavily. He said that he was too old to learn English, and he did not help with the children even though he was home all day. Jacob often got so frustrated that he screamed at the children, occasionally hitting them with a belt to get them to behave. Anna gave him an ultimatum: get a job or leave the family. Jacob finally got a menial job, and the oldest child, age 17, took over most of the family child care responsibilities. The youngest child, 8-year-old Joseph, was beginning to show signs of emotional disturbance, including hyperactivity, aggression toward his parents, oppositional and defiant behavior, and outbursts of rage. Anna told Joseph's teacher that she could no longer manage his behavior. She also explained that her only support in the United States was her husband, who left all of the disciplining to her and often undermined her authority by indulging Joseph despite his behavior. Anna had not established any relationships in her new community with people from her culture. Although she stated that she was very proud of her culture, Anna did not encourage Joseph or her other children to participate in it or use its language.

This vignette demonstrates how cultural disconnection can result in individual and familial breakdown. Without familiar resources to restore functioning, the family members resorted to ineffective coping skills (e.g., excessive drinking, withdrawal, violence, neglect). A teacher or practitioner struggling to help such a family needs to consider cultural disconnection as a major factor in the family's inability to manage the stress of relocating outside its culture. One possible intervention is connecting the family to other families from this culture that have successfully made the transition.

Other Protective Mediating Factors

In addition to a strong cultural affiliation, other protective factors—those for the individual child as well as those within the environment—can affect the child's response to extreme stress and trauma. These mediating factors include

- A secure, predictable, stable home environment

- An independent, resilient personality (children with dependent, fragile personalities are more vulnerable to emotional upheaval)

- Advanced age and developmental stage (younger children are more vulnerable and affected by their parents' own coping abilities)

- Birth order (older children may have access to more resources than their younger siblings)

- Physical and emotional well-being (physical and emotional vulnerability are risk factors for negative outcomes due to stress and trauma)

- Access to culturally responsive and validating environments in the classroom, at home, and in places of worship

- Access to accurate information and education about resources to address mental illness, addiction, abuse, and neglect

- Evidence of successful adjustment and good recovery from previous stressful events

CREATING HEALING ENVIRONMENTS FOR YOUNG CHILDREN

It is assumed that all practitioners strive to provide classroom environments that are conducive to learning and cognitive development. Addressing the overwhelming stress and trauma that many students struggle with daily presents an additional challenge—providing a healing environment. Providing such an environment not only enhances children's learning but also allows them to thrive rather than merely survive. The following elements may be part of such an environment.

- Sensitivity to changes in a child that may signal stress or trauma

- Respect for physical safety and boundaries

- Solution-focused rather than blame-oriented strategies

- Validation of feelings and experiences

- Safe opportunities to express feelings through talking, drawing, and playing

- Comfortable, familiar, and predictable routines

- Flexibility in routines when needed (e.g., special accommodations to allow a child to feel safe)

- Patience when attempting to decode the meanings and metaphors in a child's language and behaviors

- Permission for temporary regression when appropriate

Practitioners are often on the front line of intervention with young children and families who are struggling with extreme stress and trauma. Although these issues may also require intervention from mental health professionals, much can be done in the classroom to mediate some effects of stressful or traumatic experiences. Hopefully this discussion will help educators and other practitioners who strive to understand the complexities of working with children and families from diverse backgrounds. See Neighbors and Jackson (1996), Perry (1994), Perry and Hambrick (2008), van der Kolk et al. (1996), and Walsh et al. (2007) for further information.

Afterword

Isaura Barrera

At its core, this book is about recognizing the need to remember individuals for who they are and honoring their identities. Skilled Dialogue's focus on experientially anchoring understanding responds to remembering who individuals are. Its focus on 3rd Space addresses honoring multiple identities in mutual and collaborative ways.

Remembering identity and honoring the rich diversity of all identities is as important for practitioners themselves—whatever their cultures—as it is for the children and families they serve. Failing to recognize and honor diverse identities has implications that reach far beyond early childhood. Palmer's observation is critical:

> *Remembering ourselves and our power can lead to revolution, but it requires more than recalling a few facts. Remembering involves putting ourselves together, recovering identity and integrity, reclaiming the wholeness of our lives* [emphasis added]. When we forget who we are [because there is insufficient validation] we do not merely drop some data. We "dis-member" ourselves, with unhappy consequences for our politics, our work, our heart. (1997, p. 20)

Sociological and scientific data expand our understanding of these "unhappy consequences." Quinn quoted a poignant statement by a Peruvian elder: "I dream in Chamicuro, but I cannot tell my dreams to anyone. Some things cannot be said in Spanish. It's lonely being the last one" (2001, p. 9). Failure to honor culture as an integral part of identity results in the loss of more than words and behavioral rules; also lost are dreams and unique funds of knowledge that unlock perspectives otherwise unknown. In addition, data on the need to recognize and preserve diversity at the biological and environmental levels are a red flag for the need to recognize and preserve diversity at the human and cultural levels. Nabhan eloquently presented the delicate and utterly complex interdependence of "cultural diversity, community stability, and the conservation of biological diversity" (1997, p. 2).

223

Data at a human developmental level show the "dis-membering" consequences of culturally discontinuous or invalidating early environments. Validating and culturally continuous environments that support unique, individualized experiences are a crucial requirement for all children's development and well-being (Brazelton & Greenspan, 2000). The need to believe that all individuals have worth and that the world is a safe and nurturing place is basic (Janoff-Bulman, 1992). One of culture's primary purposes is to ensure and protect this need. Culturally invalidating experiences can shatter a person's sense of self and of the world's safety and meaning, leaving him or her with no secure base on which to stand.

Once diversity is recognized, its preservation must follow. Doing so, however, is seldom easy. Skilled Dialogue proposes 3rd Space as a mindset and skill that can facilitate preserving others' diverse identities without sacrificing one's own identity, which is also unique (i.e., diverse from theirs). Recognizing diversity invariably presents contradictory assumptions about how the world works and about how individuals should behave within it. Fletcher and Olwyer (1997) pointed out that accepting contradictions and mining them for their potential strengths expands one's value of oneself and of others. In conceptualizing 3rd Space in their own terms, these authors have referred to the phrase "Janusian thinking: the ability to conceive of two or more opposites existing simultaneously [and in a complementary manner]" (p. 10).

My encounters with radically contradictory roles and rules drew and continue to draw me to the study of such thinking. Three specific anecdotes illustrate this experience. The first one illustrates my discovery that the academic environment (i.e., the "English-speaking world," as I perceived it) operated by a very different set of rules than my familial "Spanish-speaking world."

- *"Always sit in the front row."*

- *"Always raise your hand even if you don't know the answer (the teacher never calls on those who raise their hands repeatedly)."*

- *"Always smile and nod your head as the teacher is talking."*

These three rules and a basic vocabulary of approximately 100 English words were my mother's gifts to me the summer before I started first grade—and my first recognition that reality might not be as seamless as I believed. As a teacher herself, my mother had some familiarity with academic environments and their demands on strong-willed Mexican American 6-year-olds who spoke only Spanish.

Consequently, as described in the second anecdote, I learned that being competent in one world was not enough in the eyes of the other world.

At age 6, I learned quickly that there was a sharp contrast between the roles and rules of the reality I had lived from birth and the roles and rules common to academic environments. The divide between these two sets of roles and rules was further reinforced as I left home for college. My father, who had lovingly shared his knowledge of the world with me as I grew up, told me in the only letter he ever wrote me that I was going into a world within which he could no longer mentor me. The message was clear: Knowledge from one world was neither valued nor useful in the other. Unlike my mother, he did not perceive himself as having both sets of knowledge.

The third anecdote describes my realization that in certain cultures it is not only possible but also advisable to split one's emotional reality from one's professional reality.

Approximately 5 years later, while I was in graduate school, the message that echoed the degree of contradiction between my worlds was "official"—it was issued by my professors as I was struggling amid rather unsettling personal events to meet the demands of rigorous clinical training as a speech-language pathologist. As a result, I sometimes exhibited less than the calm, "objective" professional demeanor expected of everyone in that environment (which should come as no surprise to anyone who knows me).

One day I was explicitly told that this could not continue. I no longer remember what exactly happened. I do remember my supervisor's instructions: Imagine a basket at the classroom door. Drop all of your frustrated, upset, and other negative emotions into that basket, and enter the room with a calm, professional demeanor. Up until that time, I had never been explicitly asked to split my subjective emotional self from my professional self. To me, the message was clear: Leave your personal way of being outside of the professional environment; only a professional role determined by others is allowed in.

In many ways, this book is an outcome of these and other similar experiences. It stems from what I discovered and came to value in my journey of "recovering identity and integrity, reclaiming the wholeness of [my] life" (Palmer, 1997, p. 20). The material presented in this book is designed to help practitioners strengthen and sustain (i.e., "remember") families' and children's identities and integrity across environments in ways that are life enhancing. As Langer stated in her book on mindful learning,

The rules we are given to practice are based on generally accepted truths about how to perform the task and not on our individual abilities. Even if we are fortunate enough to be shown how to do something by a true expert, mindless practice keeps activity from becoming our own. If I try to serve exactly like Martina Navratilova serves, will I be as good as she (apart from differences in innate gifts), given that my grip on the racket is determined by my hand size, not hers, and my toss of the ball is affected by my height, not hers, and given the difference in our muscles? (1997, p. 14)

We recommend what Langer termed "sideways learning," or "learning a subject or skill with an openness to novelty and actively noticing differences, contexts, and perspectives" (1997, p. 23) when practicing Skilled Dialogue. Ultimately, cultural competency as defined in this book cannot be prescribed.

Each situation, no matter how similar to the illustrative vignettes, will have its own unique complexities. We hope that the information in this book provides a framework for exploring those complexities in ways that are respectful, reciprocal, and responsive. These qualities can only truly emerge when, in Palmer's words,

> We embrace the promise of diversity, of creative conflict, and of "losing" in order to "win" [and] face one final fear—the fear that a live encounter with otherness will challenge or even compel us to change our lives. Otherness, taken seriously, always invites transformation, calling us not only to new facts and theories and values but also to new ways of living our lives—and that is the most daunting threat of all. (1997, p. 38)

References

Althen, G. (1988). *American ways: A cultural guide to the United States.* Yarmouth, MA: Intercultural Press.

Archer, C.M. (1986). Culture bump and beyond. In J.M. Valdes (Ed.), *Culture bound: Bridging the cultural gap in language teaching* (pp. 170–178). Cambridge, MA: Cambridge University Press.

Arnberg, L. (1987). *Raising children bilingually: The preschool years.* Philadelphia, PA: Multilingual Matters.

Artiles, A.J. (2007). *Challenges to response to intervention (RTI).* Modesto, CA: Equity and Cultural Considerations.

Artiles, A., Kozleski, E., Trent, S., Osher, D., & Ortiz, A. (2010). Justifying and explaining disproportionality, 1968–2008: A critique of underlying views of culture. *Exceptional Children, 76,* 279–299.

Artiles, A.J., & Ortiz, A. (Eds.). (2002). *English language learners with special needs: Identification, placement, and instruction.* Washington, DC: Center for Applied Linguistics.

Artiles, A.J., Trent, S.C., & Kuan, L.A. (1997). Learning disabilities research on ethnic minority students: An analysis of 22 years of studies published in selected refereed journals. *Learning Disabilities Research and Practice, 12,* 82–91.

Baca, L.M., & Cervantes, H.T. (1984). *The bilingual special education interface.* St. Louis, MO: Times Mirror/Mosby.

Baca, L.M., & Cervantes, H.T. (1998). *The bilingual special education interface* (3rd ed.). Columbus, OH: Charles E. Merrill.

Baldwin, J.R., Faulkner, S.L., Hecht, M.L., & Lindsley, S.L. (2006). *Redefining culture: Perspectives across disciplines.* Mahwah, NJ: Lawrence Erlbaum Associates.

Barrera, I. (1993). *Effective and appropriate education for all children: The challenge of cultural/linguistic diversity and young children with special needs. Topics in Early Childhood Special Education, 13*(4), 461–487.

Barrera, I. (1996). Thoughts on the assessment of young children whose sociocultural background is unfamiliar to the assessor. In S.J. Meisels & E. Fenichel (Eds.), *New visions for the developmental assessment of infants and young children* (pp. 69–84). Washington, DC: ZERO TO THREE: National Center for Infants, Toddlers, and Families.

Barrera, I. (2000). Honoring differences. *Young Exceptional Children 3*(4), 17–26.

Barrera, I., & Corso, R. (2000, December). *Cultural diversity and early childhood: A critical review of literature with implications for ECSE research, evaluation and practice.* Research Roundtable presented at the Division of Early Childhood (DEC) National Conference, Albuquerque, NM.

Barrera, I., & Kramer, L. (1997). From monologues to skilled dialogue. In P.J. Winton, J.A. McCollum, & C. Catlett (Eds.), *Reforming personnel preparation* (pp. 217–252). Baltimore, MD: Paul H. Brookes Publishing Co.

Barrera, I., & Kramer, L. (2009). *Using Skilled Dialogue to transform challenging interactions: Honoring identity, voice, and connection.* Baltimore, MD: Paul H. Brookes Publishing Co.

Bear, C. (2008, May 12). American Indian boarding schools haunt many. *NPR stories.*

Bearne, E. (2002). *Making progress in writing.* London: Routledge.

Bhagwanji, Y., Santos, R.M., & Fowler, S.A. (2000). *Culturally and linguistically sensitive practices in motor skills interventions for young children* (CLAS Technical Report #1). Champaign: University of Illinois at Urbana-Champaign, Early Childhood Research Institute on Culturally and Linguistically Appropriate Services.

Billings, J.A., Pearson, J., Gill, D.H., & Shureen, A. (1997). *Evaluation and assessment in early childhood special education.* Olympia, WA: Office of the Superintendent of Public Instruction.

Block, P. (2002). *The answer to how is yes: Acting on what matters.* San Francisco, CA: Berrett-Koehler Publishers.

Bowers, C.A., & Flinders, D.J. (1990). *Responsive teaching: Ecological approach to classroom patterns of language, culture, and thought.* New York, NY: Teachers College Press.

Bowman, B.T., & Stott, F.M. (1994). Understanding development in a cultural context. In B.L. Mallory & R.S. New (Eds.), *Diversity and developmentally appropriate practices* (pp. 119–134). New York, NY: Teachers College Press.

Brazelton, T.B., & Cramer, B.G. (1990). *The earliest relationship.* Boston: Addison Wesley.

Brazelton, T.B., & Greenspan, S.I. (2000). *The irreducible needs of children: What every child must have to grow, learn, and flourish.* Cambridge, MA: Perseus.

Bredekamp, S., & Copple, C. (1997). *Developmentally appropriate practice in early education programs.* Washington, DC: National Association for the Education of Young Children.

Brice, A.E. (2002). *The Hispanic child: Speech, language, culture and education.* Boston, MA: Allyn & Bacon.

Brown, W., & Barrera, I. (1999). Enduring problems in assessment: The persistent challenges of cultural dynamics and family issues. *Journal of Early Intervention, 12*(1), 34–42.

Buber, M., & Smith, R.G. (1958). *I and thou* (2nd Ed.). New York, NY: Charles Scribner's.

Bush, R.A.B., & Folger, J.P. (1994). *The promise of mediation: Responding to conflict through empowerment and recognition.* San Francisco, CA: Jossey-Bass.

Catlett, C., & Winton, P. (2000). *Selected early childhood/early intervention training manual* (9th ed.). Chapel Hill, NC: The Systems Change in Personnel Preparation Project's Resource Guide.

Catlett, C., Winton, P., & Santos, R.M. (2000). Resources within reason: Supporting culturally and linguistically diverse families. *Young Exceptional Children, 3*(3), 28.

Chamot, A.U., & O'Malley, J.M. (1994). *The CALLA handbook: Implementing the cognitive academic language learning approach.* Boston, MA: Addison Wesley.

Chen, G.M., & Starosta, W.J. (2005). *Foundations of intercultural communication.* Lanham, MD: University Press of America.

Cheng, L.L. (1995). *Integrating language and learning for inclusion.* San Diego: Singular.

Childs, C. (1998). *The spirit's terrain: Creativity, activism and transformation.* Boston, MA: Beacon Press.

Cintas, H.L. (1995). Cross-cultural similarities and differences in development and the impact of parental expectations on motor behavior. *Pediatric Physical Therapy, 7*, 103–111.

Clandinin, D.J., & Connelly, F.M. (2000). *Narrative inquiry.* San Francisco, CA: Jossey-Bass.

CLAS Early Childhood Research Institute. (2001, February). *CLAS annual report.* Champaign: University of Illinois at Urbana-Champaign, Early Childhood Research Institute on Culturally and Linguistically Appropriate Services.

Cole, M. (1998). Culture in development. In M. Woodhead, D. Faulkner, & K. Littleton (Eds.), *Cultural worlds of early childhood* (pp. 11–13). New York, NY: Routledge.

Collier, C. (2005). Separating language difference from disability. *National Association of Bilingual Education News, 28*(3), 13–17.

Cozzolino, L.J. (2006). *The neuroscience of human relationships: Attachment and the developing social brain.* New York, NY: W.W. Norton & Company.

Cross, S.E., Gore, J.S., & Morris, M.M. (2003). The relationship-interdependent self-construal, self-concept consistency, and well-being. *Journal of personality and social psychology, 85*(5), 933–944.

Cudahy, D., Finnan, C., Jarusiewicz, C., & McCarty, B. (2002). *Seeing dispositions: Translating our shared values into observable behavior.* Available from http://www.coehs.nku.edu/educatordispositions/...2002/.../seeingdispositions.ppt

Cummins, J. (1984). *Bilingualism and special education: Issues in assessment and pedagogy.* Philadelphia, PA: Multilingual Matters.

Cummins, J. (1989). A theoretical framework for bilingual special education. *Exceptional Children, 56*(2), 111–119.

Cummins, J. (1991). Interdependence of first- and second-language proficiency in bilingual children. In E. Bialystock (Ed.), *Language processing in bilingual children* (pp. 70–89). Cambridge, UK: Cambridge University Press.

Cummins, J. (2000). *Language, power, and pedagogy: Bilingual children in the crossfire.* Bristol, UK: Multilingual Matters.

Cushner, K., & Brislin, R.W. (1996). *Intercultural interactions: A practical guide* (2nd ed.). Thousand Oaks, CA: Sage Publications.

Damen, L. (1987). *Culture learning: The fifth dimension in the language classroom.* Boston, MA: Addison Wesley.

Darder, A. (1991). *Culture and power in the classroom: A critical framework for bicultural education.* Westport, CT: Bergin & Garvey.

DeBono, E. (1970). *Lateral thinking.* New York, NY: Harper & Row.

DeBono, E. (1991). *I am right you are wrong: From rock logic to water logic.* New York, NY: Penguin Books.

DeBono, E. (2008). *Creativity workout: 63 exercises to unlock your most creative ideas.* Berkeley, CA: Ulysses Press

DeBono, E. (2009). *Think! Before it's too late.* London, UK: Random house.

Delpit, L. (1995). *Other people's children: Cultural conflict in the classroom.* New York, NY: Free Press.

Derman-Sparks, L., Ramsey, P.G., & Edwards, O. (2003). *What if all the kids are white? Antibias multicultural education.* New York, NY: Teachers College Press.

Deskin, G., & Steckler, G. (1996). *When nothing makes sense: Disaster, crisis and their effects on children.* Minneapolis, MN: Fairview.

deVries, M.W. (1996). Trauma in cultural perspective. In B.A. van der Kolk, A.C. McFarlane, & L. Weisaeth (Eds.), *Traumatic stress: The effects of overwhelming experience on mind, body, and society* (pp. 398–413). New York, NY: Guilford Press.

Díaz-Rico, L.T., & Weed, K.Z. (1995). *The crosscultural language and academic development handbook: A complete K–12 reference guide.* Boston, MA: Allyn & Bacon.

Donovan, D.M., & McIntyre, D. (1990). *Healing the hurt child.* New York, NY: W.W. Norton.

Donovan, S., & Cross, C. (Eds.). (2002). *Minority students in special and gifted education.* Washington, DC: National Academies Press.

Dunst, C., Trivette, C., & Deal, A. (1988). *Enabling and empowering families.* Brookline, MA: Brookline Books.

Echevarria, J., & Graves, A. (1998). *Sheltered content instruction: Teaching English language learners with diverse abilities.* Boston, MA: Allyn & Bacon.

Edwards, C., Gandini, L., & Forman, G. (1995). *The hundred languages of children: The Reggio Emilia approach to early childhood education.* Norwood, NJ: Ablex.

Fantini, A.E. (2001, April). *Developing intercultural competence in the LCTLs.* Presented at the National Council of Less Commonly Taught Languages Fourth Annual Conference, Arlington, VA.

Federal Interagency Forum on Child and Family Statistics. (2011). *America's children: Key national indicators of well-being, 2011.* Washington, DC: U.S. Government Printing Office.

Fewell, R. (1996). Intervention strategies to promote motor skills. In S.L. Odom & M.E. McLean (Eds.), *DEC recommended practices: Indicators of quality in programs for infants and young children with special needs and their families* (pp. 245–248). Reston, VA: Council for Exceptional Children.

Fishman, J. (1996). What do you lose when you lose your language? In G. Cantoni (Ed.) (1996), *Stabilizing indigenous languages*. Flagstaff, AZ: Center for Excellence in Education, Northern Arizona University. Retrieved from http://jan.ucc.nau.edu/jar/SIL.pdf

Fletcher, J., & Olwyer, K. (1997). *Paradoxical thinking: How to profit from your contradictions.* San Francisco, CA: Berrett-Koehler Publishers.

Fontes, L.A. (2005). *Child abuse and culture: Working with diverse families.* New York, NY: Guilford Press.

Frankenburg, W.K., Dodds, J., Archer, P., Bresnick, B., Mashka, P., Edelman, N., & Shapiro, H. (1990). *Denver II.* Denver, CO: Denver Developmental Materials.

Freedman, J., & Combs, G. (1996). *Narrative therapy: The social construction of preferred realities.* New York, NY: W.W. Norton.

Fritz, R. (1989). *The path of least resistance.* New York: Fawcett Columbine.

Garcia, E. (2001). *Hispanic education in the United States: Raíces y alas.* Lanham, MD: Rowman & Littlefield.

Gardner, H. (1993). *Frames of mind: The theory of multiple intelligences.* New York, NY: Basic Books.

Gee, J. (2001). Identity as an analytic lens for research in education. *Review of Research in Education 25,* 99–125.

Genesee, F. (2000). Early bilingual language development: One language or two? In L. Wei (Ed.), *The bilingualism reader* (pp. 327–343). New York, NY: Routledge.

Gergen, K.J. (2009). *An invitation to social construction.* Thousand Oaks, CA: Sage Publications.

Gernsbacher, M.A. (2006). Toward a behavior of reciprocity. *Journal of Developmental Processes, 1,* 139–152. Retrieved from http://psych.wisc.edu/lang/pdf/gernsbacher_reciprocity.pdf

Goldhaber, D.E. (2000). *Theories of human development: Integrative perspectives.* Mountain View, CA: Mayfield Publishing Company.

Goleman, D. (1995). *Emotional intelligence.* New York, NY: Bantam.

Goleman, D. (2006). *Social intelligence.* New York, NY: Bantam.

Gollnick, D.M., & Chinn, P.C. (1990). *Multicultural education in a pluralistic society.* Columbus, OH: Charles E. Merrill.

Gonzalez, N., Moll, L., & Amanti, C. (Eds.) (2005). *Funds of knowledge: Theorizing practice in households and communities.* Mahwah, NJ: Lawrence Erlbaum Associates.

Gonzalez-Mena, J. (2000). *Multicultural issues in child care* (3rd ed.). New York, NY: McGraw-Hill.

Gonzalez-Mena, J., Herzog, M., & Herzog, S. (2000). *Diversity: Reconciling differences.* Crystal Lake, IL: Magna Systems.

Greenfield, P.M., & Cocking, R.R. (1994). *Cross-cultural roots of minority child development.* Mahwah, NJ: Lawrence Erlbaum Associates.

Greenspan, S. (1999). *Building healthy minds.* Cambridge, MA: Perseus.

Groome, T. (1980). *Christian religious education.* New York, NY: Harper & Row.

Guardado, M. (2003). Parental attitudes toward L1 loss and maintenance in Canada: Case studies of Spanish-speaking families. *International Journal of Learning, 10.*

Hamayan, E.V., & Damico, J.S. (1991). *Developing and using a second language.* Austin, TX: PRO-ED.

Harding, E., & Riley, P. (1986). *The bilingual family: A handbook for parents.* New York, NY: Cambridge University Press.

Harry, B. (1992). Developing cultural self-awareness: The first step in values clarification for early interventionists. *Topics in Early Childhood Special Education, 12*(3), 333–350.

Harry, B. (2002). Trends and issues in serving culturally diverse families of children with disabilities. *Journal of Special Education, 36*(3), 131–138.

Hatfield, E., Cacioppo, J.L., & Rapson, R.L. (1993). *Emotional contagion.* New York, NY: Cambridge University Press.

Haviland, W.A. (1993). *Cultural anthropology.* New York, NY: Harcourt Brace.

Hsueh, Y., & Barton, B.K. (2005). A cultural perspective on professional beliefs of childcare teachers. *Early Childhood Education Journal, 33,* 179–186.

Huber, C. (1988). *How you do anything is how you do everything.* Murphys, CA: Keep It Simple Books.

Huntsinger, C.S., & Jose, P.E. (2009). Parental involvement in children's schooling: Different meanings in different cultures. *Early Childhood Research Quarterly, 24*(4), 398–410.

Igoa, C. (1995). *The inner world of the immigrant child.* New York, NY: St. Martin's.

Individuals with Disabilities Education Act Amendments (IDEA) of 1997, PL 105-17, 20 U.S.C. §§ 1400 *et seq.*

Individuals with Disabilities Education Improvement Act (IDEA) of 2004, PL 108-446, 20 U.S.C. §§ 1400 *et seq.*

Isaacs, W. (1999). *Dialogue: The art of thinking together.* New York, NY: Crown Business Press/ Random House.

Jaffe, E. (2007). Mirror neurons: How we reflect on behavior. *Association for Psychological Science Observer, 20*(5).

Jahn, G. (2002, January 6). Second generation is also haunted by Holocaust. *Arizona Republic,* p. A24.

Jalava, A. (1988). Mother tongue and identity. In T. Skutnabb-Kangas & J. Cummins (Eds.), *Minority education: From shame to struggle* (pp. 168–169). Philadelphia, PA: Multilingual Matters.

Janoff-Bulman, R. (1992). *Shattered assumptions.* New York, NY: Free Press.

Jaworski, J. (1996). *Synchronicity: The inner path of leadership.* San Francisco, CA: Berrett-Koehler Publishers.

Josselson, R. (1994). Identity and relatedness in the life cycle. In H.A. Bosma, T.L. Graafsma, H.D. Grotevant, & D.J. de Levita (Eds.), *Identity and development* (pp. 81–103). Thousand Oaks, CA: Sage Publications.

Kahane, A. (2009). *Solving tough problems.* San Francisco, CA: Berrett-Koehler Publishers.

Kalyanpur, M., & Harry, B. (1999). *Culture in special education: Building reciprocal family–professional relationships.* Baltimore, MD: Paul H. Brookes Publishing Co.

Kame'enui, E.J., Carnine, D.W., Dixon, R.C., Simmons, D.C., & Coyne, M.D. (2002). *Effective teaching strategies that accommodate diverse learners.* Columbus, OH: Charles E. Merrill.

Katie, B. (2002). *Loving what is.* New York, NY: Harmony Books.

Kendall, F. (1996). *Diversity in the classroom.* New York, NY: Teachers College Press.

Kendrick, M. (April, 2000). Right relationships, pp. 5-9. *Queensland Advocacy Incorporated Newsletter,* Queensland, AU.

Klein, G. (1998). *Sources of power: How people make decisions.* Cambridge, MA: The MIT Press.

Klingner, J.K., & Artiles, A.J. (2003). When should bilingual students be in special education? *Educational Leadership, 61*(2), 66–71.

Klingner, J., Hoover, J.J., & Baca, L.M. (Eds.). (2008). *Why do English language learners struggle with reading? Distinguishing language acquisition from learning disabilities.* Thousand Oaks, CA: Corwin Press, Sage.

Koplow, L. (1996). *Unsmiling faces: How preschools can heal.* New York, NY: Teachers College Press.

Kramer, L.K. (1997). *Cultural perspectives on developmentally appropriate practice in a model inclusive Navajo preschool.* Unpublished dissertation.

Kritikos, E. (2003). Speech-language pathologists beliefs about language assessment of bilingual/bicultural individuals. *American Journal of Speech-Language Pathology, 12*(1), 73–91.

Landrine, H. (1995). Clinical implications of cultural differences: The referential vs. the indexical self. In N.R. Goldberger & J.B. Veroff (Eds.), *Culture and psychology* (pp. 744–766). New York, NY: New York University Press.

Landrine, H., & Klonoff, E.A. (1996). *African American acculturation.* Thousand Oaks, CA: Sage Publications.

Landurand, P.M., & Cloud, N. (1991). *How disability can affect language acquisition.* Reston, VA: Council for Exceptional Children.

Langdon, H.W., & Cheng, L.L. (2002). *Collaborating with interpreters and translators: A guide for communication disorders professionals.* Eau Claire, WI: Thinking Publications.

Langer, E. (1997). *The power of mindful learning.* New York, NY: Perseus Books.

Lanning, K.V. (1992). *Child molesters: A behavioral analysis.* Arlington, VA: National Center for Missing and Exploited Children.

Lave, J., & Wenger, E. (1991). *Situated learning: Legitimate peripheral participation.* New York, NY: Cambridge University Press.

Lawrence-Lightfoot, S. (1999). *Respect.* Cambridge, MA: Perseus.

Losardo, A., & Notari Syverson, A. (2011). *Alternative approaches to assessing young children* (2nd ed.). Baltimore, MD: Paul H. Brookes Publishing Company.

Lubeck, S. (1994). The politics of developmentally appropriate practice. In B.L. Mallory & R.S. New (Eds.), *Diversity and developmentally appropriate practices* (pp. 17–43). New York, NY: Teachers College Press.

Lynch, E.W., & Hanson, M.J. (2011). *Developing cross-cultural competence: A guide for working with young children and their families* (4th ed.). Baltimore, MD: Paul H. Brookes Publishing Co.

MacIntosh, I.S. (2001). Plan A and plan B for cultural survival. *Cultural Survival, 25*(2), 4–6.

Malina, B.J. (2001). *The New Testament world: Insights from cultural anthropology.* Louisville, KY: Westminster John Knox Press.

Markus, H.R., & Kitayama, S. (1991). Culture and the self: Implications for cognition, emotion, and motivation. *Psychological Review, 98*(2), 224–253.

Mattes, L.J. (2007). Bilingual language disorders in Spanish-speaking children. *ACA Special Education News,* Article 7-4.

Mattes, L.J., & Omark, D.R. (1984). *Speech and language assessment for the bilingual handicapped.* San Diego, CA: College-Hill.

Maynard, A.E., & Martini, M.I. (2005). *Learning in cultural context: Family, peers and school.* New York, NY: Springer.

McDermott, R., Goldman, S., & Varenne, H. (2006). The cultural work of learning disabilities. *Educational Researcher, 35*(6), 12–17.

McLaughlin, B. (1995). *Fostering second language development in young children: Principles and practices.* Santa Cruz, CA: National Center for Research on Cultural Diversity and Second Language Learning.

McLean, M. (2001). *Conducting child assessment* (CLAS Technical Report #1). Champaign: University of Illinois at Urbana-Champaign, Early Childhood Research Institute on Culturally and Linguistically Appropriate Services.

Medina, V. (1982). *Interpretation and translation in bilingual B.A.S.E.* San Diego, CA: San Diego County Office of Education.

Metz, I.B. (1991). Learning from personal experiences. In M. Anderson & P. Goldberg (Eds.), *Cultural competence in screening and assessment: Implications for services to young children with special needs ages birth through five* (pp. 8–10). Chapel Hill, NC: National Early Childhood Technical Assistance System.

Middleton-Moz, J. (1989). *Children of trauma: Rediscovering your discarded self.* Deerfield Beach, FL: Health Communications.

Miller, A. (1980). *The drama of the gifted child.* New York, NY: Basic Books.

Miller, N. (Ed.). (1984). *Bilingualism and language disability: Assessment and remediation.* San Diego, CA: College-Hill.

Mofina, R. (2001, Summer). 20,000 survivors of residential schools to seek compensation. *First Nations Drum.* Available from *http://firstnationsdrum.com/2001/12/20000-survivors-of-residential-schools-to-seek-compensation/*

Moll, L.C. (1990). *Vygotsky and education: Instructional implications and applications of sociohistorical psychology.* New York, NY: Cambridge University Press.

Moll, L., Amanti, C., Neff, D., & Gonzalez, N. (1992). Funds of knowledge for teaching: Using a qualitative approach to connect homes and classrooms. *Theory into Practice, 31*(2), 132–141.

Moll, L.C., & Greenberg, J.B. (1990). Creating zones of possibilities: Combining social contexts for instruction. In L.C. Moll (Ed.), *Vygotsky and education: Educational implications and applications of sociohistorical psychology* (pp. 319–348). New York, NY: Cambridge University Press.

Moore, S.M., & Beatty, J. (1995). *Developing cultural competence in early childhood assessment.* Boulder, CO: University of Colorado.

Nabhan, G.P. (1997). *Cultures of habitat.* Washington, DC: Counterpoint.

Nakkula, M.J., & Ravitch, S. (1998). *Matters of interpretation.* San Francisco, CA: Jossey-Bass.

National Center for Education Statistics. (2007). *Status and trends in the education of racial and ethnic minorities.* Washington, DC: U.S. Department of Education, Institute of Education Science. Retrieved from http://nces.ed.gov/pubs2007/minoritytrends/.

N.E. Thing Enterprises. (1993). *Magic eye: A new way of looking at the world.* Kansas City, MO: Andrews & McMeel.

Neighbors, H.W., & Jackson, J.S. (Eds.). (1996). *Mental health in black America.* Thousand Oaks, CA: Sage Publications.

Neisworth, J.T., & Bagnato, S.J. (2000). Recommended practices in assessment. In S. Sandall, M.E. McLean, & B.J. Smith (Eds.), *DEC recommended practices in early intervention/early childhood special education* (pp. 17–27). Denver, CO: Division for Early Childhood of the Council for Exceptional Children.

Newberg, A., D'Aquili, E., & Rause, V. (2001). *Why God won't go away.* New York, NY: Ballantine.

Newborg, J., Stock, J.R., Wnek, L., Guidubaldi, J., & Svinicki, J. (1984). *The Battelle Developmental Inventory.* Allen, TX: DLM/Teaching Resources.

Nieto, S. (2001). *Language, culture, and teaching: Critical perspectives for a new century.* Mahwah, NJ: Lawrence Erlbaum Associates.

Palmer, P.J. (1997). *The courage to teach.* San Francisco, CA: Jossey-Bass.

Pang, Y., & Richey, D. (2007). Preschool education in China and the United States: A personal perspective. *Early Child Development and Care, 177*(1), 1–13.

Paradise, R. (1994). Interactional style and nonverbal meaning: Mazahua children learning how to be separate-but-together. *Anthropology and Education Quarterly, 25*(2), 156–172.

Parette, H.P., & Petch-Hogan, B. (2000). Approaching families: Facilitating culturally/linguistically diverse family involvement. *Teaching Exceptional Children 33*(2), 4–10.

Payne, R. (2005). *A framework for understanding poverty.* Highlands, TX: aha! Process Inc.

Pennsylvania Department of Education. (1994). *Early childhood assessment guidelines* (Draft ed.). Harrisburg, PA: Bureau of Special Education.

Perez, B., & Torres-Guzman, M.E. (2002). *Learning in two worlds: An integrated Spanish/English biliteracy approach.* Boston, MA: Allyn & Bacon.

Perkins, D. (2001). *The eureka effect: The art and logic of breakthrough.* New York, NY: W.W. Norton.

Perry, B.D. (1994). Neurobiological sequelae of childhood trauma: Post traumatic stress disorders in children. In M. Murburg (Ed.), *Catecholamine function in post traumatic stress disorder: Emerging concepts* (pp. 253–276). Washington, DC: American Psychiatric Press.

Perry, B.D., & Hambrick, E.P. (2008, Fall). The neurosequential model of therapeutics. *Reclaiming Children and Youth, 17*(3), 38–43.

Perry, B.D., & Pollard, R. (1998, January). Homeostasis, stress, trauma, and adaptation: A neurodevelopmental view of childhood trauma. *Child and Adolescent Psychiatric Clinics of North America, 7*(1), 33–51.

Perry, G., & Duru, M. (2001). *Resources for developmentally appropriate practice: Recommendations from the profession.* Washington, DC: National Association for the Education of Young Children.

Philips, S.U. (1972). Participant structure and communicative competence: Warm Springs children in community and classroom. In C.B. Cazden, D. Hymes, & V. John-Steiner (Eds.), *Functions of language in the classroom* (pp. 370–394). New York, NY: Teachers College Press.

Phillips, C.B. (1994). The movement of African-American children through sociocultural contexts. In B.L. Mallory & R.S. New (Eds.), *Diversity and developmentally appropriate practices* (pp. 137–154). New York, NY: Teachers College Press.

Phillips, D., & Crowell, N. (1994). *Cultural diversity and early education: Report of a workshop.* Washington, DC: National Academies Press.

Pink, D.H. (2006). *A whole new mind.* New York, NY: Riverhead Books.

Polk, C. (1994). Therapeutic work with African-American families: Using knowledge of culture. *Zero to Three, 15*(2), 9–11.

Quinn, E.M. (2001). Can this language be saved? *Cultural survival quarterly, 25*(2), 9–12.

Quiñones-Eatman, J. (2001). *Second language acquisition in the preschool years: What we know and how we can effectively communicate with young second language learners* (CLAS Technical Report #1). Champaign: University of Illinois at Urbana-Champaign, Early Childhood Research Institute on Culturally and Linguistically Appropriate Services.

Remen, R.N. (2000). *My grandfather's blessings.* New York, NY: Riverhead.

Reyes, I. (2004). Functions of code switching in schoolchildren's conversations. *Bilingual Research Journal 28*(1), 77–98.

Rizzolati, G., Fogassi, L., & Gallese, V. (2006, November). Mirrors in the mind. *Scientific American, 295*(5), 54–61.

Rogoff, B. (2003). *The cultural nature of human development.* New York, NY: Oxford University Press.

Roseberry-McKibbin, C. (2002). *Multicultural students with special language needs: Practical strategies for assessment and intervention* (2nd ed.). Oceanside, CA: Academic Communication Associates.

Rothstein-Fisch, C. (1998). *Bridging cultures: A pre-service teacher preparation module.* Material presented at NAEYC National Institute for Early Childhood Professional Development, Miami, FL.

Rothstein-Fisch, C. (2003). *Bridging cultures: Teacher education module.* New York, NY: Routledge.

Salomon, G. (Ed.). (1993). *Distributed cognitions: Psychological and educational considerations.* Cambridge, MA: Cambridge University Press.

Sanchez, S. (1999). Learning from the stories of culturally linguistically diverse families and communities. *Remedial and Special Education, 20*(6), 351–359.

Sandall, S., Hemmeter, M.L., Smith, B.J., & McLean, M.E. (Eds.). (2005). *DEC recommended practices: A comprehensive guide for practical application in early intervention/early childhood special education.* Missoula, MT: Division of Early Childhood, Council for Exceptional Children.

Santos, R.M., Corso, R.M., & Fowler, S.A. (Eds.). (2005). *Working with linguistically diverse families* (Vol. 3). Longmont, CO: Sopris West Educational Services.

Santos, R.M., Fowler, S.A., Corso, R.M., & Bruns, D. (2000). Acceptance, acknowledgement, and adaptability: Selecting culturally and linguistically appropriate early childhood materials. *Teaching Exceptional Children, 32*(3), 14–22.

Santos, R.M., Lee, S., Valdivia, R., & Zhang, C. (2001). Considerations when selecting and using early childhood materials translated from one language to another language. *Teaching Exceptional Children, 34*(2), 26–31.

Schneider, E., Parush, S., Katz, N., & Miller, L.J. (1995). Performance of Israeli versus U.S. preschool children on the Miller Assessment for Preschoolers. *American Journal on Occupational Therapy, 49*(1), 19–23.

Seelye, H.N., & Wasilewski, J.H. (1996). *Between cultures: Developing self-identity in a world of diversity.* Lincolnwood, IL: NTC Publishing Group.

Senge, P.M., Scharmer, C.O., Jaworski, J., & Flowers, B.S. (2005). *Presence: An exploration of profound change in people, organizations, and society.* New York, NY: Currency/Doubleday.

Shafir, R.Z. (2000). *The zen of listening.* Wheaton, IL: Quest Books.

Shelton, C. (1999). *Quantum leaps.* Boston, MA: Butterworth-Heinemann.

Shem, S., & Surrey, J. (1998). *We have to talk.* New York, NY: Basic Books.

Skutnabb-Kangas, T., & Cummins, J. (1988). *Minority education: From shame to struggle.* Philadelphia, PA: Multilingual Matters.

Solomon, C.M., & Schell, M.S. (2009). *Managing across cultures: The seven keys to doing business with a global mindset.* New York, NY: McGraw-Hill.

Stettbacher, J.K. (1991). *Making sense out of suffering.* New York, NY: Dutton.

Stewart, E.C., & Bennett, M.J. (1991). *American cultural patterns: A cross-cultural perspective.* Yarmouth, ME: Intercultural Press.

Tabors, P.O. (2008). *One child, two languages: A guide for early childhood educators of children learning English as a second language* (2nd ed.). Baltimore, MD: Paul H. Brookes Publishing Co.

Takaki, R. (1993). *A different mirror: A history of multicultural America.* New York, NY: Little, Brown.

Tobin, D., Wu, J., & Davidson, D. (1989). *Preschool in three cultures: Japan, China, and the United States.* New Haven, CT: Yale University Press.

Trawick-Smith, J. (2010). *Early childhood development: A multicultural perspective* (5th ed.). Columbus, OH: Charles E. Merrill.

Trumbull, E., Rothstein-Fisch, C., Greenfield, P.M., & Quiroz, B. (2001). *Bridging cultures between home and school.* Mahwah, NJ: Lawrence Erlbaum Associates.

United Nations. (2006). *Violence against children.* Author. Available from http://www.unicef.org/violencestudy/reports/SG_violencestudy_en.pdf

Vaill, P.B. (1996). *Learning as a way of being.* San Francisco, CA: Jossey-Bass.

VanDerHeyden, A.M., & Witt, J.C. (2008). Best practices in can't do/won't do assessment. In A. Thomas & J. Grimes (Eds.), *Best practices in school psychology* (pp. 131–139). Bethesda, MD: National Association of School Psychologists.

van der Kolk, B.A., McFarlane, A.C., & Weisaeth, L. (Eds.). (1996). *Traumatic stress: The effects of overwhelming experiences on mind, body, and society.* New York, NY: Guilford Press.

Vann, G. (1960). *The heart of man.* Garden City, NY: Image Books.

Velez-Ibañez, C.G., & Greenberg, J.B. (1992). Formation and transformation of funds of knowledge among U.S.-Mexican households. *Anthropology and Education Quaterly, 23*(4), 313–335.

Ventriglia, L. (1982). *Conversations with Miguel and Maria.* Boston, MA: Addison Wesley.

Walsh, K., Blaustein, M., Knight, W.G., Spinazzola, J., & van der Kolk, B.A. (2007). Resiliency factors in the relation between childhood sexual abuse and adulthood sexual assault in college-age women. *Journal of Child Sexual Abuse, 16*(1), 1–17.

Wei, L. (1998). The why and how questions in the analysis of conversational code-switching. In P. Auer (Ed.), *Code-switching in conversation: Language, interaction, and identity* (pp. 156–176). London, UK: Routledge.

Wheatley, M.J. (2005). *Finding our way.* San Francisco, CA: Berrett-Koehler Publishers.

Wildman, J.M. (1996). *Privilege revealed: How invisible preference undermines America.* New York, NY: New York University Press.

Williams, L.R., & DeGaetano, Y. (1985). *ALERTA: A multicultural, bilingual approach to teaching young children.* Boston, MA: Addison Wesley.

Wilson, J. (2001). Looking closer. *Hope, 27,* 64.

Winzer, M.A., & Mazurek, K. (1994). *Special education in multicultural contexts.* Columbus, OH: Charles E. Merrill.

Yankelovich, D. (1999). *The magic of dialogue.* New York, NY: Simon & Schuster.

Zander, R.S., & Zander, B. (2000). *The art of possibility: Transforming professional and personal life.* Boston, MA: Harvard Business School Publishing.

Photocopiable Materials

Assessment Cultural Linguistic Response Plan

Assessment/Instructional Cultural Linguistic Response Plan

Cultural Consonance Profile

Cultural Data Table

Family Acculturation Screen

Funds of Knowledge Worksheet for Story Assessment

Guide to Identifying Cultural Data Related to Potential Culture
Bumps

Home Language Usage Profile

Instructional Cultural Linguistic Response Plan

Relative Language Proficiency (RLP) Profile

Assessment Cultural Linguistic Response Plan

Child/family: _____

Date: _____   Completed by: _____

Specific Assessment Considerations

RE: *Language and communication differences*

RE: *Data-gathering procedures*

RE: *Interpretation of assessment information*

RE: *Reporting assessment results*

Skilled Dialogue Reminders

	Choosing Relationship over Control/ Anchored Understanding of Diversity	Setting the Stage for Miracles/ 3rd Space
Respect	**Welcoming** range and validity of diverse perspectives	**Allowing** the tension of differing perspectives
Reciprocity	**Making sense** of diverse perspectives	**Appreciating** the strengths of diverse perspectives
Responsiveness	**Joining** across diverse perspectives	**Harmonizing** diverse perspectives so as to integrate and gain access to complementary strengths

Assessment/Instructional Cultural Linguistic Response Plan

Child/family: _____   Date: _____   Completed by: _____

Assessment Considerations

RE: *Language and communication differences*

RE: *Data-gathering procedures*

RE: *Interpretation of assessment information*

RE: *Reporting assessment results*

Intervention and Instruction Considerations

RE: *Language and communication differences*

RE: *Teaching and learning strategies*

RE: *Instructional content*

RE: *Teaching and learning materials*

Skilled Dialogue Reminders

Choosing Relationship over Control/ Anchored Understanding of Diversity	**Setting the Stage for Miracles/3rd Space**
Welcoming range and validity of diverse perspective(s)	**Allowing** the tension of differing perspective(s)
Making sense of diverse perspectives	**Appreciating** the strengths of diverse perspectives
Joining across diverse perspectives	**Harmonizing** diverse perspectives so as to integrate and gain access to complementary strengths

Respect
Reciprocity
Responsiveness

Skilled Dialogue: Strategies for Responding to Cultural Diversity in Early Childhood, Second Edition
by Isaura Barrera, Lucinda Kramer, and T. Dianne Macpherson
Copyright © 2012 by Paul H. Brookes Publishing Co., Inc. All rights reserved.

Cultural Consonance Profile

Child's name: _____   Date: _____   Completed by: _____

	Highly similar to early childhood environment(s)/ practitioners' profiles ←→ Highly dissimilar from early childhood environment(s)/ practitioners' profiles					

I. Communicative-Linguistic Area

						Comments
Language(s) used in child's home	5	4	3	2	1	_____
Child's relative language proficiency	5	4	3	2	1	_____
Patterns of language usage	5	4	3	2	1	_____
Relative value placed on verbal/ nonverbal communication	5	4	3	2	1	_____
Relative status of language other than English and bilingualism	5	4	3	2	1	_____

II. Personal-Social Area

Family's degree of acculturation	5	4	3	2	1	_____
Sense of self/perception of identity/competence	5	4	3	2	1	_____
Parenting/child-rearing roles and rules	5	4	3	2	1	_____
Knowledge/experience regarding power and positioning	5	4	3	2	1	_____
Values and beliefs regarding support	5	4	3	2	1	_____

III. Sensory-Cognitive Area

Funds of knowledge/concept definition/structures	5	4	3	2	1	_____
Preferred learning strategies	5	4	3	2	1	_____
Preferred problem-solving/ decision-making strategies	5	4	3	2	1	_____
Worldview	5	4	3	2	1	_____

Degree of consonance with early childhood environment(s)/practitioners' profiles

Communicative-linguistic area	High	Moderate	Low	Minimal
Personal-social area	High	Moderate	Low	Minimal
Sensory-cognitive area	High	Moderate	Low	Minimal

Comments:

Skilled Dialogue: Strategies for Responding to Cultural Diversity in Early Childhood, Second Edition by Isaura Barrera, Lucinda Kramer, and T. Dianne Macpherson

Cultural Data Table

Child's name: _____ Date completed: _____ Completed by: _____

Directions: Fill in responses to questions from the Guide to Identifying Cultural Data Related to Potential Culture Bumps.

Developmental/curricular area	Comments
Communicative-Linguistic	
Language(s) of child's primary caregiving environment(s)	
Child's relative language proficiency (degree of proficiency in English and other language[s] used)	
Patterns of language usage in child's primary caregiving environment(s)	
Relative value placed on verbal and nonverbal communication	
Relative status associated with languages other than English and with bilingualism	

(continued)

Skilled Dialogue: Strategies for Responding to Cultural Diversity in Early Childhood, Second Edition by Isaura Barrera, Lucinda Kramer, and T. Dianne Macpherson

Cultural Data Table (continued)

Personal-Social		
Degree of family's acculturation into EuroAmerican Normative Culture (ENC)		
Degree of family's acculturation into U.S. early intervention/early childhood special education (ECSE) culture		
Sense of self (e.g., relative weight on independence, dependence, interdependence)		
Perceptions and understanding of identity and competence		
Roles and rules associated with parenting and child rearing		
Knowledge and experience regarding power and social positioning		

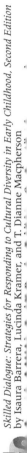

Skilled Dialogue: Strategies for Responding to Cultural Diversity in Early Childhood, Second Edition
by Isaura Barrera, Lucinda Kramer, and T. Dianne Macpherson

(continued)

Cultural Data Table (continued)

Values/beliefs/skills associated with instrumental and emotional support (e.g., gaining access to external resources, getting personal support)	
Sensory-Cognitive Funds of knowledge: what type of knowledge is valued; concept structures and definitions (e.g., how *family* is defined)	
Preferred strategies for acquiring new learning	
Preferred strategies for problem solving and decision making	
Worldview (i.e., assumptions about how the world works and about what is "right" and what is "wrong")	

Skilled Dialogue: Strategies for Responding to Cultural Diversity in Early Childhood, Second Edition
by Isaura Barrera, Lucinda Kramer, and T. Dianne Macpherson

Family Acculturation Screen

Child's name: _____ Date: _____ Completed by: _____

Degree of English spoken in child's home (High = predominant; Low = minimal)	High -▶ Low	
Level of literacy reflected in child's home (e.g., number of books, level of parent's vocabulary)	High -▶ Low	
Degree of value placed on verbal skills as compared with nonverbal communication	High -▶ Low	
Degree of familiarity with English idioms	High -▶ Low	
Parent's level of schooling in U.S. schools (High = *college*; Low = *none*)	High -▶ Low	
Familiarity with classroom rules/expectations (High = *extensive*; Low = *minimal*)	High -▶ Low	
Length of residence in United States (High = *more than 10 years*; Low = *less than 1 year*)	High -▶ Low	
Value placed on child's independence and autonomy as defined within EuroAmerican Normative Culture (ENC)	High -▶ Low	
Time spent with monolingual English speakers (High = *daily*; Low = *infrequently*)	High -▶ Low	
Amount of time spent in environments strongly reflective of ENC (e.g., schools, libraries, offices of U.S. corporations) (High = *daily*; Low = *infrequently*)	High -▶ Low	

Overall impression of degree of family's acculturation into ENC

High	Moderate	Low	Minimal

Comments:

Skilled Dialogue: Strategies for Responding to Cultural Diversity in Early Childhood, Second Edition
by Isaura Barrera, Lucinda Kramer, and T. Dianne Macpherson
Copyright © 2012 by Paul H. Brookes Publishing Co., Inc. All rights reserved.

Funds of Knowledge Worksheet for Story Assessment

Story title: _____

Publisher/source: _____

Date: _____ Completed by: _____

Instructions: Select and read a children's story. Identify the reflected fund of knowledge (i.e., the knowledge that the reader needs for optimum comprehension and learning). Use the categories below as a guide to different aspects of the story's fund of knowledge.

Concepts necessary to understand the story	Experiences described in the story
Story grammar (e.g., event sequence, plot)	Social environment(s) in which the story takes place
Composition and organization of families/communities in the story	Problem-solving approaches used by characters in the story
Language(s) (e.g., actual language[s] used, vocabulary level, structure)	Other (e.g., values, beliefs, behaviors)

Guide to Identifying Cultural Data Related to Potential Culture Bumps

Child's name: _____   Date completed: _____   Completed by: _____

Note: The questions in the second column tend to arise frequently. There may be others that are not identified on this form. Feel free to add any other questions that need to be answered. Use this guide prior to completing the Cultural Data Table.

Developmental/curricular area	Questions to answer
Communicative-Linguistic Language(s) of child's primary caregiving environment(s)	1. What language(s) are spoken in the child's primary caregiving environment(s)? 2. Which caregivers speak which language(s) with the child?
Child's relative language proficiency (degree of proficiency in English and other language[s] used)	1. How proficient is the child in understanding and using the language(s) other than English for communicating? 2. How proficient is the child in understanding and using English for communicating? 3. Would the child be considered monolingual? Partial bilingual (speaks and understands one language, only understands another)? Bilingual, dominant in one language (speaks and understands both languages but is significantly more proficient in one)? "Balanced" bilingual (similar levels of proficiency in both languages—may not be strong in either, or may be equally strong in both)?
Patterns of language usage in child's primary caregiving environment(s)	1. With what situations and topics does each language tend to be associated? 2. Which varieties of each language are spoken (e.g., if English is spoken, in which ways is it similar to or different from what is considered the "standard" variety of English)? 3. If two or more languages are used, what seems to govern which language is used when?

(continued)

Skilled Dialogue: Strategies for Responding to Cultural Diversity in Early Childhood, Second Edition by Isaura Barrera, Lucinda Kramer, and T. Dianne Macpherson

Guide to Identifying Cultural Data Related to Potential Culture Bumps *(continued)*

Relative value placed on verbal and nonverbal communication	1. To what degree is communication in the home verbal? To what degree is it nonverbal?
	2. What is the relative value placed on nonverbal communication as compared with verbal communication? Is this true in all situations, or only in some?
Relative status associated with languages other than English and with bilingualism	1. What is the social status accorded in the community to the language(s) other than English spoken in the child's home (e.g., is the accent associated with it considered a mark of distinction or of low education)?
	2. What is the social status accorded in the community to people who are bilingual? Is being bilingual considered a desirable goal?
Personal-Social Degree of acculturation into EuroAmerican Normative Culture (ENC)	1. How familiar is the child/family with ENC?
	2. How much experience does the child/family have participating in this culture?
	3. How skilled is the child/family at negotiating within this culture (e.g., accomplishing desired activities/goals)?
Degree of acculturation into U.S. early intervention/early childhood special education (ECSE) culture	1. How familiar is the child/family with early intervention (ECSE) culture (e.g., rules, expectations)?
	2. How much experience does the child/family have participating in this culture?
	3. How skilled is the child/family at negotiating within this culture (e.g., accomplishing desired activities/goals)?

Skilled Dialogue: Strategies for Responding to Cultural Diversity in Early Childhood, Second Edition
by Isaura Barrera, Lucinda Kramer, and T. Dianne Macpherson

(continued)

Guide to Identifying Cultural Data Related to Potential Culture Bumps (continued)

Sense of self (e.g., relative weight on independence, dependence, interdependence)	1. How does the family define *autonomy*? To what degree is it valued?
	2. To what degree is cooperation and group interaction/support valued?
	3. What are the characteristics of people with high credibility in the family's culture? Which characteristics/behaviors seem to be most highly valued?
Perceptions of identity and competence	1. How do family members define themselves; (e.g., by ethnic, professional, other labels; by personal attributes)?
	2. Which characteristics denote competence?
Roles and rules associated with parenting and child rearing	1. How would family members describe "good" parenting?
	2. What skills/attributes do they consider desirable in a child who is brought up well?
	3. What roles do different family members play in child rearing? Who is responsible for what?
Knowledge and experience regarding power and social positioning	1. What is the family's experience regarding social and personal power? In what situations, if any, would family members describe themselves as powerless or "at a disadvantage"?
	2. Does the family belong to and identify with a group with minority status?

(continued)

Skilled Dialogue: Strategies for Responding to Cultural Diversity in Early Childhood, Second Edition by Isaura Barrera, Lucinda Kramer, and T. Dianne Macpherson

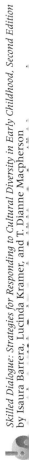

Guide to Identifying Cultural Data Related to Potential Culture Bumps *(continued)*

Values/beliefs/skills associated with instrumental and emotional support (e.g., gaining access to external resources, getting personal support)	1. How does the family obtain support? What sources are valued?
	2. When does the family believe that it is acceptable to seek instrumental support (e.g., support for getting things done)? Emotional support (e.g., personal support)?
Sensory-Cognitive Funds of knowledge: what type of knowledge is valued; concept structures and definitions (e.g., how *family* is defined)	1. What areas of knowledge does the family value and support?
	2. About what are the family members very knowledgeable?
	3. Are funds of knowledge primarily personal, communal, or institutionalized?
	4. Are funds of knowledge primarily oral? To what degree are they written?
	5. What role does the family's cultural identity (or identities) and history (or histories) play in its funds of knowledge?
Preferred strategies for acquiring new learning	1. What are the child's/family's preferred strategies for learning (e.g., modeling, questioning)?
	2. To what degree are the strategies explicit and direct? To what degree are they implicit and indirect?
	3. To what degree are the strategies oral? To what degree are they nonverbal?
	4. How do different family members go about teaching children in the home?

(continued)

Skilled Dialogue: Strategies for Responding to Cultural Diversity in Early Childhood, Second Edition by Isaura Barrera, Lucinda Kramer, and T. Dianne Macpherson

Guide to Identifying Cultural Data Related to Potential Culture Bumps (continued)

	5. Which type of intelligence tends to be favored (e.g., verbal-linguistic, visual-spatial, musical-auditory)?
Preferred strategies for problem solving and decision making	1. What are the child's/family's preferred strategies for problem solving and decision making? Do these differ according to certain characteristics of the problem or situation? If so, how?
	2. To what degree is problem solving or decision making independent? To what degree is problem solving or decision making seen as a cooperative activity? If viewed as cooperative, who gets involved in the process?
	3. To what degree are the strategies linear? To what degree are they circular or global?
	4. To what degree is problem solving deductive? To what degree is it inductive?
Worldview (i.e., assumptions about how the world works and about what is "right" and what is "wrong")	1. How does the family tend to explain events such as their child's developmental challenges?
	2. What assumptions does the family hold about how the world works (e.g., mechanistic, organic–ecological, spiritual)?
	3. What views do family members express about cultural and other differences? Do they favor the view that there is only one "right" way, or do they accept that multiple realities can exist?

Skilled Dialogue: Strategies for Responding to Cultural Diversity in Early Childhood, Second Edition
by Isaura Barrera, Lucinda Kramer, and T. Dianne Macpherson

Home Language Usage Profile

Child's name: _____   Date: _____   Completed by: _____

Person(s)	Languages used					
	Only L$_x$ Specify language other than English used in home: _____	Mostly L$_x$ (_____), some English	L$_x$ (_____) and English used equally	Some L$_x$ (_____), mostly English	Only English	Other language (specify) _____
Mother						
Father						
Siblings						
Maternal grandparents						
Paternal grandparents						
Caregiver (different from people listed above)						
Neighborhood friends/peers						
Teacher(s)						
Social peers (e.g., at child care; at preschool)						

(*Key:* L$_x$ is the language other than English used in the home.)

Comments:

Instructional Cultural Linguistic Response Plan

Child/family: _____

Date: _____   Completed by: _____

Specific Intervention and Instruction Considerations

RE: *Language and communication differences*

RE: *Teaching and learning strategies*

RE: *Instructional content*

RE: *Teaching and learning materials*

Skilled Dialogue Reminders

	Choosing Relationship over Control/ Anchored Understanding of Diversity	Setting the Stage for Miracles/ 3rd Space
Respect	**Welcoming** range and validity of diverse perspectives	**Allowing** the tension of differing perspectives
Reciprocity	**Making sense** of diverse perspectives	**Appreciating** the strengths of diverse perspectives
Responsiveness	**Joining** across diverse perspectives	**Harmonizing** diverse perspectives so as to integrate and gain access to complementary strengths

Skilled Dialogue: Strategies for Responding to Cultural Diversity in Early Childhood, Second Edition
by Isaura Barrera, Lucinda Kramer, and T. Dianne Macpherson
Copyright © 2012 by Paul H. Brookes Publishing Co., Inc. All rights reserved.

Relative Language Proficiency (RLP) Profile

Child's name: _____ Date: _____ Date of birth: _____

Chronological age: _____ Completed by: _____

Site: _____ Instrument: _____

Proficiency in language other than English (specify language: _____)

Receptive:	5	4	3	2	1
	Good; no significant errors	Mildly limited; some errors	Moderately limited; consistent/ significant errors	Severely limited; frequent and significant errors	Nonverbal and/or unintelligible
Expressive:	5	4	3	2	1

Comments:

English proficiency

Receptive:	5	4	3	2	1
	Good; no significant errors	Mildly limited; some errors	Moderately limited; consistent/ significant errors	Severely limited; frequent and significant errors	Nonverbal and/or unintelligible
Expressive:	5	4	3	2	1

Comments:

Relative Language Proficiency (Write language other than English in blanks below.)

_____ Monolingual	Receptive bilingual	Partial bilingual	Bilingual	Partial bilingual	Receptive bilingual	English monolingual

◄————————————————————————————————————►

| Has had minimal exposure to English | _____ dominant; understands some English | _____ dominant; limited English | and English about the same | English dominant; limited _____ | English dominant; understands some _____ | Has had minimal exposure to _____ |

Comments:

Guidelines for Using an Interpreter/ Translator During Test Administration

Three basic steps should occur when using an interpreter/translator while administering tests: a meeting before the testing (briefing), the testing itself (interaction), and a meeting after the assessment (debriefing). Some suggestions follow for each phase of the testing process.

BRIEFING

Prior to testing, practitioners and the interpreter/translator meet to

- Review the general purpose of the testing session

- Discuss which tests will be administered

- Discuss test validity and reliability. Care should be taken to avoid unnecessary rephrasing or radically changing test items. Interpreters/translators must also watch their use of gestures, voice patterns, and body language to avoid inadvertently providing cues

- Share information on the child being assessed

- Discuss the results of English language or other previous testing, if applicable

- Remind the interpreter/translator to write down all of the child's behaviors (e.g., gestures, facial expressions, nonverbal responses to tasks)

- Give the interpreter/translator time to organize the test materials, reread test procedures, and ask for clarification on issues, if needed

- Familiarize the interpreter/translator with terms and concepts that are specific to the test

Adapted from Medina, V. (1982). *Interpretation and translation in bilingual B.A.S.E.* San Diego, CA: San Diego County Office of Education.

INTERACTION

During actual test situations, remember that

- The practitioner is always present during the testing

- The interpreter/translator *immediately* asks questions in their prescribed order

- The practitioner writes down observations about the child during the testing

- The practitioner observes the interpreter/translator for cues of potential miscommunication or inappropriate translation:

  - Body language

  - Use of too many words or too many instructions (e.g., interpreter/translator speaks for 2 minutes after being asked to inquire about the child's place of birth)

  - Overuse of reinforcement (type and frequency) (e.g., frequent head nods to confirm correct responses)

  - Cues or prompts going beyond that required by assessment protocol

- The practitioner observes the child for

  - Use of two languages during a single task

  - False starts

  - Perseveration

  - Attention span

  - Appropriate turn taking

  - Use of gestures

  - Responses out of sequence (e.g., giving a response to a previous item or task)

DEBRIEFING

Following testing, the practitioner and the interpreter/translator meet for the following reasons:

- They review the child's correct responses and errors. The interpreter/translator gives his or her impressions of the child but does not try to diagnose the child.

- The interpreter/translator tells the practitioner what the child did and said in response to each question, including cultural or linguistic information to clarify possible reasons for responses.

- The practitioner carefully avoids professional jargon that the interpreter/translator may not understand.

- The interpreter/translator assists the practitioner in interpretation of scores, explaining which cultural or linguistic variables may have affected performance.

- The practitioner and the interpreter/translator discuss any difficulties with the testing process.

Revised Skilled
Dialogue Self-Assessment

Skilled Dialogue Self-Assessment

Choosing Relationship over Control

PRE Skill Level: 1 2 3 4   POST Skill Level: 1 2 3 4

(Circle the number above that best describes your skill level; see descriptions below.)

Setting the Stage for Miracles

PRE Skill Level: 1 2 3 4   POST Skill Level: 1 2 3 4

(Circle the number above that best describes your skill level; see descriptions below.)

LEVELS	Choosing Relationship over Control	Setting the Stage for Miracles
1	**Basic awareness:** Have a conceptual understanding of this disposition. Given scenarios, can distinguish between choosing relationship and choosing control	**Basic awareness:** Have conceptual understanding of this disposition. Given scenarios, can distinguish between Setting the Stage for Miracles and not doing so
2	**Beginning applications:** Can give examples and non-examples to illustrate this disposition	**Beginning applications:** Can generate examples and non-examples to illustrate this disposition
3	**Intermediate applications:** Can suspend my agenda in favor of relationship in at least some situations where there is no disagreement or only mild disagreement	**Intermediate applications:** Can remain open to outcomes and/or conclusions other than those I believe best or can predict based on existing data in at least some situations
4	**Skilled applications:** Can suspend my agenda in all or almost all situations even when there is significant disagreement or diversity of perspectives	**Skilled applications:** Can remain open to outcomes other than those I believe best or can predict based on existing data in most if not all situations *and* actively seek outcomes responsive to others' needs/perspectives as well as my own

(continued)

Skilled Dialogue: Strategies for Responding to Cultural Diversity in Early Childhood, Second Edition by Isaura Barrera, Lucinda Kramer, and T. Dianne Macpherson

Skilled Dialogue Self-Assessment (continued)

Welcoming

PRE Skill Level: 1 2 3 4   POST Skill Level: 1 2 3 4
(Circle the number above that best describes your skill level; see descriptions below.)

Allowing

PRE Skill Level: 1 2 3 4   POST Skill Level: 1 2 3 4
(Circle the number above that best describes your skill level; see descriptions below.)

LEVELS	Welcoming	Allowing
1	**Basic awareness:** Can describe this strategy and recognize it if given a specific scenario	**Basic awareness:** Can describe this strategy and recognize it if given a specific scenario
2	**Beginning applications:** Can give examples and non-examples to illustrate this strategy	**Beginning applications:** Can give examples and non-examples to illustrate this strategy
3	**Intermediate applications:** Can greet others with interest and warmth and believe that their behaviors/perspectives are as evidence based as my own (in at least some situations)	**Intermediate applications:** Can release my judgments and interpretations of others' behaviors or perspectives in at least some situations; that is, I can allow them to act/believe as they do without imposing my judgments or trying to correct them
4	**Skilled applications:** Consistently greet others with interest and warmth and believe that their behaviors/perspectives are as evidence based as my own even when I disagree strongly with them or do not value their perspectives	**Skilled applications:** Consistently refrain from defending/privileging my perspective and allow others to act/believe as they do without imposing my own judgments or interpretations

(continued)

Skilled Dialogue: Strategies for Responding to Cultural Diversity in Early Childhood, Second Edition
by Isaura Barrera, Lucinda Kramer, and T. Dianne Macpherson

Skilled Dialogue Self-Assessment (continued)

	Sense-Making PRE Skill Level: 1 2 3 4 POST Skill Level: 1 2 3 4 (Circle the number above that best describes your skill level; see descriptions below.)	Appreciating PRE Skill Level: 1 2 3 4 POST Skill Level: 1 2 3 4 (Circle the number above that best describes your skill level; see descriptions below.)
1	**Basic awareness:** Can describe this strategy and recognize it if given a specific scenario	**Basic awareness:** Can describe this strategy and recognize it if given a specific scenario
2	**Beginning applications:** Can give examples and non-examples to illustrate this strategy	**Beginning applications:** Can give examples and non-examples to illustrate this strategy
3	**Intermediate applications:** Can usually establish reciprocal contexts and elicit others' stories and perspectives	**Intermediate applications:** Can identify "gold nuggets" (i.e., what is of value in others' perspective/behavior) at least some of the time
4	**Skilled applications:** Can truthfully say and believe most if not all of the time that if I was in the others' shoes I would probably do/believe as they do	**Skilled applications:** Can really believe and say that I have learned something of value from others in all or almost all situations

LEVELS

(continued)

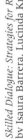

Skilled Dialogue: Strategies for Responding to Cultural Diversity in Early Childhood, Second Edition
by Isaura Barrera, Lucinda Kramer, and T. Dianne Macpherson

Skilled Dialogue Self-Assessment (continued)

Joining

PRE Skill Level: 1 2 3 4   POST Skill Level: 1 2 3 4
(Circle the number above that best describes your skill level; see descriptions below.)

Harmonizing

PRE Skill Level: 1 2 3 4   POST Skill Level: 1 2 3 4
(Circle the number above that best describes your skill level; see descriptions below.)

LEVELS	Joining	Harmonizing
1	**Basic awareness:** Can describe this strategy and recognize it if given a specific scenario	**Basic awareness:** Can describe this strategy and recognize it if given a specific scenario
2	**Beginning applications:** Can give examples and non-examples to illustrate this strategy	**Beginning applications:** Can give examples and non-examples to illustrate this strategy
3	**Intermediate applications:** Can usually identify with others' feelings, beliefs and/or others' behaviors and remember when I have felt, thought, and/or behaved in a similar fashion	**Intermediate applications:** Can usually come up with at least one "third choice" that capitalizes on both my strengths and those of others
4	**Skilled applications:** Can consistently perceive how others and I are each reflecting similar or complementary aspects of the same perspective or behavior	**Skilled applications:** Can consistently facilitate brainstorming and identify "third space" options that meet others' stated need(s) as well as my own

Skilled Dialogue: Strategies for Responding to Cultural Diversity in Early Childhood, Second Edition
by Isaura Barrera, Lucinda Kramer, and T. Dianne Macpherson

Index

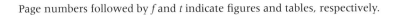

Page numbers followed by *f* and *t* indicate figures and tables, respectively.

265